Elsie McKee

D1546452

The Eucharistic Theology of
the American Holy Fairs

The Eucharistic Theology of the American Holy Fairs

Kimberly Bracken Long

WESTMINSTER
JOHN KNOX PRESS
LOUISVILLE · KENTUCKY

© 2011 Kimberly Bracken Long

First edition
Published by Westminster John Knox Press
Louisville, Kentucky

11 12 13 14 15 16 17 18 19 20—10 9 8 7 6 5 4 3 2 1

All rights reserved. No part of this book may be reproduced or transmitted in any form or by any means, electronic or mechanical, including photocopying, recording, or by any information storage or retrieval system, without permission in writing from the publisher. For information, address Westminster John Knox Press, 100 Witherspoon Street, Louisville, Kentucky 40202-1396. Or contact us online at www.wjkbooks.com.

Quotations from Leigh Eric Schmidt's *Holy Fairs: Scotland and the Making of American Revivalism* are used with permission of Wm. B. Eerdmans Publishing Co.

The facsimile page from Gilbert Tennent's sermon in appendix A is used with permission from Princeton Theological Seminary Libraries, Special Collections.

Transcriptions of Gilbert Tennent's Sermons are used with permission from Princeton Theological Seminary Libraries, Special Collections.

Book design by Sharon Adams
Cover design by Night & Day Design
Cover art © sterlsev/istockphoto.com

Library of Congress Cataloging-in-Publication Data

Long, Kimberly Bracken.
  The Eucharistic theology of the American holy fairs / Kimberly Bracken Long.
    p. cm.
  Includes bibliographical references (p.   ) and index.
  ISBN 978-0-664-23512-3 (alk. paper)
  1. Revivals—United States—History. 2. Revivals—History. 3. Lord's Supper—History.
4. United States—Church history. 5. United States—Religious life and customs. I. Title.
  BV3773.L58 2011
  234'.163097309033—dc22

2010036828

PRINTED IN THE UNITED STATES OF AMERICA

∞ The paper used in this publication meets the minimum requirements
of the American National Standard for Information Sciences Permanence
of Paper for Printed Library Materials, ANSI Z39.48-1992.

Westminster John Knox Press advocates the responsible use of our natural resources.
The text paper of this book is made from at least 30% postconsumer waste.

For Tom

Contents

Appendixes

I was so ravished with the Love of Christ that night that I could sleep little, and all next Morning and day, I was in the same frame; and saying as the Spouse of Christ, My Beloved is Mine & I am his, My beloved is white and ruddy, the Chief among 10,000, yea, Altogether lovely: and all the rest of that week, I continued rejoicing in the near views of the Sacrament in that Place, hoping I would then get my Interest in Christ and my Marriage Covenant with him sealed there.

The recollections of Catherine Cameron,
a worshiper at the revival in Cambuslang, Scotland, 1742;
in Leigh Eric Schmidt, Holy Fairs: Scotland
and the Making of American Revivalism

Acknowledgments

I owe a debt of gratitude to a number of people for their expertise and support throughout this project. Deep thanks to the Heather Murray Elkins for her encouragement and for always knowing the right questions to ask; to Robin Leaver for his keen insights and high standards; to the late Stanley Hall for his sharp eye and unfailing good humor; and to Elsie McKee for reading the manuscript so carefully and for pointing me in directions I would not have otherwise seen.

Invaluable assistance came from William O. Harris, Christine Deming, and Kenneth Henke of the Henry Luce III Library at Princeton Theological Seminary; Linda Davis and Richard Blake of the James Bulow Campbell Library at Columbia Theological Seminary; Douglas Cragg and his staff at Pitts Theological Library at Emory University. I am grateful as well to Erskine Clarke, who cheered me with his confidence in this work, and to Donald McKim, for guiding it to publication.

In all things I am buoyed by the love of those closest to me, who make space for my work and tease me away from it when necessary. To Peg and Don, Nate and Dan, Melanie and Paul, Carly and Rebekah, David and Susie, Belle and Eva—and especially, always, to Tom—my deep thanks.

Note to Reader

Unless otherwise noted, I have retained the original wording, spelling, capitalization, and punctuation of documents quoted throughout the body of this work. These particularities have also been preserved in bibliographic citations. Occasional adjustments are enclosed in square brackets.

1

Introduction

In his book *Holy Fairs: Scotland and the Making of American Revivalism*, Leigh Eric Schmidt argues that the roots of American revivalism can be found in the Scots-Irish sacramental occasions of the seventeenth and eighteenth centuries.[1] These sacramental occasions took the form of outdoor revivals that lasted for several days. Held annually during the months between May and November, they included services of preparation, preaching and exhorting, and private meditation. The week culminated in a communion service on Sunday and ended with a Monday thanksgiving service, after which people would travel back to their homes. Schmidt—along with John Boles, Paul Conkin, Marilyn Westerkamp, and Ellen Eslinger—has redefined our understanding of revivalism in this country, showing that the camp meeting, once thought to be a quintessentially American phenomenon, has its origins in the sacramental revivals of Ulster and the Scottish Lowlands.

To the contemporary ear, the term "sacramental revival" sounds like an oxymoron. What sort of eucharistic theology was at work in the midst of these events, which were marked by emotionalism and enthusiasm? This study seeks to answer that question by examining sermons, devotional writings, and catechetical materials connected to these American "holy fairs." We will see that a significant—and somewhat surprising—element of this theology is the use of language from the Song of Songs, as well as other biblical marital imagery, to describe the believer's union with Christ in communion. By considering how certain medieval writers used spousal and sexual metaphors to describe

1. Leigh Eric Schmidt, *Holy Fairs: Scotland and the Making of American Revivalism*, 2nd ed. (Grand Rapids: Wm. B. Eerdmans Publishing Co., 2001; originally published, Princeton, NJ: Princeton University Press, 1989).

the believer's relationship with Christ, examining Calvin's understanding of mystical union, and comparing the American sources with their Scottish antecedents, I will argue that the American sacramental occasions exhibited a eucharistic theology that was solidly Reformed yet included a mystical strain, expressed within the context of frontier revivalism.

In order to lay the foundation for the study, this introductory chapter will describe the ritual eucharistic pattern that was born in Scotland and transported to America, survey the history of research of American revivalism, and explain the methodology used. A brief description of the contents of each section of the study will conclude this chapter.

THE SCOTS-IRISH "HOLY FAIRS"

Historians have constructed a picture of Presbyterian sacramental occasions from church records, letters, diaries, and journalistic accounts. One important source of information is the session records of the Presbyterian Church in Booth Bay, Maine, whose first pastor, the Rev. John Murray, crossed the Atlantic from his native Ulster to lead the newly organized Scottish congregation. The records of the fledgling church were kept by the clerk of session, John Beath, whose notes from the late 1760s describe practices brought from the Scottish homeland.

Beath's account of what happened from day to day during a typical Scottish communion season makes it apparent that this event was the height of the congregation's life together. In describing the church's beginnings, he reports that one of the first things the new church did after it was formed was to take up a collection for the purpose of buying communion ware. They purchased "six cups, three large flagons, six large platters, and four large dishes, . . . 'all of the best hard metal, and most elegant fashion.'" They also purchased linen coverings for the tables that would be set up in the aisles of the church, according to Presbyterian custom.[2]

Beath goes on to provide a detailed description of the celebration of the communion season. Since this was a new congregation, the services were small and held inside the church. The rituals that were enacted, however, were the same as those that had occurred at the large outdoor communion seasons in Scotland, as well as the sacramental revivals that would spring up in

---

2. Thomas C. Pears Jr., ed., "Sessional Records of the Presbyterian Church of Booth Bay, Maine, 1767–1778," *Journal of the Presbyterian Historical Society* 16 (1935): 203–40, 243–88, 308–55. Schmidt's description of the communion seasons held at Booth Bay from 1764 to 1767 is based on these records and discussed in *Holy Fairs*, 70ff.

America. Several weeks before the communion, an announcement was made and preparations began. The pastor conducted examinations of those who intended to commune to ensure their readiness, questioning them about their understanding of Christian doctrine and the meaning of the Lord's Supper. Furthermore, he asked if they had experienced "a work of grace in their souls," and whether they were living godly lives. Would-be communicants were subjected to thorough spiritual, moral, and catechetical scrutiny to ensure their worthiness for the sacrament.[3]

A little more than a week before the fast day, the congregation gathered for a time of prayer and teaching. On the Sunday preceding the communion, called the "preparation Sabbath," services were held both morning and afternoon; in these services the preaching was focused on the Lord's Supper, "its power for the worthy and its dangers for the unworthy." The next Wednesday was a day of public fasting and humiliation. On this day,

> Sins were reviewed; each of the Ten Commandments expounded; "the great work of self-examination, and secret personal renewing their Covenant" enjoined; psalms sung; and confessions of iniquity made. At the close of this solemn, penitential service all were to return home, continuing their "fast without touching any refreshment till after the Sun was down, as it had begun at that hour [on the] preceding day."[4]

Private preparations went on through family devotions, individual meditations, "secret prayer," and self-examination, until the congregation came together again on Saturday.

On Saturday afternoon, Mr. Murray preached a sermon on "the dying love of Christ" and talked once again about who was worthy to come to the table and who must be excluded from the sacrament. Toward the end of the service, he "stood by the communion table, 'then poured out on the table a great number of small square pieces of lead,' tokens for admission to the Lord's Supper." These tokens were given out, one at a time, to each worthy communicant as the people came forward. During this process, the pastor expounded on the significance of the token as "a guard against the unworthy, a sign of the covenant and a pledge of steadfast devotion." On the following day, worshipers would give the tokens to the elders assisting in the sacrament and thereby gain admission to the table. The service ended with the singing of psalms and a benediction.[5]

---

3. Schmidt, *Holy Fairs*, 70–71.
4. Ibid., 71.
5. Ibid.

The week's rituals culminated in the Sunday communion service. The linen-covered tables were arranged in the aisles so that below the pulpit they joined with a square table on which the elements were placed and covered with a fine cloth. The service began with prayer, followed by the singing of psalms and the preaching of the sermon. Then the pastor read from 1 Corinthians 11, Paul's account of Christ's institution of the sacrament, which represented to Presbyterians the scriptural warrant for the Supper. After a verse-by-verse explication of the passage, the pastor "fenced the table" in true Presbyterian tradition, making it clear that the "ignorant, unbelieving and prophane" were excluded from the sacrament. In case some question of worthiness still remained in the minds of the worshipers, the Ten Commandments were reviewed, along with a list of characteristics of the unworthy. Then the pastor "'freely invited' all believers and 'true penitent[s]' to come and partake at the Lord's table."[6]

Drawing on Beath's records, Schmidt provides the following account of the communion celebration:

> After the table was fenced, a psalm was sung, and the worthy came to sit at the long tables. When they had seated themselves, the pastor "descended from the pulpit with his Bible and Psalm book in his hands and took his seat at the element table in the centre." The elders now uncovered the bread and wine; then the pastor read the words of institution again, "pausing at each part until he had endeavored to imitate the divine exemplar." Murray thus "took the bread and then the cup in his hand and held them up in view of all" and offered "meditations" on these elements. With the whole congregation standing and watching, the minister then consecrated the bread and wine, setting them apart "from a common to a sacred use by solemn prayer." The bread was broken and the wine poured out from a flagon into cups. At the central table the minister and elders communed; from them the bread and wine were passed along the tables until all had partaken. Murray then rose and offered further meditations and comforts as well as reminding the communicants of their "vows and resolutions" to live holy lives. As a psalm was sung, these communicants retired to their seats, and a new group filled up the tables again. The rituals of dispensing the elements were repeated as many times as necessary until all had been served.[7]

---

6. Ibid., 71–72. The practice of coming forward to commune around the table was distinctively Presbyterian. While the Westminster Directory allowed for worshipers to receive the elements while remaining seated in their pews to appease those of an Episcopalian bent, the insistence on sitting at the table to commune (as Jesus did with his disciples) was something of a rallying cry for ardent Presbyterians.

7. Ibid., 72.

Once all the communicants had partaken, the pastor gave a final exhortation, speaking to those who had communed as well as to any spectators present (both ill-prepared Christians and the unconverted), then prompting the congregation to give thanks. Services of thanksgiving would be held that afternoon and on Monday, where thanksgiving sermons were preached and the benefits of the sacrament proclaimed.[8]

After detailing the preparations for and rituals of the communion, Beath added his own comments on the aftereffects of celebrating the communion:

> There were such symptoms of the powerful and special presence of [the] God of grace, as every one might discern and we can never enough be thankful for; it was a solemn, sweet, and glorious season; many of God's children were filled with the joys of the Lord and many poor souls brought to see their need of that Saviour they had shamefully neglected, and wickedly crucified.[9]

Just as similar events had done in Scotland, the communion season of a new church in the colonies brought renewal to believers and conversion to unbelievers.

Six months after the first communion, another was held in October 1767. This time an even greater number assembled, and more than two hundred believers took part in the sacrament. Although both events were much smaller (and perhaps more sedate) than either those back home in Scotland or the large American revivals, such as the one that would be held at Cane Ridge, Kentucky, those who participated seemed to have done so with similar spiritual fervor. The congregational rituals and patterns described by John Beath are but one example of a rich and abiding tradition of sacramental occasions that emerged in Scotland in the seventeenth century and remained remarkably stable throughout the seventeenth and eighteenth centuries in both the Old and New Worlds.[10]

Thanks to Schmidt and others, the story of revivalism in America has been told in recent years with increasing nuance and greater attention to its origins in the British Isles. Nevertheless, this story has been presented from the perspective of historians and sociologists, with minimal attention to the inherent theological and liturgical issues. This inquiry, therefore, will take another look at the American holy fairs from a liturgical studies perspective. The following brief review of the literature on American revivalism will prepare for a discussion of the scope and significance of the present study.

---

8. Ibid.
9. John Beath's session records, quoted in ibid., 72–73.
10. Ibid., 72.

HISTORY OF RESEARCH

In 1972, John Boles published the first comprehensive study of the Second Great Awakening since Catherine Cleveland's *The Great Revival in the West, 1797–1805* (1916). Boles took a new approach to the story of the enthusiasm that blazed across Virginia, the Carolinas, Georgia, Kentucky, and Tennessee in the late eighteenth and early nineteenth centuries, suggesting that the events of the Second Great Awakening were the result of more than just "geography and emotion." Against the prevailing view, he argued that the Great Revival was not merely an outgrowth of life on the Western frontier but rather an expression of the gradually strengthening forces of southern evangelicalism. Boles pointed to the training and techniques that ministers received in the East, the theological shift toward Arminianism, and the move toward individualistic evangelism as formative factors; he offered a revisionist interpretation of the ecclesial schisms that resulted from this era.[11]

More than a decade later, Marilyn Westerkamp turned scholarly attention to the First Great Awakening in her book *Triumph of the Laity: Scots-Irish Piety and the Great Awakening, 1625–1760.* Arguing that the awakening was rooted in a revivalist tradition that began in Scotland and migrated to Ireland before traveling with Scots-Irish emigrants to the Middle Colonies of North America (New York, New Jersey, Pennsylvania, and Delaware), she pointed to the laity, not the clergy, as the impetus for revival.[12] In *Holy Fairs* Leigh Schmidt focused on the Second Great Awakening, further demonstrating that the eucharistic revivals in America were derived from the sacramental occasions celebrated in Scotland and Ulster in the eighteenth and nineteenth centuries. He thus offered a new interpretation of the Kentucky revivals of the late eighteenth and early nineteenth centuries, which emphasized the sacramental nature of the earliest American Presbyterian revivals and established a foundation for other scholars of American revivalism.

Subsequent studies by Paul Conkin and Ellen Eslinger built on Schmidt's work. Conkin tells the story of Cane Ridge against the backdrop of the sacramental practice of Scots-Irish Presbyterians and explains how this traditional practice evolved into what became known as the camp meeting. Eslinger's book concentrates on the social forces that were at work in shaping the camp

---

11. John B. Boles, *The Great Revival: Beginnings of the Bible Belt* (Lexington: University of Kentucky Press, 1996; originally published in 1972 as *The Great Revival, 1787–1805: The Origins of the Southern Evangelical Mind*).

12. Marilyn J. Westerkamp, *Triumph of the Laity: Scots-Irish Piety and the Great Awakening, 1625–1760* (New York: Oxford University Press, 1988).

meeting, adding another layer of understanding to a period of history that has enjoyed a certain amount of attention in recent years.[13]

In addition to these scholarly works, several dissertations have appeared since the publication of Schmidt's *Holy Fairs*, most notably John Thomas Scott's study of James McGready, "James McGready: Son of Thunder, Father of the Great Revival"; and Anthony L. Blair's "Fire across the Water: Transatlantic Dimensions of the Great Awakening among Middle-Colony Presbyterians."[14]

Within this trend of revisionist history are several matters of debate. Running through these works is a discussion about how accurate is the characterization of the huge effect of the Western frontier on American religious life, which Frederick Jackson Turner first articulated and which became the standard view. Increasingly, scholars have argued that the development of Protestant worship in general—and camp meeting revivalism in particular—was due to more than the hardships and vulnerabilities of frontier life, and that patterns retained from previous generations and former homelands were just as influential. Eslinger, in fact, has asserted that by the time of the Great Revival, the Western frontier was not so frontier-like at all; nevertheless, she points out that despite recent historical studies, the prevailing view of Turner and his contemporaries remains intact.

Another question that arises—one that is more particular to the sacramental occasions of the Scots-Irish Presbyterians—is whether the eucharistic revivals were intended to bring about the conversion of nonbelievers or the spiritual renewal of baptized Christians. Schmidt pointed out that the aspect of spiritual renewal was significant, but scholars have generally tended to view the revivals as primarily geared toward conversion. In an essay on the communion sermons of James McGready, a prominent preacher during the Great Revival, this author has suggested that the spiritual renewal of baptized Christians was at least as important as the conversion of non-Christians.[15]

Finally, Presbyterian worship has been characterized as the antithesis of sacramentality. As Leigh Schmidt points out in his preface to the new edition

13. Paul Conkin, *Cane Ridge: America's Pentecost* (Madison: University of Wisconsin Press, 1990); Ellen Eslinger, *Citizens of Zion: The Social Origins of Camp Meeting Revivalism* (Knoxville: University of Tennessee Press, 1999).

14. John Thomas Scott, "James McGready: Son of Thunder, Father of the Great Revival" (PhD diss., The College of William and Mary, 1991); Anthony L. Blair, "Fire across the Water: Transatlantic Dimensions of the Great Awakening among Middle-Colony Presbyterians" (PhD diss., Temple University, 2000; pbk. ed., Saarbrücken, Germany: LAP, Lambert Academic Publishing, 2010).

15. Kimberly Bracken Long, "The Communion Sermons of James McGready: Sacramental Theology and Scots-Irish Piety on the Kentucky Frontier," *Journal of Presbyterian History* 80, no. 1 (Spring 2002): 4. This essay appears, with adaptations, as chap. 2, below.

of *Holy Fairs* (2001), "The history of these Reformed Protestant festivals serves as an important corrective to those scholars within religious studies who continue to use Protestantism as their antiritualistic other." He goes on to explain that scholars such as Mary Douglas, Jonathan Z. Smith, Catherine Bell, and Arnold Eisen hold up Protestantism as the "great source of a modern bias against ceremony and practice." As Schmidt notes, Catherine Bell in particular considers Presbyterianism to be antiritualistic and asserts that "any notion of the divine presence" is denied in the sacraments.[16] Schmidt's work clearly took an important first step in dispelling such notions, but further investigation into the sacramental life of Presbyterians on both sides of the Atlantic would result in a more-nuanced picture of the Reformed liturgical heritage.

As stated above, none of the foundational works mentioned here is written from a theological or liturgical perspective. Although these studies all reflect a certain understanding of the theological issues inherent in American revivalism, none provides any sustained treatment of the sacramental theology at work in the eucharistic revivals that were at the center of the First and Second Great Awakenings. This study, then, will look at American Presbyterian sacramental revivals through the lens of liturgical studies. By examining the chief texts of American revivalism—sermons, devotional writings, and catechetical materials—insights will be gained into the sacramental theology at work in these events, as well as into the nature of revivalism in the American Presbyterian context.

SERMONS, DEVOTIONAL WRITINGS, AND CATECHETICAL MATERIALS AS PRIMARY TEXTS

Preaching was central to the Scots-Irish and American sacramental occasions. At every stage of the event—preparation, communion, and thanksgiving—sermons were integral to the process of self-examination, repentance, and renewal. Not only were sermons preached at these events; they also were published in multiple editions on both sides of the Atlantic and used as devotional reading.

It is not unexpected that preaching would play an important role in communion seasons since the Scots understood it to be a crucial part of ministry. Pastors in the Scottish tradition would have been guided by the Westminster Directory for Worship (1645). The section on preaching in the Westminster Directory is one of the longest, reflecting the significance of the act. Ministers

---

16. Schmidt, *Holy Fairs*, xxvi–xxvii.

are expected to approach the preaching task with a range of expertise and skill both deep and broad. One who would preach is assumed to be

> in some good measure gifted for so weighty a service, by his skill in the Originall Languages, and in such Arts and Sciences as are hand-maids unto Divinity, by his knowledge in the whole Body of The-ology, but most of all in the holy Scriptures, having his senses and heart exercised in them above the common sort of Beleevers; and by the illumination of Gods Spirit, and other gifts of edification, which (together with reading and studying of the Word) hee ought still to seek by Prayer, and an humble heart.[17]

The Directory recommends, without requiring, what would come to be known as plain-style preaching, a form by which the preacher first expounds upon some doctrine, moves to an explanation of its "use" or "application" for the hearers, then concludes with an exhortation. A variety of ways of using biblical texts is approved; the sermon may be based on a text from Scripture, focused on a particular occasion, or it may be part of an ongoing exercise of preaching through a particular chapter, psalm, or book. Preachers are to be scrupulous about making doctrinal claims. Doctrine should be truthful, expressed plainly, and if difficult to understand, related clearly to the bibli-cal text at hand. Arguments are expected to be "solid" and "convincing," and illustrations "full of light and such as may convey the truth into the Hearers heart with spiritual delight." Doctrine is not enough in and of itself, however; it must be clearly related to how hearers might make use of it, and preachers must apply it to the living of the Christian life.[18]

Although the method of preaching is not prescribed, it is expected that a minister's sermons display certain characteristics. Preaching is to be under-taken "painfully," with great care. It is to be delivered "plainly, that the mean-est may understand," as well as "faithfully, . . . wisely, . . . [and] gravely." It is important that sermons be delivered "with loving affection" and that the minister be "persuaded in his own heart" that he speaks the truth.[19]

Along with the Directory for Public Worship, the Westminster divines issued a Directory for Family Worship (1647); together these Scottish direc-tories "created an official typology of worship," stressing a "three-fold pattern of public worship, family exercise, and secret or individual devotion."[20] The

---

17. Westminster Assembly (1643–1652), *The Westminster Directory Being a Directory for the Publique Worship of God in the Three Kingdomes*, with an introduction by Ian Breward (Bramcote: Grove Books, 1980), 15.

18. Ibid., 15–16.

19. Ibid., 17–18.

20. Stanley Robertson Hall, "The American Presbyterian 'Directory for Worship': History of a Liturgical Strategy" (PhD diss., University of Notre Dame, 1990), 84.

content of both directories was echoed by a popular minister's manual written by William Steuart of Pardovan. First published in 1707, "Pardovan," as it was sometimes called, provided ministers emigrating to America with guidance for their ministries. As Stanley Hall explains, this manual drew on both directories and "was the common heritage of all the forms of Presbyterianism through the period of the Scottish and Irish emigrations that provided a base for the American churches. This is a bridge from the 1640s, to the efforts of American Presbyterians."[21]

Indeed, Pardovan includes sections on preaching, the sacraments, catechizing, and family worship, sometimes quoting verbatim from the earlier directories. Several passages clearly reflect practices associated with sacramental occasions. After citing the directives of the Westminster divines regarding the observation of the Lord's Supper, Steuart goes on to explain that "present practice" differs somewhat. The Thursday before communion is usually a fast day, he explains, and three sermons are customarily delivered. Two preparation sermons follow on Saturday, and two action sermons on Sunday, just before communion. Thanksgiving sermons follow on Sunday afternoon and on Monday. Because of the number of worshipers, there would usually be five or more ministers present. Steuart goes on to describe the actions of communion: how a table may be placed so that communicants might be easily seated around it, how the table is fenced, how the elements are sanctified and distributed, and so on.[22] His description mirrors that provided by Clerk John Beath, demonstrating that the rituals established nearly a century earlier not only prevailed in Scotland but were also carried by émigrés to the New World.

An American Directory for Worship would not be adopted until 1788. As Hall points out, the American Directory substantially reduced the amount of attention given to preaching. Fewer directions are given, and much of the counsel to the minister was eliminated. The sermon was still considered "an institution of God for the salvation of men," but more emphasis was now put on the didactic nature of preaching.[23] The preachers considered in this study would have been informed by the Westminster documents; only James McGready flourished after the American Directory was adopted. Certainly he would have been aware of the earlier directives as well as the American version, and it will be seen that his preaching was in continuity with earlier figures, both in terms of style and content.

21. Ibid., 85.
22. Walter Steuart of Pardovan, *Collections and Observations Concerning the Worship, Discipline, and Government of the Church of Scotland*, 5th ed. (Edinburgh: Edinburgh Printing Co., 1837), 138–42.
23. S. R. Hall, "American Presbyterian 'Directory for Worship,'" 121–22.

These key documents make it apparent that sermons, devotional writings, and catechetical material are important sources for discerning the eucharistic theology at work in the American sacramental occasions. It is these texts that will be the chief area of inquiry for this study. A statement of the thesis to be argued from these sources follows, after which a thorough exposition of the methodology at work in this study will be provided.

THESIS

Not only did American Presbyterians of Scots-Irish descent share the liturgical practice of annual sacramental occasions with their forbears; they also shared a vocabulary of faith regarding eucharistic theology and experience. In the sermons, devotional writings, and catechetical materials of Scottish and American clergy, one sees a eucharistic theology that emphasizes Reformed themes such as justification by grace through faith, the real presence of Christ in the sacrament, and the importance of worthy participation. Close examination of the sermons preached just before the celebration of the Lord's Supper reveals yet another common characteristic: the frequent use of language from the Song of Songs to describe the union with Christ that occurs in the Lord's Supper. In fact, union and communion with Christ—both the earthly experience of the Eucharist and the eschatological longing for final consummation—are recurring themes in public worship as well as in private devotion. This thesis will seek to answer two basic questions: (1) What does this use of language from the Song of Songs mean? (2) Where does it come from?

After a thorough examination of the homiletical, devotional, and catechetical contributions of key figures in the American and Scottish sacramental revivals, I will argue that for American Presbyterians of Scots-Irish descent, the marriage bed is a lively and frequently used metaphor for the eucharistic Table. The sacrament of the Lord's Supper is the place where Christ, the bridegroom, is wedded to the believer, the bride; it is the locus of a spiritual union that is longed for and experienced in part on earth, one that will be fully consummated in heaven. Central to this understanding of the eucharistic Table as marriage bed is the use of language from the Song of Songs, as well as other biblical marital imagery, to describe this union. These metaphors of love and desire, which are often highly emotional and evocative—even erotic—served preachers well as they wooed believers to the table, where they would seal the marriage covenant for which they had been longing and preparing.

By considering these sermons and other writings in light of Calvin's understanding of mystical union, it will be seen that this language serves to interpret a Reformed sacramental theology that reflects Calvin's views. I will also argue that the eucharistic theology of the American holy fairs expressed a spiritual vitality that echoes the mysticism of some medieval writers. The Presbyterian sacramental occasions of the American frontier, then, enacted a Reformed mystical eucharistic theology in the context of a revivalism that was both evangelical and sacramental.

METHODOLOGY

Over the past twenty years or so, liturgical scholars have paid increasing attention to a variety of elements of Christian worship, and not only to liturgical texts, as had been the practice. As Lawrence Hoffman explains, liturgies may be defined much more broadly. Liturgies are, he says, "acted-out rituals involving prescribed texts, actions, timing, persons, and things, all coming together in a shared statement of communal identity by those who live with, through, and by them."[24] Or to put it another way, "it is not the text, then, but the people who pray it, that should concern us."[25]

Other esteemed scholars share Hoffman's holistic view of liturgical methodology. Even Robert Taft, who might be considered the chief expert of liturgical textual criticism, asserts that "we must plunge into . . . the 'archeology of the everyday.'"[26] Mark Searle concurs, claiming that "the formal object of . . . liturgical studies [ought to be] the actual worship life of the living offering praying Church."[27] Building on this view of liturgical methodology, this study will use as primary sources sermons preached during communion services, as well as devotional and catechetical materials written for individuals to use at home in order to prepare for communion. These are still texts, to be sure, but they are texts broadly defined; that is, they are not the texts of liturgies, but documents that will offer a view of how Presbyterians understood and participated in the Lord's Supper in a way that liturgical texts alone could not show.

Another methodological cue is taken from Kevin Irwin, who also views liturgy as an "event" and not as texts alone.[28] Irwin differentiates between "theology of the liturgy," "theology drawn from the liturgy," and "doxological

---

24. Lawrence A. Hoffman, *Beyond the Text: A Holistic Approach to Liturgy* (Bloomington and Indianapolis: Indiana University Press, 1987), 3.

25. Ibid., 2.

26. Robert Taft, "Response to the Berakah Award: Anamnesis," *Worship* 59 (1985): 305; quoted in Hoffman, *Beyond the Text*, 2.

27. Mark Searle, "New Tasks, New Methods: The Emergence of Pastoral Liturgical Studies," *Worship* 57 (1983): 306; quoted in Hoffman, *Beyond the Text*, 2.

28. Kevin W. Irwin, *Context and Text: Method in Liturgical Theology* (Collegeville, MN: Liturgical Press, 1994), 53.

theology."[29] It is Irwin's first and second categories that are most useful for this study. In considering the theology of the liturgy, it is affirmed that how the community of believers enacts, experiences, and anticipates the mysteries of the faith is of key theological importance.[30] How this happens in the particular contexts of the Scottish and American holy fairs is significant, then, in expressing how believers worship in continuity with other communities of believers that went on before them. In this sense, this study is concerned not only with the particularities of the Presbyterian sacramental occasions, but also with those events as expressions of catholicity within the Christian faith. Furthermore, this inquiry will strive to use the liturgy, broadly defined, of the Presbyterian sacramental occasions "as a source for systematic theology in such a way that systematic theology is intrinsically connected to the act of worship."[31]

Irwin furthermore asserts that the liturgical context *is* the text, the source, for liturgical theology. For Irwin, context includes the historical evolution of rites (theologically and liturgically) as well as the contemporary celebration of those rites; context focuses not only on the texts involved but also on the actual uses of those texts, past and present. It is those rites, then, that serve as a source for theology.[32] Since Presbyterian sacramental revivals involved few liturgical texts—Presbyterians used not a prayer book but a directory for worship, which provided guidelines but few required words or acts—Irwin's method is applicable in this way as well. The context of the celebration becomes a source from which an understanding of eucharistic theology of seventeenth-, eighteenth-, and early nineteenth-century Scots-Irish and American Presbyterians might be derived.

Though these scholars have opened the door to a more far-reaching approach to liturgical sources, they also caution against too much speculation. As Bradshaw points out, sources leave much unsaid; what is commonly practiced will often be passed over without comment, since familiarity on the part of the reader is assumed.[33] Furthermore, the careful scholar will not jump to conclusions about the presumed behavior or attitudes of the people whose documents are being examined. Wayne Meeks reminds the researcher that "the sociological interpreter is tempted to infer what *must* have happened and the conditions that *must* have obtained on the basis of certain assumed

29. Ibid., 46–52.
30. Ibid., 46–48.
31. Ibid., 51.
32. Ibid., 54–55.
33. Paul Bradshaw, *The Search for the Origins of Christian Worship* (New York: Oxford University Press, 1992), 76.

regularities in human behavior." To counteract that tendency, he suggests, one might follow the advice of "the exegetical critic [who] insists that the task of the historian is only to report the facts: what the texts say, what the monuments show."[34] Meeks's warnings are useful for the liturgical theologian as well. Although the project will seek to discover insights regarding the thoughts and practices of real people at worship, the boundaries surrounding the source material will be closely guarded.

This study, then, will pay close attention to the texts that are at hand: sermons, devotional writings, and catechetical materials. Following Bradshaw's cue that "texts must always be studied in context," primary sources will be examined in light of the denominational guidelines described above.[35] Because, as Bradshaw also advises, "contextual study . . . also requires the search for another point of reference besides the text itself,"[36] American Presbyterian usages of the Song of Songs will be compared with those found in Scottish counterparts, as well as with those found in the writings of pertinent medieval, Reformation, and post-Reformation figures.

Implicit in this sort of methodology is an interdisciplinary approach. As Geoffrey Wainwright puts it, liturgical theology is best done in the "borderlands between theology and some of its neighboring human disciplines, such as the sociology of knowledge, the philosophy of language, the anthropology of ritual, the psychology of belief, and the theory of action."[37] In making the same point, Hoffman cites Daniel Stevick's statement that "to be a liturgist is not to be one sort of thing."[38] The danger in this sort of approach is that one must be diligent about setting and keeping in place the parameters of the project at hand.

One fascinating question, for instance, concerns the relationship between the use of the Song of Songs in clergy-generated materials and the use of the same sort of language by worshipers in their accounts of experiences of spiritual union with Christ in the Eucharist. Furthermore, the use of such vividly sensual language as that of the Song of Songs to express theological concepts as well as ecstatic experience raises questions regarding the involved preachers and worshipers' attitudes toward sexuality. Such questions necessarily go beyond the parameters of this study. Although it would be tempting to do a

34. Wayne A. Meeks, *The First Urban Christians: The Social World of the Apostle Paul* (New Haven, CT, and London: Yale University Press, 1983), 5.

35. Ibid., 77.

36. Ibid., 78.

37. Geoffrey Wainwright, "A Language in Which We Speak to God," *Worship* 57 (1983): 309; quoted in Hoffman, *Beyond the Text*, 2.

38. Daniel Stevick, "Responsibility for Liturgy," *Worship* 50 (1976): 301–2; quoted in Hoffman, *Beyond the Text*, 17.

thoroughgoing study of the sociological, cultural, and psychological dimensions of the Presbyterian sacramental occasions, this study will focus on examining the eucharistic theology at work in those events, with an eye trained on the use of imagery from the Song of Songs and related biblical material.

In order to draw conclusions about the eucharistic theology of the American holy fairs in general, and to discern the meaning and sources of marital imagery for mystical union in particular, this study will take something of an *ad fontes* approach. Just as the humanists and Reformers of the sixteenth century called for a return to ancient and biblical sources in order to reach an authentic Christianity,[39] this author seeks to follow the trail of sources from American manifestations back to their Scottish roots. Since the events surrounding Cane Ridge have been so central in interpreting the American religious experience, this inquiry will examine the themes of mystical union, Christ as lover, and preacher as advocate—tracing them from the Kentucky frontier at the dawn of the nineteenth century, back to the Middle American colonies and the kirks of Scotland in the mid-eighteenth century. I hope that the reader will be persuaded that the founts of both medieval and Reformation understanding, piety, and spiritual experience fed the streams that eventually flowed to the American holy fairs.

This journey of sorts will be undertaken, however, only after considering how the themes of mystical union and spiritual marriage were expressed from the medieval era through the eighteenth century. Furthermore, a review of Calvin's understanding of these same themes will be considered in order to provide a framework for the study of the American sources. As these currents are traced back to their sources, and conclusions are drawn regarding the eucharistic theology of the American sacramental revivals, it will become evident that although the Reformed theological perspective was expressed and defended with vigor, the medieval spiritual inheritance was also significant. Although it is sometimes tempting to assume that Reformation-era theologians made a clean break from their medieval predecessors, the attentive scholar will recognize that the Reformers were informed by their theological and spiritual ancestors of the Middle Ages.

Philip Schaff argued in the mid-nineteenth century that the church is not well served by overlooking, much less castigating, certain eras in its history. "We gather with fond affection the flowers of the Christian life, out of all times and generations, and adorn with them our own altars," Schaff once wrote. He stressed that the church does well to embrace "all the treasures that

---

39. Bard Thompson, *Humanists and Reformers: A History of the Renaissance and Reformation* (Grand Rapids: William B. Eerdmans Publishing Co., 1996), 30–31.

history brings within our reach, even though derived in part from the so called dark ages themselves."[40]

Although it might seem far-fetched to claim that preachers on the American frontier would have been steeped in medieval mysticism (and indeed, that is not the claim being made here), it does seem clear that the river of American sacramental revivals was fed by an array of tributaries of the church: medieval, Reformed, and evangelical.

There is not one obvious way to tell the story presented by this study, and the ordering of chapters is problematic. A certain abruptness must be acknowledged between parts 1 and 2, as attention moves from laying the groundwork in the medieval and Reformation eras to examining revivals on the Kentucky frontier. The present schema has been adopted in order to resist making quick assumptions regarding the influence of earlier theologians on later preachers. It is also hoped that the continuities observed here will suggest avenues for future research.

TELLING THE STORY: OUTLINE
OF THE ARGUMENT

This inquiry will begin with a brief survey of the use of the themes of mystical union and spiritual marriage from the medieval era to the eighteenth century. Chapter 2 will consider the broad range of sources in which this metaphorical language is prominent, while pointing out continuities between pre- and post-Reformation traditions. Among the sources considered are medieval devotional materials, Luther's theological writings, the works of early Reformed scholars, Puritan preaching and devotional writings, Moravian hymnody, and Methodist hymns and sermons.

Calvin's understanding of union with Christ will be explored in chapter 3. These observations will enable the reader to see that Calvin's theological views on the Eucharist, union with Christ, and practical concerns regarding preparation for communion are reflected in the preaching and devotional writings of Scots-Irish Presbyterians in both the Old and New Worlds. Calvin's own use of marital imagery to describe union with Christ will be examined in the *Institutes*, the *Short Treatise on the Lord's Supper*, commentaries, and other writings. Sermons of Theodore Beza on the Song of Songs will also

---

40. Philip Schaff, "What Is Church History? A Vindication of the Idea of Historical Development," in *Reformed and Catholic: Selected Historical and Theological Writings of Philip Schaff*, ed. Charles Yrigoyen Jr. and George M. Bricker, Pittsburgh Original Texts and Translations Series 4 (Pittsburgh: Pickwick Press, 1979), 137.

be examined, with an eye to their use of the book's love poetry to describe the believer's understanding and experience of communion. I will argue that Calvin's sacramental theology and Beza's preaching on the Canticles form a strong theological foundation for their Scots-Irish and American heirs, whose own vigorous and colorful preaching exhibited both spiritual vitality and intellectual rigor.

Part 2 of this study will focus on the American sacramental revivals and the Scottish events that preceded them. The examination will begin with a key figure in the sacramental occasions during the time of the Great Revival, James McGready, a Presbyterian minister of Scots-Irish descent who was schooled in the "Log College" tradition.[41]

Chapter 4 will examine McGready's communion sermons, which reflect a Reformed theological heritage as well as a concern with vital religious experience. His ministry on the Kentucky frontier represents the waning of the Scots-Irish pattern of celebrating sacramental seasons and anticipates what would become the American camp meeting. In McGready's sermons one hears of believers meeting Christ in the sacrament of holy communion after having longed for such union. This union is not complete, however; it is only the earthly foretaste of the consummation to come in heaven. This eschatological thrust is combined with an exuberance about the experience of believers at the earthly table, where Christ the bridegroom and his believer-bride are joined in eucharistic marriage.

These themes resonate even more loudly in the preaching of Gilbert Tennent, one of the most influential Presbyterians of the First Great Awakening. Born in Ulster, the son (and student) of the founder of the Log College, Tennent was a minister in the then-frontier land of New Jersey, and later served as pastor of Second Presbyterian Church in Philadelphia. Tennent found himself continually involved in controversies of the fledgling American Presbyterian church, seeking to inhabit a middle ground between his Reformed theological heritage and his convictions about "experimental" religion. Although Tennent

---

41. The labeling of certain time periods as "the Great Revival" or "the Great Awakening" has been questioned by historians over the last two decades. In his essay "Enthusiasm Described and Decried: The Great Awakening as Interpretative Fiction," *Journal of American History* 69 (September 1982): 306–9, Jon Butler argued against singling out one period of awakening and asserted that such labels are imposed in an exercise of historical interpretation. More recently, Frank Lambert, in *Inventing the "Great Awakening"* (Princeton, NJ: Princeton University Press, 1999), has continued the conversation by giving assent to Butler's basic argument while contending that revivalists of the period themselves imagined the construct, if not the term. He and other scholars have since built on the notion that people of the time did indeed live through profound religious experiences while also acknowledging that media accounts and detractors played a role in shaping how the time period was perceived. The fine points of that discussion are beyond the scope of this inquiry, although it is useful to note that the conversation is ongoing.

preached sermons of all kinds and at all sorts of occasions, his sacramental sermons are of interest here; they will be examined in chapter 5. His communion sermons brim with enthusiastic and even erotic language when he describes the mystical union that takes place at the eucharistic Table between Christ and the believer. The mode of expression that was hinted at in McGready's preaching is seen in full bloom in that of Tennent.

In order to trace the theological, liturgical, and homiletical inheritance of these two ministers, chapter 6 will explore the sermons, devotional writings, and catechisms of John Willison, a contemporary of Tennent who wrote more on the sacraments, and was more widely published, than any other Scottish Presbyterian of his time. In Willison's vast output, numerous examples of language from the Song of Songs and other biblical marital imagery can be seen. In his sermons, devotional books, and catechisms, Willison freely uses the metaphors of lover and spouse to describe mystical union with Christ in communion, thereby providing both clergy and laity with language for prayer as well as for learning. Because Willison's works were published for more than a century and a half in both America and Scotland, his influence on Presbyterians of Scottish heritage was significant, and his value to this study is great.

In the final chapter (7), conclusions will be drawn regarding the eucharistic theology of the American sacramental occasions. We will see that for Americans involved in holy fairs, the interests of revivalism were mitigated by the Reformed concern for intellectual rigor, biblical scholarship, and a theological tradition inherited from Calvin and Beza, as well as the spiritual influence of a particular strain of medieval mysticism. Furthermore, I will contend that for the Scots-Irish and American Presbyterians, the eucharistic Table was akin to the marriage bed, the locus of mystical union for Christ and his covenanted believers. Finally, the insights gained from the study of this segment of American Presbyterian liturgical history will point to implications for the renewal of Reformed worship in the twenty-first century.

PART I

Medieval and Reformation Antecedents

2

Mystical Union and Spiritual Marriage

From the Middle Ages to the Eighteenth Century

Before beginning a close examination of American Presbyterian sources, it is instructive to take a look at the uses of the metaphor of mystical union, the imagery of spiritual marriage, and language from the Song of Songs, examining examples from the medieval era through the eighteenth century. Even a brief and selective survey shows that this language and imagery pervade the theological and devotional works of Christians over the centuries. Although this collection of examples is far from exhaustive, one is able to see how these linguistic themes enliven the theological imagination of the church throughout the ages. Evidence of an allegorical interpretation of the Song of Songs is seen as early as the third century in the writings of Hippolytus of Rome, who lived around 200 CE. Although only fragments of his commentary on the biblical book are extant, there is evidence that he saw the lovers of 1:4 as Christ and those whom he had married and brought into the church. Origen (who flourished in the middle of the third century and was probably influenced by Hippolytus) favored an interpretation that assigned the role of bride to the church, but he also sometimes referred to the individual believer's soul as being in union with Christ.[1] Various patristic authors favored allegorical interpretations of the book as well. Attention to the Song of Songs peaked in the twelfth century, however, as numerous monastics and mystics delved into the book; the Cistercian monk Bernard of Clairvaux (1090–1153) represents the culmination of this surge of interest.

---

1. Marvin H. Pope, *Song of Songs*, Anchor Bible (New York: Doubleday, 1977), 114–15; Roland Murphy, *The Song of Songs* (Minneapolis: Augsburg Fortress, 1990), 17.

BERNARD OF CLAIRVAUX AND
OTHER MEDIEVAL FIGURES

Bernard's most notable work was a series of eighty-six sermons on the Song of Songs, which treat only the first two chapters of the book.[2] Rather than taking an exegetical approach, Bernard "primarily explored the spiritual dimensions of human experience,"[3] and so the language of the Song was used to explore any number of spiritual and theological concerns as well as that of spiritual union. As Michael Casey explains, Bernard's approach to the book was essentially eschatological; the Song is about the love between Christ (the Word) and the church (or the soul), but that love can only be fully realized in the life to come. In this life, then, the soul longs for union with Christ, and spiritual marriage is a prominent metaphor for understanding Christian devotion.[4] Casey points to sermon 83 (ca. 1152) as the most significant expression of Bernard's understanding of spiritual marriage:

> What can be a source of greater pleasure than such a close union of wills? What can be more desirable than the love by which you, O soul, are not satisfied with human teaching, but go directly to the Word, remaining joined to the Word, familiarly relating and discussing whatever falls within the mind's grasp and the range of bold desire?

Such a soul has really entered into a spiritual and holy contract of marriage.

> Perhaps, instead of "contract," I should say "contact," since there is here, without a doubt, question of an embrace. This is because when two will the same things and reject the same things, they become one spirit.[5]

Casey goes on to explain that for Bernard, "spiritual marriage takes place when the soul, undeterred by its limited capacity to love, gives itself totally to responding to its experience of the love of God."[6] The soul is first loved by Christ, the Word, and it is only in reflecting that love that the soul can reciprocate. "Happy is the one who is thus anticipated by the blessing of such sweetness!" cries Bernard. "Happy is the one to whom it is given to experience the great pleasure of this embrace!" This love is one "which is both strong and

---

2. Pope, *Song of Songs*, 122–23.

3. Murphy, *The Song of Songs*, 28.

4. Michael Casey, *Athirst for God: Spiritual Desire in Bernard of Clairvaux's Sermons on the Song of Songs* (Kalamazoo, MI: Cistercian Publications, 1988), 190–91.

5. Bernard of Clairvaux, *Sermo super Cantica canticorum* 83.3; quoted in Casey, *Athirst for God*, 195–96.

6. Casey, *Athirst for God*, 198.

intimate, which joins two not into one flesh, but into one spirit, so that they are no longer two, but one."[7] This is but a tiny sampling of Bernard's writings on spiritual desire and mystical union with Christ, yet it gives us a glimpse of the spirituality that is entwined with the theology.

More than two hundred years after the death of Bernard, French scholar Jean Gerson (1363–1429) picked up the themes of spiritual marriage and mystical union in his own writings. Throughout his life as a theologian and mystical writer, Gerson sought to combine theological inquiry with affective knowledge of God. One of the key figures to which he turned in that endeavor was Bernard of Clairvaux. In his sermon on the feast of Saint Bernard (probably preached in 1402), Gerson took for his text a line from the Song of Songs—"Sustain me with flowers, refresh me with apples, because I am languishing with love" (2:5; cf. Vg.)—using them as "a summation of Bernard's life and desire to experience the love of God."[8] Gerson was interested in constructing a "mystical theology" that included an understanding of mystical union. For Gerson, this union does not presume the dissolving of the soul into the divine or the loss of the creaturely self. Rather, the soul desires God, moves toward God "through fervent and pure love," and experiences God "through the embrace of unitive love," which gives wisdom, "a savory knowledge of God."[9] It is not surprising, then, that Gerson found inspiration in the writings of Bernard in general and the Song of Songs in particular.

It lies beyond the bounds of this study to survey thoroughly the medieval landscape regarding the understanding of mystical union and the use of the imagery of spiritual marriage. Yet it is useful to point out that, as Caroline Walker Bynum explains, the language of "nuptial mysticism," or *Brautmystik* ("the use of nuptial and erotic imagery to describe the soul's union with God"), is common in medieval literature. From the twelfth century onward, one finds more and more "female erotic and sexual experience used to describe the soul's union with Christ."[10] One additional example, from the writings of Hildegard of Bingen (1098–1179), is particularly interesting since here the author places marriage to Christ within the context of the Eucharist. In describing a vision she writes:

---

7. Bernard of Clairvaux, *Sermo super Cantica canticorum* 83.6; quoted in Casey, *Athirst for God*, 199.

8. Jean Gerson, *Early Works*, translated and introduced by Brian Patrick McGuire, preface by Bernard McGinn (New York and Mahwah, NJ: Paulist Press, 1998), 26.

9. Steven E. Ozment, *Homo Spiritualis: A Comparative Study of the Anthropology of Johannes Tauler, Jean Gerson and Martin Luther (1509–16) in the Context of Their Theological Thought* (Leiden: E. J. Brill, 1969), 78–79.

10. Caroline Walker Bynum, *Jesus as Mother: Studies in the Spirituality of the High Middle Ages* (Berkeley: University of California Press, 1982), 138–41, 171.

> And after these things, I saw the Son of God hanging on the Cross, and the aforementioned image of a woman coming forth like a bright radiance from the ancient counsel. By divine power she was led to Him, and raised herself upward so that she was sprinkled by the blood from his side; and thus, by the will of the Heavenly Father, she was joined with Him in happy betrothal and nobly dowered with his body and blood.[11]

Commenting on this vision, Roman Catholic scholar Owen F. Cummings explains that here "the church is imaged as a bride prepared for marriage to her husband. Christ crucified is the husband of the church, and Lady Church's dowry is his body and blood. Every time the eucharist is celebrated, this event is remembered by the Father as the dowry of Lady Church." He further reports that this same vision is represented in a miniature painted under Hildegard's supervision: "in medieval dress and under the image of marriage, the indissoluble union of Christ and church are affirmed."[12]

Yet medieval Christians heard this sort of physical—even sexual—language differently than do contemporary Christians. In dealing with medieval interpretations of the Song of Songs, Ann E. Matter explains that commentaries "portray the human soul as the female member of the love relationship, and consistently portray this soul, no matter the gender of the body, as the female character of the love story." Gender, then, is not the key issue here; "medieval Christians thought about physicality with a complex of associations which are not immediately recognizable to us. An effort of cultural translation is thus called for in the analysis of these texts." What is important to remember, she counsels, is that to the medieval way of thinking, "spiritual union is also corporeal. . . . This tradition understood the Song of Songs as the *epithalamium* [wedding song] of a spiritual union which ultimately takes place between God and the resurrected Christian—both body and soul."[13]

This language of spiritual marriage is not restricted to the Middle Ages, however. Though it is wise to be cautious about claiming direct influence between particular medieval and Reformation figures, it is possible to see continuities in language and imagery, suggesting that the boundaries between pre- and post-Reformation figures—and between those who would eventually be known as Roman Catholics and Protestants—are not as impenetrable

11. Hildegard of Bingen, *Scivias* [2.6], trans. Mother Columba Hart, OSB, and Jane Bishop (New York and Mahwah, NJ: Paulist Press, 1990), 237.

12. Owen F. Cummings, "Mystical Women and the Eucharist," *Antiphon* 5, no. 3 (2000): 12.

13. Ann E. Matter, *The Voice of My Beloved: The Song of Songs in Western Medieval Christianity* (Philadelphia: University of Pennsylvania Press, 1990), 141–42.

as the polemics of the era suggest.[14] Not surprisingly, the theme of mystical union abounds in the works of figures of the Catholic Reformation, most notably Teresa of Avila (1515–82) and St. John of the Cross (1542–91). Both describe a "spiritual betrothal" that would ultimately be consummated "in the indescribable bliss of the 'spiritual marriage.'"[15] John of the Cross authored his *Spiritual Canticle* (and its second redaction), a poem based on the Song of Songs, accompanied by a commentary on that poem. He depicts the soul's movement through three stages: "the Purgative, the Illuminative, and the Unitive." The beginning stanzas reflect the soul's seeking and cleansing; the second, the soul's spiritual betrothal to God. In the third and final section, he describes the soul's union, or marriage, with the divine, a "beatific state, to which only the soul in that perfect estate aspires."[16]

It was not only Roman Catholic writers who continued writing in the tradition of the medieval mystics. Nor was it only persons identified as "mystics" who used the metaphors of betrothal and marriage to describe the soul's relationship with the divine. Some of the church's most prominent Protestant theologians also relied on these expressions to explain their understanding of the believer's union with Christ, as well as to elucidate the doctrine of salvation.

MARTIN LUTHER

Perhaps it should come as no surprise that Martin Luther, who might be considered something of a bridge between two theological worlds, draws on the imagery of spiritual marriage in order to describe the soul's mystical union with Christ. His *Brief but Altogether Lucid Commentary on the Song of Songs* was the result of a series of twenty-four lectures he gave in Wittenberg during the years 1530 and 1531. Seeking to apply new exegetical methods, Luther rejects the allegorical interpretations of the Song that had prevailed for centuries, asserting instead that the Song reflects the relationship between God and the kingdom of Solomon (a relationship that could be extended to apply to the

14. Recent efforts in liturgical studies and church history have focused on identifying continuities as well as change in the religious practices of medieval and post-Reformation churches. See, e.g., Karen Maag and John D. Witvliet, eds., *Worship in Medieval and Early Modern Europe: Change and Continuity in Religious Practice* (Notre Dame, IN: University of Notre Dame Press, 2004).

15. E. W. Trueman Dicken, "Teresa of Avila and John of the Cross," in *The Study of Spirituality*, ed. Cheslyn Jones, Geoffrey Wainwright, and Edward Yarnold, SJ (New York: Oxford University Press, 1986), 374–75.

16. John of the Cross, *The Complete Works of Saint John of the Cross, Doctor of the Church*, vol. 2, trans. and ed. E. Allison Peers, new ed. (London: Burns, Oates, & Washbourne, 1953), 185.

church). In spite of his efforts to rely on the new historical criticism, however, he occasionally falls back on allegorical explanations, relating the bride of the Song to both the church and the individual soul.[17]

Perhaps more significant for this study, however, is his treatise *The Freedom of a Christian* (1520). Referring to Ephesians 5:31–32, Luther asserts that the soul is united with Christ "as a bride is united with her bridegroom. By this mystery, as the Apostle teaches, Christ and the soul become one flesh." Since they are one flesh, "there is between them a true marriage," which means that Christ the bridegroom takes on all of the evil and sin of the bride. "By the wedding ring of faith," Luther writes, "[Christ] shares in the sins, death, and pains of hell which are his bride's. . . . He makes them his own and acts as if they were his own and as if he himself had sinned; he suffered, died, and descended into hell that he might overcome them all."[18]

Luther's understanding of spiritual marriage, then, is tied to his doctrine of salvation by grace through faith, rather than to a description of spiritual or mystical experience. Nevertheless, the imagery he uses is vivid and evocative. At times he uses language from the Song of Songs to make his point:

> Who can understand the riches of the glory of this grace? Here this rich and divine bridegroom Christ marries this poor, wicked harlot, redeems her from all her evil, and adorns her with all his goodness. Her sins cannot now destroy her, since they are laid upon Christ and swallowed up by him. And she has that righteousness in Christ, her husband, of which she may boast as of her own and which she can confidently display alongside her sins in the face of death and hell and say, "If I have sinned, yet my Christ, in whom I believe, has not sinned, and all his is mine and all mine is his," as the bride in the Song of Solomon [2:16] says, "My beloved is mine and I am his."[19]

Luther makes use of marital imagery in his commentary on Isaiah 53, where, as Bengt R. Hoffman observes, "the language of the Bible and the mystic's conjugal imagery fit well together." "True faith," Luther writes, "states this, 'My beloved is mine, and I embrace him with gladness.'" Furthermore, as Hoffman points out in his discussion of Luther's sermon on Matthew 22:1–14 (1537), "Life with Christ is like 'a secret wedding.'" Writes Luther:

---

17. Murphy, *The Song of Songs*, 33–35.

18. Martin Luther, *The Freedom of a Christian*, trans. W. A. Lambert, rev. Harold J. Grimm, from the American Edition of Luther's Works 31, in *Three Treatises* (Philadelphia: Fortress Press, 1986), 286–87.

19. Ibid., 287.

> Now life is like a hidden, secret, spiritual wedding that cannot be seen by mortal eyes and cannot be grasped through intellectual reasoning. Only faith can grasp it, by holding fast to the Word. It is in such a way that faith hears of this wedding—yet understands it only in a dim fashion, since the flesh is so reluctant.

Again, in the same sermon, Luther proclaims that "as a bride in heartfelt trust relies on her bridegroom and regards her bridegroom's heart as her own, so you ought to trust in Christ's love and not doubt that He has the same devotion to you as you have to your own heart."[20]

EARLY REFORMED FIGURES

The Song of Songs is used widely by early Reformers in sermons, lectures, commentaries, liturgies, and other writings. In the early part of the sixteenth century, scholars from a variety of traditions commented in some way or another on the Canticles. In the Reformed tradition, three figures stand out: Konrad Pellikan (1478–1556), Pierre Robert Olivétan (ca. 1506–38), and Theodore Bibliander (ca. 1504–64).

Konrad Pellikan, the first Christian scholar to produce a Hebrew grammar, was one of the best Hebraists of the first half of the sixteenth century.[21] He was among several Christian Hebrew scholars of the time who translated and commented on the Song of Songs.[22] His commentary presents the Canticles as an *épithalame*: a series of fourteen wedding poems sung between God and the faithful soul, or between God and the church. Pellikan asserts that Solomon, who was divinely inspired when he wrote the songs, turned poems about natural love into contemplations of the goodness of God toward the faithful.[23] For Pellikan, the beauty of the young women (1:8) represents the church as a multitude of faithful souls, who are created in the image of God,[24] and the longed-for kiss of the beloved (1:2) corresponds to the desire that the faithful might receive the grace of God given in Jesus Christ.[25]

---

20. Bengt R. Hoffman, *Theology of the Heart: The Role of Mysticism in the Theology of Martin Luther*, ed. Pearl Willemssen Hoffman (Minneapolis: Kirk House Publishers, 1998), 99–100.

21. Max Engammare, *"Qu'il me baise des baisiers de sa bouche"* [Song 1:2]: *Le Cantique des cantiques à la Renaissance*; Étude et bibliographie (Geneva: Librairie Droz, 1993), 171.

22. Ibid., 154.

23. Ibid., 275.

24. Ibid., 276.

25. Ibid.

In notes written in 1543, Pellikan points to the Canticles as prophesying the incarnation of the Son of God, especially as developed in the eighth chapter of the Song. Other images and words illustrate the relationship between the spouse and the espoused, that is, between Christ and the church.[26] Although Pellikan's commentaries contain only the spiritual sense of the Song of Songs, he acknowledges the difficulty of interpreting the book[27] and gradually adopts a more allegorical approach.[28]

The work of Olivétan shows some of the same struggle, as exhibited in two radically different interpretations of the book. A scholar of both Hebrew and Greek, Olivétan produced two sets of notes on the Song of Songs, one set in 1535 and another in 1538. His first interpretation focuses on the sensuality of the text; basing his work on a historical and literal approach, he views the Canticles as relating to the love of Solomon for his spouse. He refers to the "spouse and his virgins" without ever naming Christ or the church, opting for an interpretation shared by few Christian scholars save Castellio (see below).[29] After discussing the book with a cousin, however—none other than John Calvin—Olivétan's comments on the Song of Songs change drastically. Now desire is for eternal faith, and beauty is interpreted as eschatological joy. Now, Olivétan asserts, the Canticles describe a divine and spiritual love between Christ and his spouse, the church.[30]

Like the debate between Calvin and Castellio that would follow a few years later, the shift in Olivétan's exposition of the Song of Songs depicts the tensions inherent in interpreting biblical love poetry. As scholar Max Engammare wryly comments, although a solely literal interpretation of the book was rare, here and there commentators would remark on the sensual quality of the book. As he puts it, "These commentators remain sexual men, not insensitive to female beauty omnipresent in and between the verses of the biblical poem: 'the kisses of her mouth' may touch certain sensual cheeks."[31]

Theodore Bibliander was also among the finest Christian biblical scholars of the time. The translator of the Canticles for a new Latin edition of the Bible in Zurich, he also added interpretive notes, as did Pellikan. Both sets of marginal notes include variants of translation, biblical parallels, and some spiritual comments. Bibliander gives a nod to the literal sense of the text by providing the significance of certain words in Hebrew and the contexts in which they might be used. (For example, in a note on 7:3 he mentions that

26. Ibid., 278.
27. Ibid., 320–21.
28. Ibid., 349.
29. Ibid., 287.
30. Ibid., 290–91.
31. Ibid., 317–18.

mandrakes are associated with love.) Nevertheless, he simply provides the Hebrew text and draws no conclusions.[32]

In his magisterial work on the interpretation of the Song of Songs in the first half of the sixteenth century, Engammare concludes that the ecclesiastical approach has certainly dominated, an observation borne out by these few brief examples.[33] These scholars were influenced by humanism, to be sure, as evidenced in the seriousness with which they studied the original biblical texts. At the same time, they moved away from more-mystical understandings and toward more-ecclesial ones, often seeing the Canticles as "an initiating journey for beginners in the faith." As Engammare puts it, "Our authors are moderns."[34]

THE CALVIN-CASTELLIO DEBATE

In spite of the attention that other early Reformed scholars gave to the Song of Songs, John Calvin never wrote a commentary on the Canticles. He was not unconcerned with the book, however, as shown by the debate between him and his Genevan associate Sebastian Castellio. Beginning in 1544, the two scholars engaged in a public debate over hermeneutics. Was the Song of Songs to be interpreted literally or allegorically? Castellio, who favored an interpretive approach that relied on human reason and moral principles, concluded that the book was a rather racy love poem written by Solomon. As such, he questioned its place in the biblical canon but never went so far as to reject it outright. For his part, Calvin understood the Canticles allegorically, reading the book as an analogy of faith. Even though both scholars agreed on the importance of the words of the text, and on not moving too quickly to a christological interpretation, they never did see eye to eye on the overall interpretive scheme.

After three years of arguing over the Song of Songs (as well as the question of Christ's descent into hell in the Apostles' Creed), Castellio left Geneva. As Pope puts it, the dispute "made Geneva too small for the two of them." He reports that "Calvin issued a statement on Castellio's departure: 'Our principal dispute concerned the Song of Songs. He considers that it is a lascivious and obscene poem, in which Solomon has described his shameless love affairs.'"[35] Although one might characterize Calvin's remark as inflammatory,

---

32. Ibid., 197–99.
33. Ibid., 487.
34. Ibid., 316–17.
35. Pope, *Song of Songs*, 126–27.

it is an indication that he accepted the church's long tradition of allegorical interpretation, a tradition put forth by Bernard and other early and medieval scholars.

In fact, Calvin drew on the work of Bernard, and especially from his commentary on the Song of Songs. Just how he used this work and that of earlier medieval theologians, as well as a more-thorough discussion of Calvin's understanding of mystical union (and that of his Genevan successor, Theodore Beza), follows in chapter 3.

THE PURITANS

It is clear from the many Puritan sources available to the contemporary reader that the language of mystical union and spiritual marriage did not die out with the Reformers. The Puritans produced numerous commentaries on the Song of Songs and greatly admired that of Bernard; as Gordon Wakefield points out, they were "not afraid to talk of rapes, ravishments, and ecstasies." Charles Hambrick-Stowe explains that Puritan authors were well acquainted with the classic devotional works of the pre-Reformation church; most popular among them seemed to be the works of Augustine and Bernard, along with Thomas à Kempis's *The Imitation of Christ*, which began to be published in Protestant editions. In fact, Hambrick-Stowe observes that "the Puritan devotional writing that blossomed in the early seventeenth century was modeled on earlier Roman Catholic devotional literature." Among the characteristics that found an echo in later works was the use of language from the Song of Songs:

> The sensual imagery of the Song of Songs nourished devotional writing among all parties, and the image of the garden particularly emerged as a metaphor for the devotional setting. As the beloved came to his spouse in the garden, so Christ came to the devout soul in meditation and prayer. "I have come into my garden, my sister, my spouse: I have gathered my myrrh with my spice; I have eaten my honey-comb with my honey; I have drunk my wine with my milk: eat, O friends; drink, yea, drink abundantly, O beloved" (5:1). . . . Catholic manuals used in their titles such phrases as "A Paradise of Prayers," "The Flowers of Lodowickes," "The Garden of Our Blessed Lady." Protestants followed with "The Flower of Godly Prayers," "A Garden of Spiritual Flowers," and "A Posie Gathered out of Mr. Dod's Garden."[36]

36. Charles Hambrick-Stowe, *The Practice of Piety: Puritan Devotional Disciplines in Seventeenth-Century New England* (Chapel Hill: University of North Carolina Press, 1982), 28–29.

Even a sampling of Puritan sources shows the influence of earlier devotional traditions. In Thomas Shepard's sermon "Behold the Happiness of those Espoused to Christ" (from his series The Parable of the Ten Virgins, preached between 1636 and 1640), Christ is the husband and woos believers to a match, an espousal. Similarly, in "Containing Motives and Arguments to Persuade Us Unto the Love of Christ, and to Be Espoused to Him," Shepard asserts that the love of Christ "is a conjugal love"; Christ is a suitor who "makes love to thee." In "Consider How Christ Will Love You," Shepard takes the marriage imagery even further, describing how Christ the husband will protect, comfort, enrich, and counsel his believer-bride, from whom he will never part.[37]

Thomas Watson (1620–86) uses similarly vivid imagery in his sermon "Mystic Union Between Christ and the Saints," which is based on Song of Songs 2:16, "My beloved is mine and I am his." Immediately he makes a doctrinal statement: "There is conjugal union between Christ and believers," and then launches into an exposition of his claim. In Watson's economy, "God the Father gives the Bride, God the Son receives the Bride, and God the Holy Spirit ties the knot in marriage." The saints are married to Christ, "the best Husband, 'the chiefest among ten thousand (Song 5:10),'" who is met in heaven fully, but on earth is met in preaching and at the Table:

> See the reason why the saints so rejoice in the Word and sacrament, because here they meet with their Husband, Christ. The wife desires to be in the presence of her husband. The ordinances are the chariot in which Christ rides, the lattice through which he looks forth and shows his smiling face. Here Christ displays the banner of love (Song 2:4). The Lord's Supper is nothing other than a pledge and earnest of that eternal communion which the saints shall have with Christ in heaven. Then he will take the spouse into his bosom. If Christ is so sweet in an ordinance, when we have only short glances and dark glimpses of him by faith, oh then, how delightful and ravishing will his presence be in heaven when we see him face to face and are for ever in his loving embraces![38]

The sacramental note is also sounded in the meditations of Edward Taylor, whose poems express a fervent longing for Christ. "Edward Taylor, perhaps more than any other New England Puritan, knew what it was to yearn for

---

37. Thomas Shepard, *The parable of the ten virgins opened & applied: Being the substance of divers sermons on Matth. 25.1, 13 . . . by Thomas Shepard, late worthy and faithfull pastor of the church of Christ at Cambridge in New-England* (London: Printed by J. H. for John Rothwell and Samuel Thomson, 1660).

38. Thomas Watson, *The Godly Man's Picture, Drawn with a Scripture Pencil, or Some Characteristic Marks of a Man who Is Going to Heaven* (1666; reprint, Edinburgh: Banner of Truth Trust, 1992), 246–47.

the soul's unitive state with Christ as mystic Lover, which we associate with Teresa or John of the Cross," explains Hambrick-Stowe.[39] His "Preparatory Meditations Before My Approach to the Lord's Supper" (1682) begin with this ardent expression:

> What Love is this of thine, that Cannot bee
>   In thine Infinity, O Lord, Confinde,
> Unless it in thy very Person see,
>   Infinity, and Finity Conjoyn'd?
>   What hath thy Godhead, as not satisfide
>   Marri'de our Manhood, making it its Bride?
>
> O, Matchless Love! filling Heaven to the brim!
>   O're running it: all running o're beside
> This World! Nay Overflowing Hell; wherein
>   For thine Elect, there rose a mighty Tide!
>   That there our Veans might through thy Person bleed,
>   To quench those flames, that else would on us feed.
>
> Oh! that thy Love might overflow my Heart!
>   To fire the same with Love: for Love I would.
> But oh! My streight'ned Breast! my Lifeless Sparke!
>   My Fireless Flame! What Chilly Love, and Cold?
>   In measure small! In Manner Chilly! See.
>   Lord blow the Coal: Thy love Enflame in mee.[40]

Other of Taylor's meditations are based on verses from the Song of Songs ("Let Him Kiss Me with the Kisses of His Mouth" and a "Reflexion" on Canticles 2:1, "I am the rose of Sharon"). Here again, the believer is sick with love, begging kisses from Christ, and sighing with longing for the Lord/Lover who meets the faithful soul in the feast.

A thorough exposition of the use of mystical marriage in Puritanism would require its own full-length study.[41] The sermons of Richard Sibbes, Lewis Bayly's spiritual classic *The Practice of Piety*, and *Mystical Marriage* by Sir Francis Rous (the author of metrical psalms endorsed by the Westminster divines) are among the myriad Puritan works that engage metaphors of love, sex, and marriage to describe the soul's union and communion with Christ. These

---

39. Charles E. Hambrick-Stowe, ed., *Early New England Meditative Poetry: Anne Bradstreet and Edward Taylor* (New York and Mahwah, NJ: Paulist Press, 1988), 13.

40. Ibid., 158–59.

41. In fact, one such study can be found in Jonathan Jong-Chun Won, "Communion with Christ: An Exposition and Comparison of the Doctrine of Union and Communion with Christ in Calvin and the English Puritans" (PhD diss., Westminster Theological Seminary, 1989), in which the author examines the writings of William Perkins, Richard Sibbes, John Cotton, Thomas Goodwin, and John Owen.

themes appear in less-public works as well. As Leslie Lindenauer has shown, the letters and diaries of colonial Puritans are also full of marital imagery to describe the relationship between Christ and believers. The rhetoric of spiritual marriage, then, was not only the property of clerics and academics, but of common people as well.[42]

THE MORAVIANS

For the Moravians of Germany, England, and America in the seventeenth and eighteenth centuries, hymnody was a significant expression of theology. Among the storehouse of vivid images they used was that of spiritual marriage. The theology of Nikolaus Ludwig, Count von Zinzendorf, was foundational for the Moravian community, and as Craig Atwood explains, the metaphor of marriage figures in his writings:

> Zinzendorf focused intently on the atoning death of Jesus and made the blood and wounds of Christ the primary object of devotion for his followers. This blood mysticism was joined to the idea of the soul's mystical marriage to Christ. All believers, men and women, were to be brides of Christ. Furthermore, Zinzendorf and his followers also worshipped the Holy Spirit as "mother." This language of motherhood and the soul's marriage to the crucified Jesus offended many of Zinzendorf's contemporaries, including John Wesley, George Whitefield, and Gilbert Tennent.[43]

The Moravian leader also saw the conversion experience as akin to falling in love and marrying:

> And as soon as they are with him, there is an embrace, a kiss, a heart, thus he draws like a magnet, rises them all up to himself, lays them all deep in his holy side, so that a soul in that hour and at that moment when she has experienced it can say: much happiness to eternal life, if only my whole life could remain like this![44]

While marital imagery was used in general terms to describe the relationship between Christ and the believer, it was also employed to depict the

---

42. Leslie J. Lindenauer, *Piety and Power: Gender and Religious Culture in the American Colonies, 1630–1700* (New York: Routledge, 2002), 44.

43. Craig C. Atwood, *Community of the Cross: Moravian Piety in Colonial Bethlehem* (University Park: Pennsylvania State University Press, 2004), 7.

44. Ibid., 92.

mystical union that occurs in communion. In one hymn, simply titled "Love," one observes both maternal and spousal images at work:

> Right inward must the soul remain,
> And suck Love's breasts for her nutrition,
> retiring so from Lust as Pain,
> To soft Composure's sweet fruition.
> If now the En'my finds that those
> Ignoble Objects will not suit us,
> Which to our Bridegroom he'd oppose,
> Who is so exquisitely beauteous:
> Then does he try his might
> To cause a gloomy night
> If possible, our eyes to cover,
> that we, in shadows dull,
> Can't see the beautiful,
> And gracious Face of our soul's Lover.[45]

Another hymn, "O du seelen-Brautigam," begins with marital imagery, naming Christ as "Bridegroom of the soul."[46] Two other hymns name Christ as Bridegroom, Husband, and Lamb, and the believer as spouse, sinner, and child.[47] Throughout these hymns one hears the language of union and the assertion that the marriage between Christ and the believer is completely consummated only in heaven.

"Mein Freund ist mir, und ich bin Ihm" (cf. Song 2:16) sings of desire for the Bridegroom while also incorporating a favorite Moravian image, that of the side hole (the wound in Jesus' pierced side).

> My Friend's to me, and I'm to him
> A fix'd unturning Cherubim;
> Ever each other looking on,
> Much as He likes, and as I can.
>
> He loveth me most tenderly,
> And I love Him much more than me;
> He turns to me with Heart on fire,
> And I to Him with chaste desire.

---

45. [Moravian Church], *A Collection of Hymns of the Children of God in all Ages, from the Beginning till now. In Two Parts. Designed chiefly for the Use of the Congregations in Union with the Brethren's Church* (London: Printed; and to be had at all the Brethren's chapels, 1754), nos. 152, 107. 1754 MORA, Archives and Manuscript Department, Pitts Theology Library, Emory University.

46. Ibid., nos. 154, 107.

47. Ibid., nos. 155, 107–8, 156, 109.

He seeks within my Heart to rest,
And my Cry's always to his Breast:
He longs to be within my soul,
And I within his dear Side's hole.

My spirit's Desire appeases he,
I dwell in Him, and He in me!
He comes to me with Kiss of grace,
And I to him with blushing Face.

His thoughts are taken up with me,
And mine with him continually:
The sweetest sound to me's his Name,
And I am his delightful Theme.

He is my Bridegroom, I his Bride,
My soul's to him in marriage ty'd;
Nothing shall sep'rate Him from me,
Nor me from him eternally.[48]

The language of marriage and longing are connected with the Lord's Supper in "Schmucke dich, O liebe seele":

Trim my lamp, O Soul betrothed!
Sin and darkness be quite loathed;
Come into the Light where clearest,
Duly mind what Dress thou wearest.
For the gracious Lord by token,
Has thee as his guest bespoken:
He who Heav'n's Expanse can manage,
Will now rest in thy poor Cottage.

Hasten, as for brides is fitting,
Give thy Bridegroom soon the meeting,
Who knocks soft with Grace's hammer
On the door of thy Heart's chamber.
Ope the Spirit's Portals speedy,
With thy heart's Address be ready,
"Come my Friend! (say) let me kiss thee,
Hold thee fast, and ne'er dismiss thee."

How do I wish spirit's hunger
Lamb! to taste thy Goodness linger:
O how use I oft with crying,
After this Food to be sighing!

---

48. Ibid., nos. 467, 272.

O how use I to be thirsting
For the Drink from life's Prince bursting!
All my Bones with God connected,
This I wish through Christ effected.[49]

These are but a few examples of the usage of marital imagery that is wide-spread in Moravian hymnody, but they show the presence of an idiom that has prevailed since medieval times.[50]

THE WESLEYS, WHITEFIELD, AND WATTS

The eighteenth century saw a great deal of spiritual fervor on both sides of the Atlantic. Although John Wesley would later be critical of mysticism in general, and the Moravians in particular, he was influenced by a wide variety of mystical writers and by his contacts with Moravians early in his ministry. During his ill-fated journey to Georgia, he engaged in conversations with A. G. Spangenburg and translated Moravian hymns. Eventually he would incorporate into his own theological and spiritual program what he called the "gold" of the mystics.[51] Charles Wesley, who came to the communion table and "sealed his marriage vows,"[52] penned with his brother the hymns that express the core of their eucharistic theology. Although the Wesleys do not make extensive use of marital imagery, they speak of the "banquetting house" (cf. Song 2:4), and the "marriage-feast."[53] An understanding of eschatological hope in which

---

49. Ibid., nos. 468, 272.

50. At least one minister of the gospel, John Watson (1725–83), was scandalized by the Moravian hymn texts. He expressed his opinions in his *Letter to the clergy of the church known by the Name of Unitas Fratrum, or Moravians, Concerning a Remarkable book of hymns Us'd in their Congregations' pointing out several inconsistencies, and Absurdities in the said Book* (London: printed for J. Payne, and sold by R. Whitworth, printer and bookseller in Manchester, 1756); 1756 WATS, Archives and Manuscripts Department, Pitts Theology Library, Emory University. Watson was particularly offended by the hymns about the wound in Christ's side; after quoting two stanzas of one such text, he writes, "Really, Gentlemen, bad as the Performances of Sternhold and Hopkins may be deem'd, this, and the greatest Part of your Book is incomparably worse." After quoting lines from several hymns using marital imagery, he declined to include more, because "I am really asham'd to transcribe" them (25).

51. A. Raymond George, "John Wesley and the Methodist Movement," in Jones, Wainwright, and Yarnold, *The Study of Spirituality*, 456.

52. John C. Bowmer, *The Sacrament of the Lord's Supper in Early Methodism* (London: Dacre Press, 1951), 189.

53. J. Ernest Rattenbury, *The Eucharistic Hymns of John and Charles Wesley*, ed. Timothy J. Crouch, 2nd American ed. (Akron, OH: OSL Publications, 1996), 34, 58.

communion is a foretaste of heavenly bliss can be heard in sixteen hymns that fall under the category of "the sacrament is a pledge of heaven." Hymn 93 speaks of the "rapturous joy and love and praise" the believer will experience in heaven and compares the earthly banquet with the heavenly one:

> The wine which doth His passion show,
> We soon with Him shall drink it new
>   In yonder dazzling courts above;
> Admitted to the heavenly feast,
> We shall His choicest blessings taste,
>   And banquet on his richest love.
> We soon the midnight cry shall hear,
> Arise, and meet the Bridegroom near,
>   The marriage of the Lamb is come;
> Attended by His heavenly friends,
> The glorious King of saints descends
>   To take His bride in triumph home.[54]

The Eucharist is "a soul-transporting feast," and this "mystic banquet" leads to heaven's glory. All glories are not in the next life, however; even in this life, believers experience something of heaven's rapture:

> The light of life eternal darts
>   Into our souls a dazzling ray,
> A drop of heaven o'erflows our hearts,
>   And deluges the house of clay.
>
> Sure pledge of ecstasies unknown
>   Shall this Divine communion be;
> The ray shall rise into a sun,
>   The drop shall swell into a sea.[55]

All around Britain and America, meanwhile, George Whitefield was drawing crowds by the hundreds, even thousands, preaching sermons such as "Christ the Believer's Husband," in which he asks his listeners to recall an experience of spiritual delight:

> Canst thou not remember, when, after a long struggle with unbelief, Jesus appeared to thee, as altogether lovely, mighty and willing to save? And canst thou not reflect upon a season, when thy own stubborn heart was made to bend; and thou wast made willing to embrace him, as freely offered to thee in the everlasting gospel? And canst thou

54. Ibid., 183.
55. Ibid., 186.

not, with pleasure unspeakable, reflect on some happy period, some certain point of time, in which a sacred something (perhaps thou could not then well tell what) did captivate, and fill thy heart, so that thou could say, in a rapture of holy surprise, and ecstasy of divine love, "My Lord and my God! My beloved is mine, and I am his; I know that my Redeemer liveth"; or, to keep to the words of our text, "My Maker is my husband [Isaiah 54:5]."[56]

The marital imagery served Whitefield in a variety of ways. In "Christ the Best Husband," preached to "a society of young women," he urged his listeners to accept Christ's offer of marriage, where they will find "mutual choice," "mutual affection," "mutual union," and "mutual obligation." Borrowing language from the Song of Songs, he tells them of their Savior's love for them:

And the Lord Jesus Christ desireth to see this beauty in his spouse, for he cries out, "O my dove, thou art in the clefts of the rock, in the secret places of the stairs, let me see thy countenance, let me hear thy voice, for sweet is thy voice, and thy countenance is comely." He calleth his spouse his love, being the dear object of his love; and he admireth her loveliness; he repeats it twice in one verse, "Behold thou art fair, my love, behold thou art fair." Thus you see he describes their beauty. And then, my sisters, we have wonderful expression of Christ to his spouse, "Thou hast ravished my heart, my sister, my spouse, thou hast ravished my heart with one of thine eyes, with one chain of thy neck." Thus you see how pleased the Lord Jesus Christ is with his spouse; and will not you, therefore, be espoused unto the Lord Jesus? I offer Jesus Christ to all of you; if you have been never so notorious for sin, if you have been as great a harlot as Mary Magdalen was, when once you are espoused to Christ, you shall be forgiven.[57]

Clearly the metaphors of marriage, espousal, and courtship were ones Whitefield drew on with energy and conviction.

Wherever Whitefield went, the people who gathered sang the hymns of Isaac Watts, whose *Hymns and Spiritual Songs* (1707) had become widely used. Watts is well known for his psalm paraphrases and his prolific hymn writing, but fewer know his paraphrases of the Song of Songs. Hymns 66 through 78

---

56. George Whitefield, *The Works of the Reverend George Whitefield, Late of Pembroke-College, Oxford, and Chaplain to the Rt. Hon. The Countess of Huntingdon, containing all his sermons and tracts which have been already published: With a select collection of letters written to his most intimate friends, and persons of distinction in England, Scotland, Ireland, and America, from the year 1734 to 1770, including the whole period of his ministry. Also, some other pieces on important subjects, never before printed, prepared by himself for the press. To which is prefixed, an account of his life, compiled from his original papers and letters*, vol. V (London: Printed for Edward and Charles Dilly, in the Poultry, 1772), 180–81.

57. Ibid., 69–70.

represent his metrical versions of most of the contents of the biblical book. Like the metrical psalms, the hymns on the Song of Songs incorporate christological themes; Jesus is the lover of the soul. Hymn 66, "Christ the King at his Table," based on selected verses from the first chapter of the Song of Songs, begins thus:

> Let him embrace my Soul, and prove
> Mine Interest in his heavenly Love:
> The Voice that tells me, *Thou art mine*,
> Exceeds the Blessings of the Vine.

The third verse identifies the Lover:

> *Jesus*, allure me by thy Charms,
> My Soul shall fly into thine Arms:
> Our wandering Feet thy favours bring
> To the Fair Chambers of the King.[58]

Hymn 67, based on Song of Songs 1:7, includes two verses that are clearly additions to the original text; they link the bride who seeks her spouse in the pastures to the one who seeks her lover in the sacrament:

> The Footsteps of thy Flock I see;
> Thy sweetest Pastures here they be;
> A wondrous Feast thy Love prepares,
> Bought with thy Wounds, and Groans, and Tears.
>
> His dearest Flesh he makes my Food,
> And bids me drink his richest Blood;
> Here to these Hills my Soul will come,
> Till my Beloved lead me home.[59]

In each title of the hymn, the church is identified as the spouse, yet the language of the hymns is intimate and personal, implying that it is not only the corporate body, but also the individual soul, who is espoused to Christ. Watts's paraphrases also include the same eschatological emphasis that the hymns of the Wesley brothers exhibit. Hymn 77 ends with these lines:

> In Paradise within the Gates
> An higher Entertainment waits;

---

58. Selma L. Bishop, *Hymns and Spiritual Songs of Isaac Watts, 1707–1748: A Study in Early Eighteenth Century Language Changes* (London: Faith Press, 1962), 60.

59. Ibid., 62.

Fruits new and old laid up in store,
Where we shall feed, but thirst no more.[60]

Watts's eucharistic hymns comprise book 3 of his *Hymns and Spiritual Songs*. Tucked into these reflections on the sufferings of Christ and the rhapsodizing about amazing love and the delights of the table—we find a reminder of the marital relationship:

Lord, how Divine thy Comforts are!
  How heavenly is the Place
Where *Jesus* spread the sacred Feast
  Of his redeeming Grace!
There the rich Bounties of our God
  And sweetest Glories shine,
There *Jesus* says, that, *I am his,*
  And my Beloved's mine.[61]

SUMMARY

In briefly surveying the use of marital imagery and language from the Song of Songs to describe mystical union, it has become clear that the usages that will be observed in the American Presbyterian sources are not at all unique. In fact, such a review indicates that Presbyterians were aware of the theological and spiritual movements that had preceded them and were going on around them. What is interesting about the Presbyterian expressions, however, is that the focus seems to be more clearly on the Lord's Supper as the locus of this communion with Christ. Although the American Presbyterians would have been in line with Calvin—who, as shall be demonstrated in the following chapter, understood union with Christ to happen in a general sense as well as in the specific context of communion—the chief use of marital imagery and language from the Song of Songs appears to be in preparation for the celebration of the Eucharist. This study, therefore, does not argue for the uniqueness of the Presbyterian expressions, but rather places them in the context of a history of interpretation, while acknowledging the particularity of the eucharistic context of American sacramental revivals.[62]

60. Ibid., 76.
61. Hymn 11, "Pardon Brought to Our Senses," in ibid., 358.
62. Research remains to be done on the use of the Song of Songs and other marital imagery throughout the history of Christian worship. One fascinating area of inquiry that is yet to be explored is the use of these metaphors in the Communion manuals of other traditions, notably Lutheran and Anglican.

After this cursory survey of a particular hermeneutical landscape, we will now turn our attention to John Calvin and his successor in Geneva, Theodore Beza. As the father of the Reformed tradition, Calvin was the theological ancestor of the American Presbyterian revivalists. His understanding of mystical union with Christ, particularly in the context of the Lord's Supper, is crucial to establishing an interpretive framework within which the American Presbyterian sources might be considered. For his part, Beza not only continued the theological tradition of Calvin but also produced a book of sermons on the Song of Songs. These sermons reflect the continuation of an allegorical interpretation of the book, while also making connections between the Canticles and the church's practice of communion.

An examination of sermons by Scots-Irish preachers who were involved in Scottish and American eucharistic revivals will show that their preaching was firmly grounded in a Reformed understanding of salvation, upholding the importance of repentance and renewal in the Christian life, emphasizing preparation for worthy participation in the Lord's Supper, and affirming that Christ is present in both Word and sacrament. In urging their hearers to make, or renew, a covenant with Christ at the Table, these preachers relied on the metaphor of spiritual marriage. Drawing on the Song of Songs and other biblical marital imagery, they sought to woo their hearers to union with Christ in communion. At this juncture, therefore, it is necessary to examine Calvin's own understanding of union with Christ as well as the metaphors he and Beza employ in their discussions.

3

John Calvin, Theodore Beza, and Mystical Union

After considering how the themes of mystical union and spiritual marriage were expounded upon by representative figures in the church's history, our attention now turns to Calvin's understanding of these topics and the metaphors he uses to discuss them. Several related subjects in Calvin's thought will also be considered. Calvin saw Word and sacrament as interdependent and thought that both effected union with Christ. His understanding of piety as a balance of cognition and emotion, or intellectual understanding and spiritual worship, is also tied to his views of mystical union. A discussion of Calvin's own brand of "mysticism" will conclude this inquiry into the reformer's thought. In part 2 of this study we will see that the theological foundation Calvin establishes, as well as the metaphorical language employed by his successor, Theodore Beza, are all expressed in the writings of the American and Scottish preachers considered here. This review of these Genevan reformers, then, will help to lay the groundwork for an examination of the preaching that took place at American sacramental occasions.

CALVIN'S UNDERSTANDING OF UNION WITH CHRIST

Union with Christ is a significant theme in Calvin's writings. Since he views mystical union as Trinitarian in nature, he does not distinguish carefully between union with God and union with Christ: believers are "united to Christ; and become one with God,"[1] all through the "work of the Holy Spirit."[2] Although Calvin frequently speaks of union with Christ in the context of his discussions on faith, he also asserts that this union is accomplished in the sacraments of baptism and the Lord's Supper, as well as in the preaching of the Word.

In Calvin's view, believers are united with Christ in two ways, one complete and one partial. Christ is first given in baptism, as believers are engrafted into the body, which is both the church and Christ himself.[3] This union is once and for all, yet also effected over and over again, as Christ continues to grow and dwell in those who receive him. This insight is crucial for the study at hand: it points to the necessity of ongoing repentance and renewal as a feature of the believer's union with Christ, as well to the eschatological thrust that has been observed in all of the preachers to be considered. The Christian life is one of "continual effort and exercise in the mortification of the flesh," says Calvin; the believer is "to hasten to God and yearn for him in order that, having been engrafted into the life and death of Christ, he may give attention to continual repentance."[4] This ongoing turning and returning to Christ is not an endless pursuit, but one that strains toward a goal. "Even on this earthly pilgrimage we know the sole and perfect happiness," Calvin counsels his readers, "but this happiness kindles our hearts more and more each day to desire it, until the full fruition of it shall satisfy it."[5] Tamburello helpfully elucidates this point: "For Calvin . . . there is one sense in which union with Christ is complete in the present life. . . . At the same time, [he] looks to the final resurrection as the ultimate locus of union with God."[6] In other words, the believer is united with Christ, once and for all, in baptism; yet she is also continually renewed, and union is repeatedly effected, until the final consummation.

One way that the union of Christ and the believer is continually effected—and perfected—is through the celebration of the Lord's Supper; in fact, as

1. John Calvin, *The Gospel according to St. John 11–21 and the First Epistle of John*, ed. David W. Torrance and Thomas F. Torrance, trans. T. H. L. Parker, Calvin's Commentaries (Edinburgh and London: Oliver & Boyd, 1961), 314.

2. John Calvin, *Commentary on the Epistle of Paul the Apostle to the Corinthians*, trans. John Pringle, vol. 1 (Grand Rapids: Wm. B. Eerdmans Publishing Co., 1948), 406; idem, *Institutes of the Christian Religion* [4.15.6], ed. John T. McNeill, trans. Ford Lewis Battles, Library of Christian Classics 20–21 (Philadelphia: Westminster Press, 1960), 1307–8.

3. Calvin, *Institutes* 4.15.6; idem, *Corinthians*, 1:406; idem, *Commentaries on the Epistles to Timothy, Titus, and Philemon*, trans. William Pringle (Grand Rapids: Wm. B. Eerdmans Publishing Co., 1948), 333.

4. Calvin, *Institutes* 3.3.20.

5. Ibid., 3.25.2.

6. Dennis Tamburello, *Union with Christ: John Calvin and the Mysticism of St. Bernard*, Columbia Series in Reformed Theology (Louisville, KY: Westminster John Knox, 1994), 89–90.

Brian Gerrish points out, Calvin's understanding of mystical union between believers (or the church) with Christ is "a pivotal theme in his doctrine of the Lord's Supper."[7] For Calvin, the mystical union that believers enjoy with Christ in communion is as important as the union that is effected in baptism.[8] In the meal, believers who are already engrafted into the body "may grow more and more together with him, until he perfectly joins us with him in the heavenly life."[9] Both sacraments, notes Ronald Wallace, have the same purpose in Calvin's view: "to testify, and to assist in effecting our union with the body of Christ." He explains further that "baptism . . . mainly bears witness to our initiation into this union, while the Lord's Supper is a sign of our continuation in this union."[10]

Calvin calls union with Christ "the special fruit of the Lord's Supper" and describes it thus:

> Godly souls can gather great assurance and delight from this Sacrament; in it they have a witness of our growth into one body with Christ such that whatever is his may be called ours. As a consequence, we may dare assure ourselves that eternal life, of which he is the heir, is ours; and that the Kingdom of heaven, into which he has already entered, can no more be cut off from us than from him; again, that we cannot be condemned for our sins, from whose guilt he has absolved us, since he willed to take them upon himself as if they were his own. This is the wonderful exchange which, out of his measureless benevolence, he has made with us; that, becoming Son of man with us, he has made us sons of God with him; that, by his descent to earth, he has prepared an ascent to heaven for us; that, by taking on our mortality, he has conferred his immortality upon us; that, accepting our weakness, he has strengthened us by his power; that, receiving our poverty unto himself, he has transferred his wealth to us; that, taking the weight of our iniquity upon himself (which oppressed us), he has clothed us with his righteousness.[11]

Lest the reader imagine that he describes some theological abstraction, Calvin insists that this union is "a mystery felt rather than explained."[12] It is, first of all, a true sharing in the body of Christ. Really partaking of the bread

---

7. B. A. Gerrish, *Grace and Gratitude: The Eucharistic Theology of John Calvin* (Minneapolis: Fortress Press, 1993), 72.

8. Ronald S. Wallace, *Calvin's Doctrine of the Word and Sacrament* (Grand Rapids: Wm. B. Eerdmans Publishing Co., 1953), 150.

9. Calvin, *Institutes* 4.17.33.

10. Wallace, *Calvin's Doctrine of the Word and Sacrament*, 150.

11. Calvin, *Institutes* 4.17.2.

12. Ibid., 4.17.4.

that is Christ's body matters, since his life passes into us and is made ours, "just as bread when taken as food imparts vigor to the body." Furthermore, in partaking, believers "embrace Christ not as appearing from afar but as joining himself to us that he may be our head, we his members."[13] This is not only a spiritual communion, Calvin cautions, but one with the very flesh and blood of Christ.

> I urge my readers not to confine their mental interest within these too narrow limits, but to strive to rise much higher than I can lead them. For, whenever this matter is discussed, when I have tried to say all, I feel that I have as yet said little in proportion to its worth. And although my mind can think beyond what my tongue can utter, yet even my mind is conquered and overwhelmed by the greatness of the thing. Therefore, nothing remains but to break forth in wonder at this mystery, which plainly neither the mind is able to conceive nor the tongue to express.[14]

CALVIN'S USE OF THE METAPHOR OF MARRIAGE

In commentaries, sermons, and the *Institutes*, Calvin refers to Ephesians 5:28–33, in which marriage between a man and a woman is compared to the bond between Christ and the church. Brian Gerrish explains that

> Calvin was fascinated by the notion of a sacred wedlock that makes us flesh of Christ's flesh and bone of his bone, and he noted that verse 32 says, "This is a great mystery, and I take it to mean Christ and the church." In his commentary on Ephesians 5:28–33, he calls it a "remarkable passage on the mystical communion [*de mystica communicatione*] that we have with Christ."[15]

Indeed, Calvin relies on Ephesians 5:28 (and the embedded reference to Genesis 2:23) to refute the Roman church's claim that marriage is a sacrament, insisting that Paul intended "to teach how Christ loved the church as himself, nay, how he made himself one with his bride the church." He continues:

> For when Eve (who he knew was formed from his rib) was brought into his sight, he said, "She is bone of my bones, and flesh of my flesh" [Gen. 2:23, Vg.]. Paul testifies that all this was spiritually fulfilled in

13. Ibid., 4.17.5; 4.17.6.
14. Ibid., 4.17.7.
15. Gerrish, *Grace and Gratitude*, 73; cf. Calvin, *Institutes* 3.1.3; 4.19.35.

Christ and in us, when he says that we are members of his body, of his flesh, and of his bones, and thus one flesh with him. Finally, he adds this summation: "This is a great mystery." And that nobody may be deceived by an ambiguity, he explains that he is not speaking of carnal union of man and woman, but of the spiritual marriage of Christ and the church. Truly, indeed, this is a great mystery, that Christ allowed a rib to be removed from himself to form us; that is, when he was strong, he willed to be weak, in order that we might be strengthened in his strength; so that we ourselves should no longer live, but he should live in us [Gal. 2:20].[16]

Dennis Tamburello further notes that in his sermon on Ephesians 5:31–33, "it is clear . . . that Calvin wishes to speak of a spiritual union between Christ and believers, effected by the Spirit . . . [that] embraces both the body and soul of the believer." Similarly, in his commentary on 1 Corinthians, Calvin says little about 6:17 ("But anyone united to the Lord becomes one spirit with him") "except that 'the union [*coniunctionem*] of Christ with us is closer than that of husband and wife;' and that believers 'are not only one flesh with Christ, but also one Spirit [*non una tantum caro sunt cum Christo, sed unus etiam spiritus*].'"[17] This union, Tamburello continues, "is so intimate that Calvin sees it as the ground of faith's certitude."[18]

Calvin also compares the believer's union with Christ to marriage in his exposition on the second commandment.

God very commonly takes on the character of a husband to us. Indeed, the union by which he binds us to himself when he receives us into the bosom of the church is like sacred wedlock, which must rest upon mutual faithfulness [Eph. 5:29–32]. As he performs all the duties of a true and faithful husband, of us in return he demands love and conjugal chastity.[19]

Calvin reiterates his explanation of mystical union in arguing against Osiander's view of incarnation. By drawing on the same passage from Ephesians, he asserts, Paul used the image of marriage to depict "the holy union that makes us one with Christ."[20] The point to be made here is that in a variety of contexts, Calvin consistently uses the metaphor of marriage to describe Christ's union with the church—both the church as a corporate body and individual believers—following Paul's example in Ephesians.

16. Calvin, *Institutes* 4.19.35.
17. Tamburello, *Union with Christ*, 88.
18. Ibid., 89.
19. Calvin, *Institutes* 2.8.18.
20. Ibid., 2.12.7.

WORD AND SACRAMENT
AS THE LOCUS OF UNION

For Calvin, both Word and sacrament are the locus of union, the means by which the believer is brought into communion with Christ. In his sermon on Ephesians 5:25–27, Calvin describes the sacraments as "a ladder to us so that we may seek our Lord Jesus Christ, and so that we may be fully convinced that he lives in us and we are united to him."[21] In both baptism and the Lord's Supper, he says, God "has prescribed a way for us, though still far off, to draw near to him."[22] One might say, then, that for Calvin the goal of Christian life is union with God in Christ, achieved through the power of the Holy Spirit, and that the sacraments are divine gifts provided to effect that union for believers. It is not only the sacraments, however, that lead believers to union with Christ. As Gerrish points out, Calvin sees the Word as serving the same purpose. "The word is not simply information about God," he asserts; "it is the instrument through which union with Christ is effected and his grace is imparted."[23] In preaching as well as the sacraments, then, God works through the Spirit to continue and improve the spiritual marriage between Christ and believers.

Gerrish rightly acknowledges the didactic tone that often characterizes Calvinism, "an arid intellectualism that turns the worshipping community into a class of glum schoolchildren." Yet he recognizes another strand as well, "which points to a mystery that defies understanding: communion with Christ. For the word of God is not only a reassuring doctrine, but also a powerful instrument of the Spirit, and it is both these things together."[24] He goes on to explain that "Calvin felt no antagonism between what we may call the 'pedagogical' and the 'sacramental' functions of the word." Preaching, he says, is a link between these two functions. It is a public event in which God uses the human voice to create faith in its hearers. Recalling Calvin's claim that Christ himself speaks through human agents, and that the power of the keys is in his word (of which humans are the ministers), Gerrish asserts that the gospel is not only the "promise and decision of God," but it also "unites us in one body with Christ."[25] Preaching, then, is not only a telling, but also a doing. As Gerrish puts it, "It is crucial to Calvin's interpretation that the gospel is not

---

21. Tamburello, *Union with Christ*, 99.
22. Calvin, *Institutes* 4.1.1.
23. Gerrish, *Grace and Gratitude*, 76.
24. Ibid., 82.
25. Ibid., 83; cf. Calvin, *Institutes* 4.11.1.

a mere invitation to fellowship with Christ, but the effective means by which communion with Christ is brought about."[26]

Calvin affirms this idea in his *Short Treatise on the Lord's Supper* (1541): "Just as God has set all fulness of life in Jesus, in order to communicate it to us by means of him, so he has ordained his Word as instrument by which Jesus Christ, with all his benefits, is dispensed to us."[27] As Gerrish explains, Calvin was already clear on this point in the first edition of the *Institutes* (1536). Arguing against the use of indulgences, he said, "For Christ is offered to us by the gospel with all the abundance of heavenly goods, with all his merits, all his righteousness, wisdom, grace, without exception." The statement remained unchanged in later editions, and in 1559 Calvin added, "And believers know what the value of the fellowship [κοινωνία, *koinōnia*] of Christ, which, as the same apostle [Paul] testifies, is in the gospel offered us to enjoy."[28] "What is most remarkable about these utterances," Gerrish observes, "is that they ascribe to the proclaimed word of God the power and efficacy that the medieval church credited to the seven sacraments." He points out that Calvin himself speaks of the "sacramental word," by which he means "the word that constitutes, or makes, a sacrament," but also "a proclamation that . . . as an efficacious means of grace, *is* a sacrament."[29]

Calvin also attributes the same character to the sacrament that he does to the Word: "Now what is said of the Word fitly belongs also to the sacrament of the Supper," he says, "by means of which our Lord leads us to communion with Jesus Christ." Since preaching and teaching alone are not enough to overcome "our infirmity," God

> has desired to attach to his Word a visible sign, by which he represents the substance of his promises, to confirm and fortify us, and to deliver us from all doubt and uncertainty. Since then it is a mystery so high and incomprehensible, when we say that we have communion with the body and blood of Christ, and since we on our side are so rude and gross that we cannot understand the smallest things concerning God, it was of consequence that he give us to understand, according as our capacity can bear it. For this reason, the Lord instituted for us his Supper, in order to sign and seal in our consciences the promises contained in his gospel concerning our being made partakers of his body and blood.[30]

26. Gerrish, *Grace and Gratitude*, 84; cf. Calvin, *Institutes* 3.5.5.

27. John Calvin, *Short Treatise on the Holy Supper of Our Lord and Only Saviour Jesus Christ*, in *Calvin: Theological Treatises*, Library of Christian Classics 22, translated with introduction and notes by J. K. S. Reid (Philadelphia: Westminster Press, 1954), 143.

28. Gerrish, *Grace and Gratitude*, 84; Calvin, *Institutes* 3.5.5.

29. Gerrish, *Grace and Gratitude*, 84–86.

30. Calvin, *Short Treatise*, 144.

For Calvin, then, Christ is communicated to the believer in Word and sacrament, in both aural and visual proclamation. "When we hear the sacramental word mentioned," says Calvin, "let us understand the promise, proclaimed in a clear voice by the minister, to lead the people by the hand wherever the sign tends and directs us."[31] In other words, preaching and sacrament work in tandem: both lead to, or effect, communion with Christ.[32] This is no mechanistic view of either preaching or the sacraments, but rather an understanding that God, through the power of the Holy Spirit and the faith of the believer, makes use of both Word and sacrament to make Christ present—to create space, as it were, for that mystical union of believer and Christ, bride and Bridegroom.

CALVIN'S "SUM OF PIETY"

In his view of mystical union—and in his theological program in general—Calvin is as interested in the spiritual life of believers as he is in the articulation of doctrine. As Gerrish puts it, Calvin (like Erasmus) believed that "true theology is a matter not of marshalling formal arguments more clever and subtle than those of one's opponents, but of grasping the poetics of scriptural discourse and letting it make a better person out of you." For Calvin, "theological understanding and practical piety" were inseparable.[33]

Gerrish points to the expansive subtitle of the first edition of the *Institutes* as a case in point: *Instruction in the Christian Religion, Embracing an Almost Complete Summary of Piety and What It Is Necessary to Know in the Doctrine of Salvation: A Work Most Worthy of Being Read by All Who Are Devoted to Piety, and Recently Published* (1536). From the beginning, it seems, Calvin is presenting his readers with a *pietatis summa* and not a *summa theologiae*. This intention appears to have remained key to his work; in a section added to the 1559 edition, Calvin proclaims that God cannot be known "where there is no religion or piety." And piety, he explains, is "that reverence joined with love of God which the knowledge of his benefits induces."[34] As Gerrish observes, "Piety and its renewal as faith in Christ—this is the subject of Calvin's *pietatis summa*."[35]

---

31. Calvin, *Institutes* 4.14.4.
32. Gerrish, *Grace and Gratitude*, 108–9.
33. Ibid., 17.
34. Calvin, *Institutes* 1.2.1.
35. Gerrish, *Grace and Gratitude*, 19–20.

Serene Jones echoes a similar view in her rhetorical reading of Calvin: "According to [Calvin's] definition, true knowledge of God does not consist of a simple intellectual assent to God's existence. Rather, it involves trust, obedience, and worship."[36] She argues persuasively that this definition is reflected not only in the content of the *Institutes*, but also in its form, as Calvin moves back and forth between classroom and pulpit. She describes the theologian's rhetorical style as "waves":

> By mixing and blending a series of rhetorical forms, Calvin constructs waves of appeal that wash over the reader. These waves begin in the calm voice of exposition. They then build in intensity as the temper of sermonic and polemical passion takes over. At the climactic moment of the discussion, they crash upon the reader in a wondrous display of doxological elation. And finally, having moved the reader to the heights of *pietas*, the waves recede into the steady tone of exposition. But in the course of this one short chapter, Calvin is not content to sweep the reader away only once: As if to drive home the power of godly piety and familiarize the reader with its force, Calvin repeats the wave pattern four times, creating the rhetorical effect of a relentless play between turbulence and rest, between affective exaltation and intellectual assent.[37]

The reader, then, is led not only to knowledge, but also to "feeling" and "embracing" that knowledge;[38] in short, understanding leads to worship, erudition to awe.

Calvin exhibits this balance of cognition and affect in his exposition on the real presence of Christ in the sacrament:

> Now, if anyone should ask me how this takes place, I shall not be ashamed to confess that it is a secret too lofty for either my mind to comprehend or my words to declare. And, to speak more plainly, I rather experience than understand it. Therefore, I here embrace without controversy the truth of God in which I may safely rest. He declares his flesh the food of my soul, his blood its drink [John 6:53–58]. I offer my soul to him to be fed with such food. In his Sacred Supper he bids me take, eat, and drink his body and blood under the symbols of bread and wine. I do not doubt that he himself truly presents them, and that I receive them.[39]

36. Serene Jones, *Calvin and the Rhetoric of Piety*, Columbia Series in Reformed Theology (Louisville: Westminster John Knox, 1995), 147.

37. Ibid., 122.

38. Ibid., 130.

39. Calvin, *Institutes* 4.17.32.

Here, intellectual inquiry gives way to mystery, and Calvin freely admits that there is room for both—even the necessity for both—in the life of faith.[40] For Calvin, the sum of piety is indeed the "ordered union of knowledge and spirituality."[41]

CALVIN'S MYSTICISM?

In *The Spirituality of John Calvin*, Lucien Joseph Richard suggests that Calvin's rejection of scholastic theology led him to embrace the humanists' approach to the theological task. In this approach—exemplified by Erasmus, whose influence upon Calvin has been well documented—"theology and spirituality were one."[42] The integration of spirituality and theology, Richard explains, "established, at the outset of the Reformation, a deep yearning among serious people for a religion of inward experience."[43] Dennis Tamburello pushes this line of thinking further, arguing that there is even a mystical strand evident in the writings of John Calvin. In *Union with Christ: John Calvin and the Mysticism of St. Bernard*, Tamburello examines Calvin's understanding of mystical union and compares it with that of Bernard of Clairvaux, a medieval theologian for whom mystical union figures significantly, and one to whom Calvin often refers. Though a thorough exposition of Tamburello's work is not possible here, it is useful for the discussion at hand to summarize his argument.

Since the term "mysticism" can be used in a variety of ways, Tamburello appeals to the definition offered by French humanist Jean Gerson, who defines mystical theology as "experiential knowledge of God attained through the union of spiritual affection with Him."[44] Elaborating on Gerson's definition, Tamburello observes that it "exemplifies the focus on 'union with God' that became prominent in the late medieval period." This union is "spiritual,

---

40. Calvin appeals to this sense of mystery in describing the life of faith in general, and not only in reference to the sacraments. See, e.g., his discussion of the nature of faith in *Institutes* 3.2.14ff.

41. Iain S. Maclean, "The First Pietist: An Introduction and Translation of a Communion Sermon by Jodocus van Lodenstein [on Song 1:4, 'The King Brought Me into His Inner-Room']," in *Calvin Studies VI: Colloquium on Calvin Studies at Davidson College and Davidson Presbyterian Church, Davidson, North Carolina, January 1992*, ed. John H. Leith (Davidson, NC: Davidson College, Colloquium on Calvin Studies, 1992), 15.

42. Lucien Joseph Richard, *The Spirituality of John Calvin* (Atlanta: John Knox Press, 1974), 187.

43. Ibid., 73. Calvin was not unique in this; the Middle Ages saw considerable interest in *Frömmigkeitstheologie*, or devotional-spiritual theology.

44. Tamburello, *Union with Christ*, 11.

not essential—a 'union of will'"; in other words, Gerson does not understand union as the absorption of the soul into the divine being, as do some mystics. Furthermore, for Gerson mystical union "always has a cognitive component. The content of mystical union 'will be in an experiential mode [*experimentalis*] but it will also be knowledge [*cognitio*].'" This means that Gerson's mystical experience is not reserved for contemplatives, but is available to any faithful believer. Finally, mystical union is not an individualistic prospect, but one that takes place in the context of the church and its sacraments.[45] Working with this definition, which is particularly useful because it is a medieval construct rather than a modern one, Tamburello argues that Calvin's work shows a knowledge of, and affinity with, the medieval mystical tradition.

Gerson's definition is a fascinating one, and as Jill Raitt observes, "if one grants Tamburello this definition, then indeed both Bernard and Calvin may be compared and found to be closer on this point than many scholars might have anticipated."[46] It would be difficult to argue, however, that Gerson's definition of mysticism is representative of the medieval era, however; perhaps more than anything, Tamburello has demonstrated a certain affinity between Gerson and Calvin.

In fact, Tamburello makes some significant concessions. He readily confesses that Calvin did not seem to view himself as a mystic, nor did mysticism seem to be of major concern to him in his work. Furthermore, although Bernard will usually correlate union with love, Calvin connects union with faith.

Finally, Tamburello makes an important distinction when he concedes that Calvin was less interested in contemplative forms of mysticism than was Bernard. Rather, "Calvin's mysticism was a fact of Christian existence, the fruits of which were expressed primarily in the active love of God and neighbor." While mysticism involves more than contemplation, the differences between the two theologians on this point "explain why we would continue to call Bernard a mystic while withholding the title from Calvin."[47] Raitt concurs that this is "a major difference." As she explains, "Bernard finds contemplation, best fostered in monasteries, the most direct road to the experience of God. Calvin eschews both monastic life and contemplation, finding union with God available in God's Word, preached and sacramentally received."[48]

Calvin does make it clear that he is interested in Christian experience: intellectual knowledge of God is not enough. As Tamburello puts it, "The

---

45. Ibid., 11–12.

46. Jill Raitt, "Union with Christ: John Calvin and the Mysticism of St. Bernard," *Journal of Religion* 76, no. 1 (January 1996): 116.

47. Tamburello, *Union with Christ*, 104.

48. Raitt, "Union with Christ," 117.

promotion of *piety* is what concerns him most deeply."[49] Tamburello's argument for the presence of a mystical strand in Calvin's thought is tantalizing, but in the end one must acknowledge that if mysticism is defined as Christian experience, then every Christian qualifies as a mystic.[50] Perhaps "spirituality" or "religious experience" are better terms to apply to Calvin's understanding of the Christian's apprehending of the mysterious union with Christ.

A further caution comes from Anthony N. S. Lane's work on the relationship between Calvin and Bernard. Lane readily acknowledges that Calvin made significant use of Bernard and appreciated his work. He points out, however, that Calvin only appropriated the medieval theologian's writings several years after the initial 1536 edition of the *Institutes*. By 1543, Calvin seems to have become familiar with Bernard and appeals to him primarily as confirmation of his orthodoxy. As Lane puts it, "Calvin saw him as witness to Augustinian truth during the Middle Ages."[51] Although it is clear that the Genevan reformer held a certain esteem for the Cistercian monk, the additions of citations from Bernard that increased over time "testify to Calvin's deepening appreciation of Bernard, not to Bernard's significant influence upon his theology."[52] After carefully examining which Bernardine sources Calvin used and how he used them, Lane concludes that Calvin is highly selective in the material he chooses. Although he quotes often from the sermons on the Canticles, he "ignores the specifically mystical teachings of Bernard." In Lane's view, Calvin draws on the parts of Bernard that support his own claims, but these citations do not represent the core of Bernard's thought.[53] Apparently, then, though one can certainly affirm that Calvin knew of and appreciated Bernard's work, he does not work with the same understanding of mysticism.

Two observations are in order at this juncture. First, Calvin's "mysticism" is primarily an outward rather than an inward phenomenon. As Tamburello rightly points out, Calvin is not focused on contemplation but rather on experiencing, and responding to, the grace of God. An experience of grace has ethical implications, as the believer responds in gratitude both in worship (in prayer, song, and the Eucharist) and in the world (in acts of charity). Furthermore, Calvin's understanding of the spiritual life concerns the individual believer only in the context of the community of faith. Though he is careful to place the locus of union with Christ in the experience of the individual believer (and not in that of the institutional church), that believer

49. Tamburello, *Union with Christ*, 104.

50. Elsie McKee, personal correspondence, December 29, 2007.

51. Anthony N. S. Lane, *John Calvin: Student of the Church Fathers* (Edinburgh: T&T Clark, 1999), 98.

52. Ibid., 97.

53. Ibid., 100.

comes to union with Christ through the agency of the church: first in baptism, where union is initiated, then repeatedly in the Lord's Supper, where union is renewed and strengthened.

Second, Calvin's concern with religious experience is a critical counterbalance to the intellectual component that he values in the life of faith. "Religious experience" for Calvin may be less about transports of ecstasy than it was for some medieval mystics and more about acknowledging mystery. Or to put it another way, Calvin's "mysticism" involves the experience of coming face-to-face with the divine reality in a way that transcends the power of words to explain it. That acknowledging of mystery leads not only to a feeling, but also to awe, which in turn is transformed into doxology. Thus, for Calvin, piety is indeed the "union of knowledge and spirituality"; faith seeks understanding, and understanding falls down before mystery in wonder and praise.

Both Calvin's theological understanding of mystical union and his view of Christian experience will find echoes in the preaching of two key American Presbyterian figures, James McGready and Gilbert Tennent, and in the writings of Scottish Presbyterian minister John Willison, whose work will be examined in part 2 of this study. A close reading of their sermons and devotional writings will reveal similar themes: an understanding of union with Christ as an experience that is available to every believer, one that involves not the absorption of the soul into a divine being, but rather a combination of feeling and understanding that is made manifest in the soul's marriage to the bridegroom Christ. This union is not the purview of lone spiritual seekers, but rather that of Christians worshiping in community, particularly in the context of sacramental occasions.

It is clear that in spite of his use of marital imagery to describe union with Christ, Calvin does not employ the vivid language of the Song of Songs. This expression does come to light, however, in the work of his successor, Theodore Beza, to whom attention now turns.

THEODORE BEZA'S "MYSTICAL MARRIAGE"

French Reformed scholar Theodore Beza (1516–1605) represents a fascinating link between his theological mentor, John Calvin, and the Scots-Irish preachers who are the focus of this study. Calvin called Beza to head a new academy in Geneva in 1557, where he joined the clergy of that city. He was elected moderator of the Company of Pastors of that city upon Calvin's death in 1564, and he continued to serve in that capacity until 1580. As the theological colleague and heir of Calvin, he represented Reformed interests at several colloquies held in France during the 1560s and 1570s.

Not surprisingly, Beza's own eucharistic theology echoes that of Calvin's. As Calvin insisted, the Holy Spirit effects salvation in Jesus Christ through faith; Word and sacraments are means through which faith is born and nurtured.[54] Like Calvin, he regarded preaching as the necessary accompaniment to the sacraments, considering both to be elements of the Word.[55]

Jill Raitt has provided a detailed analysis of Beza's eucharistic theology, and only the salient points of her study will be rehearsed here. Especially noteworthy for the purposes of this inquiry is her discussion of what happens when "the faithful take the bread of life and the cup of salvation":

> By the power of the Holy Spirit, they enter into communion, *koinōnia*, with Christ. . . . The purpose of the sacraments is, by the power of the Holy Spirit, to effect that most intimate union of the faithful with Christ. This then is the fifth point of *De controversiis*, in which Beza speaks of the mystical marriage effected between the communicants and Christ in the Supper. In this section, Beza's references are biblical and the scholastic terminology and argument fall away as he draws upon St. Paul and the *Song of Songs*. His references are also homely as he speaks of the contract between a man and his wife and then that between Christ and the Church. And just as from the carnal union of that man and woman children are born, so from the spiritual union of Christ and his faithful, holy children are born.[56]

Indeed, for Beza, the "end of the sacraments is a mystical union or marriage; it is the *koinōnia* of which Paul wrote."[57]

BEZA'S SERMONS ON THE CANTICLES

Although Calvin's own work made little direct use of the Song of Songs, the language and imagery of the Canticles is clearly present in the preaching of his successor, Beza. Most significant, perhaps, is Beza's collection of sermons on the first three chapters of the Song of Songs, published in French in 1586 and in English translation the following year.[58] The collection numbers

54. Jill Raitt, *The Eucharistic Theology of Theodore Beza: Development of the Reformed Doctrine* (Chambersburg, PA: American Academy of Religion, 1972), 15.

55. Ibid., 21.

56. Ibid., 68.

57. Ibid., 71.

58. Theodore Beza, *Master Bezaes Sermons Upon the Three First Chapters of the Canticle of Canticles: Wherein are handled the chiefest points of religion controversed and debated between us and the adversarie at this day, especially touching the true Jesus Christ and the true church, and the certain & infallible marks both of the one and of the other*, translated out of French into English by John

thirty-one sermons in all and begins with an apology for why one ought to preach from the Canticles. He bases his argument on the conviction that the book, like Psalm 150, is to be taken in *"a spirituall sense"* for *"there is no appearance or shewe of reason to take it as some have done, for a marriage song of Salomon and Pharoes daughter."* Nevertheless, Beza does not shy away from the vivid language of the Song of Songs. His sermons certainly make use of an allegorical interpretative approach, yet the language also reflects the ardor and passion of the Canticles. In his second sermon, for example, he expounds on 1:2, "Let him kisse me with the kisses of his mouth." All the while making connections between the Song of Songs, the Gospels, and the Epistles, Beza explains the incarnation:

> The Sonne of God hath kissed us, by joining himself in such wise and so near to us, that the man whom we hath taken unto himself, is not only the image of God his Creator, as was the first Adam, but is true God & true man in one onlie person: and that in such sort, that this joining and uniting himself with our nature neither is nor shall bee ever severed or broken: by this means his mouth hath ever, & doth yet remain, as it were glued upon ours, by this holy kisse of his.[59]

Furthermore, Beza insists that if Jesus Christ is the Bridegroom of the church, and that, if he is "to make her flesh of his flesh, and bone of his bones, as it is spoken, *Eph 5.30*, there must be between him and his Church a matrimonial conjunction, whereof the spouse speaketh in this place."[60]

Beza goes on to explain carefully the nature of this union. It is, in the first place, "in this present life, which is made by the promise of the Bridegroome, and received by faith of the spouse," through the gospel which is preached and sealed by baptism and the Lord's Supper. But this is only an initial circumstance; Christians aspire to and eventually will enjoy "this real & entire actual union, whereunto we shal come in the later day, when that which we are already by hope neither vain nor uncertain shal be then perfitly effectuated." When the spouse speaks of desiring "the kisses of his mouth," then, she speaks not only of an earthly union with his "corporall presence" but also of "the true consummation of this marriage . . . in heaven."[61] The Christian life, then, is one of craving the kisses of the Bridegroom—not just one, but many, for the

---

Harmar, Her Highes professor in the Greeke Toung in the Universitie of Oxford and Felowe of the Newe College there (Oxford: Joseph Barnes, 1587).
   59. Ibid., 20.
   60. Ibid., 20–21.
   61. Ibid., 21.

church desires "continuance & increase of faith, hope, & charity, & all other graces necessary to salvation."[62]

Perhaps Beza feared that his readers would be moved too profoundly by his vivid imagery from the Canticles, because the third sermon begins with a caution: every person knows, he says, that the spouse does not speak "as a fond passionate bodie, but as one which is indeed sage and sober."[63] Yet his discourse continues to make good use of the language of the Canticles and of Paul's marital metaphor. For whom did Christ take on all sin? "For us his enemies, out of whom hee hath chosen, and made to be borne this beloved spouse, to the end that being ravished with the Apostle, we should cry out at this most high, most great, and most profound secret of secrets, *Ephes. 3.18 and 5.32. O the profound riches of the wisdom and knowledge of God.*"[64] Indeed, the spouse savors "such a sweetnes, being altogether ravished," and desires nothing else than the Bridegroom's kisses.[65] Again, Beza does not shy away from the marital metaphors as he speaks of "the joyning and coupling of this Bridegrome with this spouse"[66] or lauds the beauty of "the Bridegroome which is Jesus Christ, . . . comparing himself unto two flowers the *Rose* and the *Lilly*." He relates the red of the rose to the wounds of Christ, and the white lily to his purity, urging the faithful to present to God, either in daily worship or in the "holy supper," this rose and this lily that their prayers might be acceptable. These perfumes are "pleasing and acceptable to God. . . . And this is it which we have to consider in this Bridegrome to be thereby stirred up and moved to joyne our selves every day nearer and nearer with him."[67]

Although the sermons are not primarily eucharistic, Beza does, from time to time, include eucharistic themes in his exposition of the Song of Songs. In the second sermon on the second chapter where he considers 2:4 ("He brought me into the place of the banquet, and his banner over me was Dilection or Love.") he explains that Christ provides not only meat but also drink. "In him alone wee must wholly and entirely seeke after and find our whole sustenance and spiritual nourishment," he proclaims.

> Which he would also shew us visibly & sensibly in the bread of the holie Supper, which is a certain & sure testimonie of the partaking of the bodie which was given for us: and in the wine which is the sacrament of the precious blood shed for us, not to be set before our visible

---

62. Ibid., 22.
63. Ibid., 28.
64. Ibid., 30.
65. Ibid., 31.
66. Ibid., 200.
67. Ibid., 210–11.

eie (seeing it cannot now be seene but by the eies of faith) but to bee truly communicated after a spirituall fashion unto a spirituall and eternal life. The like is to bee understood of the ordinarie preaching and administration of the word, in which also Jesus Christ presenteth himselffe wholly unto us, to be received as it were by the hand of faith.[68]

Later in the same sermon, Beza not only describes the benefits of the Lord's Supper but also exhorts believers to worthy participation, connecting the banqueting hall of the Canticles with the invitation to the feast in Luke 14:17.

And who is he who being admitted into the house of some great Lord, to sit with him at his table, would willingly & wittingly bring thither with him any filthinesse or villany? . . . We ought not to go, but to runne, nay to fly thither: & yet not so at random, but that we first prepare our selves, through a true contrition, and consideration both of the death of him who inviteth us unto this banquet, . . . that we bring thither a mind apt and ready to be taught, an heart full of appetite of this heavenly foode: in a woorde, a most ardent desire of receiving, eating, liking and digesting so precious a meate, to shew afterwards the fruits & effectes thereof, within and without our house, at home and abroad, farre and neare, by all our actions aswel of the body as also of the mind.[69]

References to the Lord's Supper are sprinkled throughout Beza's thirty-one sermons on the Canticles. These are expository sermons on the biblical texts, and so explication of understanding or experience of union with Christ in communion is not his primary theme. Nevertheless, it is significant that while using an allegorical approach in his preaching on the Canticles, Beza does from time to time interpret portions of the book as expressing what Christians believe and experience in the celebration of the sacrament.

There is no record of Beza's sermons having been published in English in later editions; only the 1587 London edition is extant. Only one other French edition was published, in 1615. It is impossible to speculate how influential these sermons might have been, or to know whether the Scots-Irish preachers who are the focus of this study would have been familiar with the sermons. Nevertheless, Beza's preaching does show a certain continuity of expression with medieval and early Reformation figures. Here in the Genevan legacy, represented in Beza's work, is Calvin's theology of the Eucharist joined with the marital imagery of earlier scholars and mystics.

68. Ibid., 223.
69. Ibid., 223–24.

While no direct link can be assumed between Beza and Scots-Irish preachers in the British Isles or in America, the American manifestations of the holy fairs will evidence a rich Reformed theological and liturgical heritage. The sermons from these occasions will reflect several streams of continuity: an allegorical approach to interpreting the Canticles, a Reformed understanding of union with Christ in communion, and a decidedly mystical strain in describing the Christian's spiritual experience of the sacrament. In the American sacramental occasions, believers approach the eucharistic Table, coming to communion as to the marriage bed, seeking a union with Christ that embraces mind, heart, and will.

PART 2

The American Experience

4

James McGready

Communion Sermons
on the Kentucky Frontier

During the first decade of the nineteenth century, a wave of evangelical fervor rolled through Kentucky, Tennessee, Virginia, the Carolinas, and Georgia. Known as the Great Revival, this period of awakening sparked a second wave of revivalism in America and saw the birth of a new form of worship: the outdoor camp meeting. Interpreters of the American religious experience traditionally have understood the Great Revival as an innovation of frontier missionaries: Presbyterian, Methodist, and Baptist ministers who followed the settlers westward. These preachers were thought to have taken the evangelical spirit of the First Great Awakening (1625–1760) and reshaped it into a powerful preaching technique, which they used with intentionality and great emotional force to convert unsaved souls.[1] Historians have seen this preaching as the product of a new brand of revivalist, who was less concerned with theological depth and eloquent expression than with eliciting a dramatic response to his sermons.

In the past two decades, however, scholars have brought to light the relationship between the revivals of the late eighteenth and early nineteenth century and Scots-Irish sacramental occasions. Paul Conkin, in his study of the revival at Cane Ridge, Kentucky, remarks that "little if anything that happened in this great revival was new, without precedents that stretched back

---

1. See, e.g., Sydney E. Ahlstrom, *A Religious History of the American People* (New Haven, CT, and London: Yale University Press, 1972); John B. Boles, *The Great Revival: Beginnings of the Bible Belt* (Lexington: University of Kentucky Press, 1996; originally published in 1972 as *The Great Revival, 1787–1805: The Origins of the Southern Evangelical Mind*); and Winthrop S. Hudson, *Religion in America*, 4th ed. (New York: Macmillan Publishing Co., 1987).

through two centuries, to Carolina, to Virginia, to Pennsylvania, and ultimately to Ulster and Scotland."[2] It is Leigh Eric Schmidt, however, who most fully explores this relationship, in his seminal work *Holy Fairs: Scottish Communions and American Revivals in the Early Modern Period*. By examining personal accounts, church records, histories, and sermons, he shows that the revivals stretching from western Pennsylvania to the southeastern United States in the late eighteenth and early nineteenth centuries were based on the patterns and rituals that the Scots brought with them to the New World. Although the American manifestation naturally bore its own unique marks, Schmidt argues that it is the Scottish influence that is most significant:

> Still what historians have long seen simply as the first flowering of America's own camp meetings—as the supreme example of what Peter Mode called the "frontierization" of American Christianity—from a different angle and longer historical view looks decidedly less distinctive, less exceptionally American. Throughout much of the West and the South—including western Pennsylvania, the valley of Virginia, backcountry North Carolina, Kentucky, and Tennessee—the old forms of renewal, based upon the sacramental practices of Scotland and Ulster, were often preserved for another generation or more. Agrarian settlements in these areas, removed from the older, more developed communities of the eastern seaboard, tended to become the bearers of Presbyterian tradition. The old rituals and customs—the fencing of tables, communion tokens, Scottish psalmody, preparatory meetings, fast days, thanksgiving services, action sermons, sitting at the long linen-covered tables, the great crowds, outdoor preaching from the tent—often endured in these regions into the 1820s and 1830s and in some cases even longer. For the Presbyterians, the South and West were indeed bastions for this Old World festival.[3]

In order to illustrate this relationship, Schmidt focuses on one particular figure in the Great Revival, James McGready (1763–1817), a Presbyterian minister who has been credited with holding the first American camp meeting. As a young man, McGready experienced the sacramental revivals held in western Pennsylvania, where the Scottish traditions were observed scrupulously: the Thursday fast, the Saturday preparation service, the celebration of the Lord's Supper that began Sunday morning and continued throughout the day, and the Monday service of thanksgiving were all held. The old psalms were sung, the tables were fenced, and tokens were required for admission to the sacrament, just as they had been in Scotland.[4] In the years to come,

---

2. Paul K. Conkin, *Cane Ridge: America's Pentecost* (Madison: University of Wisconsin Press, 1990), 63.

3. Schmidt, *Holy Fairs*, 65–66.

4. Ibid., 61.

McGready would go on to lead similar revivals in North Carolina and Kentucky. In the late 1790s he settled in Logan County, Kentucky, to serve as the pastor of three small churches, congregations that would soon become part of one of the most turbulent periods in this history of American revivalism.

Throughout this period, Schmidt explains, "the traditional pattern of the sacramental season would provide the guiding form" for revivals on the frontier. The Kentucky revivals, which would come to be known as the first camp meetings, would also represent the last significant wave of communion seasons, for American revivals would eventually lose their sacramental character altogether.[5] By tracing McGready's involvement in the Great Revival, however, Schmidt illustrates the dependence of the Kentucky revivals on their Scottish precursors and highlights the profoundly sacramental character of the earliest American camp meetings.

John Thomas Scott's study of McGready further underscores the connection between early American camp meetings and holy fairs, pointing to the stream of continuity that flows from Ulster through the Tennents to McGready.

> The Scottish, Ulster, and American experience of the Presbyterian Church from the Reformation to the [First] Great Awakening set the historical context for James McGready. . . . [When he began his ministry,] he had longstanding and powerful Presbyterian traditions on which to draw—the sacramental occasion, a two-hundred-year-old history of Scottish and Ulster revivalism, and the revivalism of the Tennents during the Great Awakening. These ideas and practices were communicated and transmitted to McGready through a series of like-minded ministers operating small schools on the frontier.[6]

Scott goes on to argue that in McGready we see a Calvinist revivalist who was more of a traditionalist than a progressive, one who did not invent the new form of worship that became known as the camp meeting, but rather drew on a long and rich Scottish tradition.[7]

McGready was a rather imposing figure—a large man, six feet tall, with prominent features. Historian John Boles writes that "his grave appearance and piercing eyes chained one's attention; his voice seemed unearthly, coarse, and tremulous. Thunderous tones and jerky gesticulations increased

---

5. Ibid., 63.

6. John Thomas Scott, "James McGready: Son of Thunder, Father of the Great Revival" (PhD diss., The College of William and Mary, 1991), 28–29. Scott's findings are summarized in an essay of the same title in *American Presbyterians* 72, no. 2 (Summer 1994): 87–95, http://www .cumberland.org/hfcpc/McGreJTS.htm.

7. Scott, "James McGready" (PhD diss.), 250–51.

his hypnotic ability to sway an audience."[8] Barton Stone, the pastor of the congregation at Cane Ridge who himself later became a leading revivalist in Kentucky, once described McGready's manner as "'the perfect reverse of elegance.'"[9] If McGready's gyrations and vocalizations were inelegant, his preaching style was not. His use of biblical language and allusions shows a broad knowledge of Scripture, and the construction of his sermons reflects an intellectual integrity. Taken as a whole, his preaching exhibits a strong grounding in Reformed theology, and the sacramental sermons reveal a thorough and sophisticated theology of the Lord's Supper.

McGready represents a fascinating era in the history of Protestant worship in America, and his sermons are a valuable resource since so few examples of preaching from the time are available to contemporary historians. (Of the extant sermons of Barton Stone, for example, none can be dated to this period.)[10] The eucharistic revivals over which he presided were among the last in America and represent the culmination of a long-standing eucharistic practice among Scots-Irish Presbyterians. The preaching of the previous generation will show even more continuity with the Scots-Irish tradition; yet even here, in the communion sermons of James McGready, one can see a well-developed Reformed sacramental homiletic that echoes Calvin's theology, the piety of his Scots-Irish forebears, and a view of union with Christ in the sacrament—a homiletic that bears the marks of both Calvin and the medieval mystics who came before him.

A SACRAMENTAL HOMILETIC

The first camp meeting in America took place in 1800 at Gasper River, Kentucky, under the leadership of James McGready. People came from as far away as one hundred miles to take part in what (along with the revival at nearby Red River) John Boles called "the first really extraordinary manifestations of divine power" of the movement that would culminate in the sacramental gathering at Cane Ridge in 1801.[11]

Much of what scholars know about the Great Revival is derived from letters written by McGready's own hand. *Western Missionary Magazine* serialized his accounts of the remarkable events taking place in Kentucky, and his narratives captured the attention of Protestant Christians in the eastern states who

8. Boles, *The Great Revival*, 39.
9. Scott, "James McGready" (PhD diss.), 65.
10. Eslinger, *Citizens of Zion*, 216.
11. Boles, *The Great Revival*, 52.

were interested in evangelistic efforts on the frontier. McGready's accounts were so vivid, in fact, that when the Methodist bishop Francis Asbury was traveling, he would sometimes read one of McGready's missives instead of preaching a sermon, to great effect.[12]

In addition to the letters and narratives, there is one collection of sermons titled *The Posthumous Works of the Reverend and Pious James McGready*.[13] Edited and published by the Rev. James Smith in 1837, the volume contains nearly forty sermons. As Smith points out in his preface, the sermons are incomplete and sometimes seem to end abruptly. This is due to the modified plain style of preaching that McGready employed; after expounding on the exegetical and doctrinal content of his text, McGready would launch into the application section, which would be delivered extemporaneously. Since the applications were never written down, they are not available to the modern-day inquirer. As Smith repined, "This omission is the more to be lamented as in his applications he is said to have been particularly interesting, forcing the truth home upon the consciences of his hearers with almost irresistible efficacy."[14]

These samples of McGready's preaching are particularly instructive, for not only do they provide a glimpse of preaching during the Great Revival, but they also show that such preaching was not just the emotionally manipulative, theologically diluted rantings of uneducated frontier preachers, as it has sometimes been characterized. Rather, one hears in McGready's sermons an adherence to Reformed doctrine and a Calvinist understanding of salvation, in addition to a concern for the conversion experience (or "new birth") of the Christian. Furthermore, these sermons allow modern-day readers to see the exhorting, convicting, cajoling, and even nurturing preacher working to prepare his listeners for an encounter with Christ at the eucharistic Table.

THEOLOGICAL FRAMEWORK

The sacramental emphasis of McGready's preaching is one facet of his theological framework that is both Reformed and evangelical. John Opie Jr. calls McGready the "theologian of frontier revivalism" and asserts that although his preaching style could be "coarse and inelegant," it showed theological depth. Says Opie, "McGready did not subordinate theological sophistication to religious experience. Rather, revival conversions depended upon a full and

---

12. Conkin, *Cane Ridge*, 35–36.

13. James McGready, *The Posthumous Works of the Reverend and Pious James McGready, Late Minister of the Gospel in Henderson, Kentucky*, ed. James Smith (Nashville: J. Smith's Steam Press, 1837).

14. Ibid., iv.

orthodox theological structure, and he criticized the anti-intellectualism of his contemporaries."[15]

McGready was steeped in Scots-Irish Reformed theology from birth. He was born in the Pennsylvania countryside sometime around 1760, where his family lived in a Scots-Irish settlement in the western part of the state. In 1778 the family moved to Guilford County, North Carolina, where there was also a significant Scots-Irish community, and became part of a Presbyterian congregation there. Even as a child working on the farm, young James seemed to have a religious bent, and in the early 1780s he returned to Pennsylvania in the company of an uncle to pursue a theological education.[16] In a series of schools modeled on William Tennent's Log College,[17] he studied with Presbyterian ministers who taught him three essential tenets of New Side Presbyterianism: the theology of Calvin, the belief in the necessity of a conversion experience, and an evangelical style of preaching.[18]

McGready's first real experience of revivalism came after he had been licensed to preach by Redstone Presbytery and was traveling back to North Carolina to be near his family. While at Hampden-Sydney College in Virginia, he heard the powerful preaching of the college president, John Blair Smith (another New Side Presbyterian), and this experience gave him the direction for his own preaching ministry.

Although McGready believed in the necessity of being born again to new life—even (perhaps especially) among those who already believed themselves to be Christian, he fought against the Arminian leanings of most of his revivalist colleagues. He insisted on the sovereignty of God, who acts in grace to redeem humankind, and denied the belief that conversion was chiefly a matter of humans making a choice for God out of sheer willpower. As Opie puts it, McGready "contradicts the historian's stereotype by being simultaneously a successful frontier revivalist and a subtle theologian who believed that the depreciation of total depravity and irresistible grace softened the impact of a revival and undermined the radical character of conversion."[19]

Ellen Eslinger gives further insight about how McGready held his Calvinist theology in tension with his concern for religious experience. Conversion was not expected to occur overnight, but as a result of a process of transformation. Instant conversions would have been

---

15. John Opie Jr., "James McGready: Theologian of Frontier Revivalism," *Church History* 34 (1965): 445.

16. Boles, *The Great Revival*, 36.

17. See chap. 5 for a more detailed explanation of Tennent's academy.

18. Scott, "James McGready" (PhD diss.), 46.

19. Opie, "James McGready," 446.

inconsistent with Calvinism, which held that humankind was thoroughly depraved and regeneration was possible only as a gift of God's grace. This gift would be granted not as a result of any human merit but only through God's mercy and love. Therefore, grace would arrive in "God's own sovereign time, and for that time the sinner must wait."[20]

These same emphases are seen in the sermons that McGready preaches in order to prepare people for communion. The goal of much of his preaching was the worthy participation in the sacrament: exhorting people to make themselves ready before coming to the table to meet their Lord. The purpose of sacramental revivals was twofold: to bring about the conversion of unbelievers, and to renew and revitalize the faith of those already in the church through communion. Combined with McGready's evangelical fervor was a rich and deep understanding of the Lord's Supper, and his sermons reflect a full eucharistic theology.

EUCHARISTIC THEMES
IN MCGREADY'S PREACHING

A review of McGready's communion sermons reveals that two parallel objectives are simultaneously at work. One is to proclaim the gospel to unbelievers, who may be aroused by the Spirit, experience conversion, and come for the first time to the Lord's Table. Another—and equally important—objective is to perpetuate a rhythm of religious experience for believers, a rhythm of repentance, renewal, and release that is acted out in rituals of exhortation, self-examination, and communion. The sacramental revival, then, is an occasion for both sinners and saints, where those who are already in the fold are renewed, and those who stand on the outside and looking in are urged to come inside.

None of the sermons collected in *The Posthumous Works* is dated, although James Smith states that McGready preached most of them during the period of revival in 1800. Nearly a quarter of the sermons collected include eucharistic references.[21] One sermon, "A Sacramental Meditation," appears to be an

---

20. Eslinger, *Citizens of Zion*, 191.

21. The sermons (in McGready, *Works*) containing eucharistic references are "Christ the Author and Finisher of the Life of Grace," "The Believer Embracing Christ," "A Sacramental Meditation," "The New Birth (I)," "The New Birth (II)," "The Saving Sight," "The Meeting of Christ and His Disciples," "The Believer's Espousal to Christ," and "Hindrance of the Work of God."

action sermon, that is, a sermon preached at a communion service. "The Hindrance of the Work of God" seems to be a preparatory sermon, preached on a day before the celebration of the sacrament. Another preparatory sermon, "The Meeting of Christ and His Disciples," is a particularly thorough exposition of eucharistic doctrine. Together these sermons exhibit McGready's well-developed eucharistic theology. Five other sermons, while not communion sermons per se, include specific references to the sacrament and round out the eucharistic homiletic that is at work. An examination of this group of sermons reveals that McGready's eucharistic theology is not only in line with the Reformed understanding of the Lord's Supper in general, but also echoes the prominent themes of the Scottish holy fairs of his ancestors.

Overview of eucharistic themes. Taken as a body, McGready's sermons reflect a Reformed view of the Lord's Supper. Although he never sets out to preach what one might call a "doctrinal" sermon, McGready weaves sacramental language and allusion throughout his preaching. He speaks of Christ's meeting the believer at the Communion table, and of both feeding on Christ and being fed by Christ. The Table is the place of strengthening for the saints, where they receive encouragement and the assurance of their place in heaven. It is the place where believers enjoy communion not only with Christ but also with one another, including those who have died. We observe how *infrequently* McGready touches on themes of forgiveness or atonement; the passion is discussed in detail in only two sermons, "A Sacramental Meditation" and "The Meeting of Christ and His Disciples," and forgiveness is mentioned just once, in the latter sermon. McGready is much more interested in describing the Lord's Table as the anticipation of the heavenly banquet and the promise of the life to come—and in preparing his listeners to come to that Table as worthy participants.

Readiness for the sacrament is discussed primarily in the two preparation sermons. Since the days of Calvin and Knox, Presbyterians have stressed the depravity of humankind, the need for salvation in Christ, and the importance of being prepared to come to his Table. McGready is true to his theological heritage. In "The Hindrance of the Work of God," for example, he enumerates the various conditions that keep Christians from being ready to commune: those who do not pray, those who profane the Sabbath by drinking and dancing, those who take part in the worship of the church but "do not enjoy the light of God's countenance in the performance of every duty," those who do not examine their hearts. He chastises any who are lukewarm in their faith and service, wander from the fold, or backslide. Yet he does so not to keep people from the Table, but rather to encourage them to remedy their spiritual problems:

When the child of God is called upon to draw near to Christ in the ordinances of divine appointment—to sit at the table of the Lord. O, says the soul, I dare not approach so near to God in my present frame of mind. If my heart was melted and broken for sin,—or if I had such and such heavenly feelings, I could approach. And thus he stays at a distance from Christ, waiting for a proper frame; and preparing himself to come nigh to his Lord. When such is the case, beyond all doubt an accursed thing is indulged in that soul, and unless it be removed, he and God can have no communion with each other. True, no person ought by any means approach the Lord's table, without some solid scriptural evidence of a saving change of heart, or a vital union to Christ by faith. But to whom should the soul apply for a proper frame of mind except to Christ himself. First come to Christ and then come to a communion table.[22]

One can deduce from this excerpt that when preaching to the great crowds who gathered for sacramental services, McGready is not only seeking to persuade the unbeliever, but is also addressing the already-baptized Christians who come to the camp meeting for spiritual renewal. As with his spiritual ancestors who preached preparatory sermons at the holy fairs, he sees his task as both preaching for awakening the unsaved and revitalizing the saved.[23]

While the necessity of preparing oneself for the sacrament is strongly stressed in these two sermons, it is the quality of gracious giftedness that is most apparent in the sacramental sermons as a whole. Although worthiness is certainly an emphasis at the services of preparation that precede the sacrament, McGready exults in preaching about the joys and comforts that come from meeting Christ at the Communion table, as seen in the sermons examined below.

The Saving Sight. While he rarely uses the language of "real presence," McGready's descriptions of the communion that believers enjoy with Christ as they meet him at the Table implies an understanding of a spiritually present reality. In "A Sacramental Meditation," he points to various theophanies in Scripture—the voice of God in the burning bush, the cloud on Sinai, the judgment at the last day—then proclaims:

Well, God is as really present at a sacramental table as he was in the burning bush at Horeb, or on Mount Sinai, or as he will be at the judgment of the great day. Then, as Moses did at the burning bush, turn aside and see this great sight, here you may behold all the perfections

22. McGready, *Works*, 466–67.

23. See Schmidt, *Holy Fairs*, 71–72, for a description of a similar sermon preached at one of the earliest Scottish communities in America.

of God shining with amiable brightness in the face of Jesus Christ; here you may view the infinite love of God towards our guilty race finding vent through the breaking heart and bleeding veins of the dying Jesus, and flowing to the chief of sinners. Here you may see mercy and truth meeting each other, righteousness and peace kissing each other in the salvation of guilty sinners of Adam's race.[24]

There is nothing here of Calvin's sense of being lifted to heaven to be with Christ, but rather that of Christ's meeting the believer at the Communion table.[25] In fact, "meeting Christ" is the central theme in McGready's eucharistic preaching. As Keith Watkins explains, "He states unequivocally and often that at the sacramental table Christians meet Christ. By this language he means that in the Eucharist there is a direct, sensible encounter with the fullness of Deity."[26] He quotes McGready as saying, "The sacrament of the supper is one of the most affecting institutions of heaven, and one of the nearest approaches to God that can be made on this side of eternity, in which believers are permitted to hold intimate conversation with our blessed Jesus."[27]

McGready often uses the metaphor of sight to describe this sacramental meeting. In his parlance, the Christian's goal is to "see Jesus," to enjoy spiritual communion with the Lord. His sermon "The Saving Sight" is devoted to explaining the metaphor that also is used extensively in "The Hindrance of the Work of God," "A Sacramental Meditation," and "The Meeting of Christ and His Disciples." He begins "The Saving Sight" thus:

> Man ever delights to behold, to contemplate and admire, that object which possesses his highest esteem, which holds the ascendency in his affections. The miser loves to look at his gold, to handle it, and count it—and that, because it is his portion and his happiness. The man of the world delights to see his beautiful farms, his flocks and herds, and large possessions; because his chief happiness is bound up in them. The drunkard loves to look upon the bottle and the intoxicating bowl.—The very sight of them warms his heart and elevates his mind; because in them is contained his chief pleasure and the greatest satisfaction which he enjoys in life. So, also, the real Christian, the new born child of God, loves to see Jesus and behold his glory, and with joy, delight, and wonder, to admire and adore his soul attracting beauty and loveliness; and for this reason—he is the centre of his love,

---

24. McGready, *Works*, 176.

25. Keith Watkins, "The Sacramental Character of the Camp Meeting," *Discipliana* 54 (Spring 1994): 15.

26. Ibid., 9.

27. McGready, *Works*, 175; quoted in Watkins, "The Sacramental Character," 9.

his portion, his inheritance, and the soul and substance of his happiness. Christ, in his esteem, is the fairest among ten thousand and
altogether lovely. He fills his heart and his affections—he is dearer
to his soul than life itself, with all its pleasures and comforts; and his
greatest happiness on earth, is to "*see Jesus*"—to have sweet communion and fellowship with him, and to feel his love shed abroad in his
heart; yea, the very heaven after which his soul longs and pants, is to
"*see Jesus*"—to see him forever and be like him.[28]

He insists that when Christians "do not enjoy his presence, . . . they feel
an empty void within, the world could never fill. Nothing but a view of Jesus
can afford them happiness." This experience of "seeing Jesus" is what every
Christian strives for:

> Indeed, the believer's great object, from the moment of his conversion
> till the hour of his death is, that he may see Jesus—that he may behold
> his glory and enjoy sweet sensible communion with him here below;
> and that he may see him eternally as he is, and forever enjoy him in
> the world of glory and blessedness above.[29]

At the table, the Christian "sees" the whole story of redemption. When
McGready is using the metaphor of sight, he refers to the passion of Christ,
and his descriptions of the sufferings of Christ in these passages are vivid
indeed. In "The Meeting of Christ and His Disciples," McGready depicts the
crucifixion in response to the question "When Jesus meets with his disciples
at his table, what appearance will he make?"

> They shall see him as did the penitent thief on the cross; they shall
> see him as the penitent Col. Gardiner [presumably someone known
> to those gathered at Race Creek], and thousands of repenting and
> believing sinners have seen him; they shall behold him exhibited
> hanging on the cross, all drenched in blood and tears; while the crim-
> son streams of blood divine flow from the wounds inflicted by the
> scourges, nails, thorns and spear. —You will behold him in the gar-
> den, sweating—"*great drops of blood falling down to the ground*"; ye will
> see him at Pilate's bar, insulted and scourged: and, methinks you will
> hear those groans which awaked the dead—the groans of an incarnate
> God, which shocked the universe! —Methinks you will see that face,
> brighter than the light of ten thousand suns, spat upon, black and
> mangled, swelled with strokes and red with gore, and expressive of
> love and indescribable anguish: you will hear him addressing you in

28. McGready, *Works*, 348; cf. Song 5:10, 16; Ps. 42:1.
29. McGready, *Works*, 349, 350.

such language as this, O sinners! See what I suffer for you—at how dear a price I purchased for your pardon, salvation and eternal life! Behold how much I love you.[30]

Not only does the communicant witness Christ's suffering, but also Christ's glory:

> When you meet with Jesus, you shall see many crowns upon his head; you shall see him riding upon the white horse of the everlasting gospel, clothed, with a vesture dipped in blood, and a name written upon his vesture and on his thigh—KING OF KINGS, AND LORD OF LORDS. —You shall see him with millions of crowns—one for every pardoned and believing rebel: and every genuine conversion adds one to their number. And shall not Christ gain a new crown in Henderson county, at Race creek, on the fourth Sabbath in July, 1810?[31]

At the table, the believer experiences the fullness of God's revelation in Jesus Christ: "You shall see him clad with all the glories of the Godhead. . . . You shall see him as your Prophet, Priest and King—your Father, your Redeemer, your Shepherd, and your guide—your strong hold, your hiding place and sure defence—your righteousness, your hope, your joy—your peace, your heaven, and your ALL."[32] It is at the table, too, that the Christian sees the promise of the life to come and receives assurance that divine glory awaits the faithful.

In these brief excerpts, one notices McGready's use of Scripture; the language from Revelation, which he uses often, is among his favorites. He also sounds classical Reformed themes (e.g., Christ as Prophet, Priest, and King) as he exhorts his hearers to prepare themselves for this meeting at the Table and urges them toward conversion to new life.

McGready echoes a theme of Calvin's when, through the metaphor of sight, he asserts that Christ is visible in both Word and sacrament. At times, he explains, "Christ is to be seen in his word. . . . The Bible is the treasury in which this pearl of Great price is hid, and all that is wanting is spiritual eyes to see it in every page and in every sentence." Yet at other times, he continues, worshipers see the Lord in the sacrament, when Christ "meets them at his table. Then he appears to their view, clad in the dyed garments of salvation— in his vesture dipped in blood."[33] It is through both "word and ordinances"

---

30. Ibid., 362.
31. Ibid., 363.
32. Ibid., 363–64.
33. Ibid., 353, 354.

that "Christ and his people meet and hold communion"; through these the believers are strengthened, increasing in grace and deepening their knowledge of truth.[34]

McGready often expresses this partnership of Word and sacrament by referring to the Emmaus story. In Emmaus, he explains, one sees that "a saving view of Christ" is "simply a divine illumination of the mind."[35] The Spirit reveals Jesus to believers in both Scripture and ordinance, "opening their understanding" and showing to them "their title to heaven."[36] His references to the story make it clear that he expects his listeners to immediately recognize the allusion and understand his use of it.

Watkins asserts that McGready uses sight verbs (see, view, behold, etc.) in two ways: first, to describe spiritual experience; and second, to refer to physical experience. Not only is Christ presented before believers in the sacrament, but his presence with people is also exhibited outwardly by the falling, crying, and groaning often displayed by worshipers at sacramental revivals. He points to a passage from "The Meeting of Christ and His Disciples" to illustrate his point: "When Christ meets with his children, he cannot be hid—strange things are to be seen when he comes into a congregation, and meets his people in the administration of his supper, or in the ordinances of his house."[37] Watkins comments that "the tumultuous character of the sacramental assemblies is clearly implied as empirical evidence that Christ is meeting sinners in the administration of the Eucharist."[38]

This study will not explore in detail the demonstrative behaviors of revival worshipers that others have described so well.[39] We simply observe that accounts of the ecstatic worship experienced during the Great Revival sound quite similar to descriptions of those who attended the Scottish sacramental seasons. Furthermore, some of the most interesting features of McGready's preaching appear to be directly related to the piety and focus of the holy fairs that his Scots-Irish ancestors brought with them to America: the eschatological emphasis in the sacramental sermons, and the use of language from the Song of Songs to describe the relationships between Christ and the believer.

The eschatological emphasis of sacramental revivals. Leigh Eric Schmidt points out that in the sacramental piety of eighteenth-century Scotland, emphasis

34. Ibid., 64.
35. Ibid., 353.
36. Ibid., 64.
37. Ibid., 375.
38. Watkins, "The Sacramental Character," 10–11.
39. Boles, Conkin, Eslinger, and Schmidt all give thorough descriptions of the enthusiastic worship of revival goers. McGready's own accounts in his missives to *Western Missionary Magazine* and *New York Missionary Magazine*, as well as that included in his *Works*, are particularly vivid.

shifted from remembering the suffering of Christ to "awaiting the mystical marriage to the Bridegroom." In other words, the Lord's Supper was highly eschatological in focus, and worshipers looked forward more than they looked backward.

> The Eucharist not only re-presented the Last Supper and the Passion, but also anticipated the great feast with Christ in heaven as well as his triumphal return. Eschatology was the final grand theme of the sacramental occasion. The saints, no matter how wrapped up in Christ's love, were still waiting for something more.[40]

Worshipers came to the table to anticipate the banquet they would one day enjoy in heaven, and approached the sacrament as a little heaven on earth.[41] The sacramental occasion itself, as well as the devotional activities that surrounded it, "lifted the saints out of the world—'a strange Country, a Place of their Pilgrimage'—and gave them glimpses of *the other World above*'—'their Country and their Home.'" Renewed and strengthened, believers could carry on, knowing that the experiences of union with Christ which they enjoyed on earth would one day "yield to 'full, satisfying, and everlasting' communion in heaven."[42]

An examination of McGready's sacramental sermons reveals that he is undoubtedly an heir to the piety of the holy fairs. One of the themes most prominent in his preaching is that of the Lord's Supper as a foretaste of heaven. At the Table, Christ gives those who commune "a taste of heaven, or a faith's view of their everlasting home."[43] This theme is woven together with that of sight when McGready proclaims,

> Because a sight of Jesus is a foretaste of heaven, of the immortal glory of the heavenly state, and of its enjoyments; gives him upon earth joy unspeakable and full of glory; and bright hopes of joy above; such as *"eye hath not seen, nor the ear heard, neither have entered into the heart of man"*: and gives a blessed assurance of dwelling forever in the presence of the Lord—there to feast upon heavenly food, and drink of the water of life, springing from the foot of the throne of God and the Lamb.[44]

40. Schmidt, *Holy Fairs*, 166.

41. Early American Methodists expressed the same view. See Lester Ruth, *A Little Heaven Below: Worship at Early Methodist Quarterly Meetings* (Nashville: Abingdon Press, 2000).

42. Schmidt, *Holy Fairs*, 168.

43. McGready, *Works*, 65.

44. Ibid., 358.

Heaven is actually "brought down to earth" at the communion table, which is "spread with the dainties of Paradise: the bread of life, the hidden manna, and the grapes of Eschol, with all the rich blessings purchased by the death of Jesus Christ."[45]

At the Scottish communions and the American revivals that followed, worshipers celebrated at "the *lower* Table" in this life, just as they would one day commune at "the *higher* Table." When they reached that goal, their pilgrimage would be complete, for "heaven was the sacramental season perfected."[46] McGready uses this same language when he prepares his congregation for the impending sacrament:

> It is in this dress, in this glorious white robe, that you must appear at Christ's earthly table, next Sabbath day. And in this glorious white robe you shall appear at the upper table on the top of Mount Zion, in the fields of Paradise under the shadow of the tree of life. It is this that covers all the ransomed millions, redeemed out of all nations, and kindreds, and tongues, and people upon the earth.[47]

Thus are the themes of preparation, pilgrimage, and promise braided together in his exhortation.

Eschatological themes sound throughout McGready's sermons. He tells his listeners that the sacrament is "a heavenly meeting. It will bear some faint resemblance to the glorious and happy meeting which will shortly take place between Christ and his followers, in the Paradise of God—in the heavenly city of the New Jerusalem. Christ is there, and his presence constitutes heaven."[48] Furthermore, at the sacrament worshipers not only meet with Christ, but they also enjoy communion with those who have died in the faith:

> And when our Lord's table is spread in the wilderness, and he holds communion with his saints, I think it is rational and scriptural to suppose, that the angels are hovering over the table and the assembly, rejoicing with Christ over the dear bought purchase of his blood, and waiting to bear joyful tidings to the heavenly mansions. And while they are sitting at the table, and communing with their Lord, it is more than probable, that some of their Christian friends and brethren, who once sat with them at the same table, and under the same sermons—with whom they spent many happy days and nights before, but now have left the world and gone home to the church triumphant

---

45. Ibid., 178.

46. Schmidt, *Holy Fairs*, 168. Recall the eucharistic hymns of the Wesleys mentioned in chap. 2.

47. McGready, *Works*, 371.

48. Ibid., 368.

above; —I say it is more than probable, that some of these will be mingling with the angelic band around the *"heirs of salvation."*[49]

McGready's use of the psalms and the Song of Songs. In urging his listeners toward the table, McGready's often uses the language of Psalm 42 to describe the believer's desire for communion. The language of "longing" or "panting" appears in several sermons and echoes the piety of the holy fairs. In the following excerpt from "The Saving Sight," one notices allusions not only to the Psalm 42 but also to the Song of Songs as McGready describes the Christian's yearning for Christ:

> Every view of Christ leaves an anxious longing and thirst for him. This will appear evident from the example of Moses, who, although he lived in the nearest intimacy with his God—though Jehovah conversed with him face to face, as a man converses with his friend: all this does not satisfy him. He prays for closer communion and brighter discoveries. Lord, *"I beseech thee to show me thy glory."* This is the case of the spouse, when she is in his banquetting house under the banner of his love, she desires closer fellowship with him. *"Stay me with flagons, comfort me with apples; for I am sick of love."* And this is the experience of every Christian. In a word, a view of Christ breaks the hard heart—warms the frozen heart—and gives life to the dead soul; —heals all diseases of the sin sick soul—subdues the power of sin—quickens the new nature—and renders obedience easy. It fills the soul with joy and comfort—gives it a taste of heaven upon earth—and qualifies it for immortal glory.[50]

In "The Meeting of Christ and His Disciples," McGready compares "the soul who would meet Jesus" to "the spouse in the song of Solomon [who] seeks him from ordinance to ordinance—through the streets and lanes of the city."[51] This phrase captures the sense of longing and waiting that is central to the use of language from that book. As Schmidt explains, the Canticles voice the theme of longing as well as that of fulfillment. Although their souls were married to Christ in the Supper, "final union eluded them. Their sacramental piety recognized that lack, affirmed the need to wait, and offered foretastes of the glories to come. Whatever consummation of faith they experienced in this world was but prelude to a grander fulfillment in heaven."[52]

---

49. Ibid., 369.
50. Ibid., 357; cf. Song 2:4–5.
51. McGready, *Works*, 360.
52. Schmidt, *Holy Fairs*, 166.

Yet even on earth, believers experience the overwhelming love of God in communion. In "A Sacramental Meditation," McGready describes the astonishment of heaven's citizens who "see the omnipotent Jehovah seated at his table and holding communion with the worthless sons and daughters of Adam, embracing them in his arms and *kissing them with the kisses of his mouth*." Here at the table the "pardoned sinner" sees "the smiles of his lovely face," feels the love of God in the heart, and is moved to repentance. One hears the theme of sight combined with language from Song of Songs when McGready declares that when communicants see God's glory in the face of Christ at the Table, they are struck with awe. Just as a king provides a banquet in his palace, so God "entertains his children in his own house," and the spouse is heard to say, "He took me into his banqueting house and his banner over me was love." The believer at the Table, then, is at once a child of God and a lover of Christ, aware of one's own sinfulness ("black as the tents of Kedar"), and yet overwhelmed by love. Christ "embraces them in his arms, holds them in his bosom, and presses them to his heart."[53]

McGready makes extensive use of marital themes in "The Believer's Espousal to Christ," in which he compares the conversion of a sinner to "the time of the soul's espousal to Christ." He explains the relationships in full detail:

> The word espousal is expressive of marriage and all the accompanying circumstances and solemnities. Here it is applied to the union of the soul to Christ in conversion, and with propriety too, inasmuch as the marriage covenant and the mutual love peculiar to the married state, are frequently used in scripture to represent that union and its happy consequences—the Lord Jesus being called by the endearing epithet of bridegroom, and the believing soul the bride or spouse. Saith the Spirit to the soul, "Thy maker is thine husband: the Lord of hosts is his name." The figure is very appropriate and expressive. For,
>
> 1st. As the proposals of marriage are made by the bridegroom and not the bride, so Christ first proposes the spiritual union to the soul.
>
> 2nd. In marriage the bridegroom and bride give themselves cheerfully to each other, and are no more twain, but one flesh; so in the spiritual covenant, Christ and the believing soul are so closely united, that the believer becomes one body and one spirit with Christ, and as our Lord expresses it, he is one with Christ, and he is one with the Father. The union is strong. The soul is so completely identified with Christ, that it is declared, "That neither death, nor life, nor angels, nor principalities, nor powers, nor things present, nor things to come, nor height nor depth, nor any other creature shall be able to separate" it from him.

53. McGready, *Works*, 178; cf. Song 1:2, 5; 2:4.

3rd. As the bridegroom and bride become one, in marriage, he is bound for all debts or demands against the bride; and she at the same time is jointly possessed and legally entitled to share in the wealth and property of the bridegroom.[54]

He extols the virtues of the Bridegroom by using language from the Song of Songs. "The bridegroom is beauty itself. . . . He is fairer than the sons of men—the 'rose of Sharon and the Lilly of the valley.' He 'is white and ruddy, the chiefest among ten thousand'—he is altogether lovely."[55] In comparison, "the soul whom he courts to become his bride, is a mass of depravity and moral filth—fit for the vengeance of eternal fire."[56]

In comparing the loveliness of Christ to the ugliness of the lover whom Christ seeks, McGready describes the desperate state of the sinner in need of salvation. Yet he also uses the metaphor of courtship and marriage to describe the conversion experience; here again echoes of the Canticles are heard. When "the sinner beholds Christ by faith, and all the glorious beauty of the bridegroom, he cries out" in rapture and praise. "This is the day of the soul's espousal to Christ," McGready declares, "when with praise, gratitude, and wonder it falls before the Eternal All, and in language of ravished delight, exclaims, Oh Jesus, thou art sufficient. 'Whom have I in heaven but thee? And there is none upon the earth that I desire besides thee.'"[57]

He goes on to describe the joys and delights of first love to those of the newly converted Christian—and the shame and sadness of the backsliding believer to one whose love has cooled—all in an effort to persuade those who have stayed away from the Communion table to come back to the embraces of their first love. He calls to mind the first sacrament that was celebrated in Henderson County, Kentucky, when "many . . . appeared to manifest, the kindness of their youth and love of their espousal, and seemed to go after the Lord. . . . Every evening and morning, the woods resounded with their importunate prayers and cries to God. At the table of the Lord, they appeared to feel heaven upon earth."[58] Less than a decade has passed since that time, he says, and yet those once-fervent believers now fail to pray privately, or gather for worship; they are absent from the Lord's Table. He leaves his listeners with a question: "And now let every backsliding soul seriously inquire, as if in sight of the bar of Jehovah—was my soul espoused to Christ? Was it

54. McGready, *Works*, 440–41.
55. Ibid., 442; cf. Song 2:1; 5:10, 16.
56. McGready, *Works*, 442.
57. Ibid., 445; cf. Song 4:9; Ps. 73:25.
58. McGready, *Works*, 447–48.

Christ or was it some subtle deception of the Devil."[59] Presumably an extemporaneous application section follows this thudding conclusion; one might easily imagine McGready then cajoling believers to come back to their first love, meeting him at the Table, to experience once again "heaven upon earth." Images of marriage and espousal are used, then, to describe the relationship of the converted soul to Christ, as well as to depict the experience of the sacrament, where lover meets spouse with joy, thanksgiving, and praise. Here it is possible to see a parallel with Calvin's understanding of union with Christ as being both once and for all (in baptism) as well as an ongoing, renewable experience (available in the Lord's Supper).

Near the end of his ministry, while serving a church that is no longer thriving, McGready preached a sermon titled "The Meeting of Christ and His Disciples." In it he leads his listeners gently along; although he exhorts his hearers to prepare themselves to come to the Table, there is little mention of hell. Rather, he dwells on the benefits and joys of the sacrament, encouraging his listeners to seek Christ and to remember him, assuring them that they will indeed see their Lord. And when they do meet him at the Table, he tells them, they will enjoy such sweet communion that they will be "refreshed with the new wine of Canaan and . . . filled with joy unspeakable."[60]

McGready preached this sermon at Race Creek in Henderson County, Kentucky, in the last community he served as pastor. It was 1810, seven years before his death. By this time he had grown too old-fashioned for his day; the sacramental seasons were waning, and a new camp meeting revivalism was beginning to take hold. Yet here near the end of his life and ministry, McGready presents his most thoughtful, complete, and eloquent statement of eucharistic theology and Christian faith. It is, perhaps, a fitting culmination to the tradition that he inherited from his ancestors. It is to that inheritance that attention is now turned. In the sermons of Gilbert Tennent, a prominent figure of the First Great Awakening in America, the themes identified in McGready's preaching are even more apparent, and the metaphors of spiritual marriage and union with Christ are even more pronounced.

59. Ibid., 448.
60. Ibid., 375.

5

"A Conjugal Love"

Gilbert Tennent's
Eucharistic Preaching

While a bevy of ministers fueled the revivals of America's First Great Awakening, Gilbert Tennent (1703–64) stands among them as one of the most significant figures of the day. He was particularly influential in the mid-Atlantic region, where Scots-Irish immigrants had settled in large numbers, serving first as a minister in the Raritan Valley of New Jersey (then frontier land) and later as pastor of Second Presbyterian Church in Philadelphia. Throughout his ministry, Tennent's sacramental preaching reflected the Scots-Irish tradition of which he was part, a tradition that not only emphasized the necessity of carefully examining and preparing oneself before participating in the Lord's Supper, but one that also exulted in the joy of meeting Christ at the Table. His sermons are full of vivid images of betrothal and marriage, as well as poetic love language from the Song of Songs, which he employs to woo the faithful believer to the consummation that is communion. Although this imagery is observed in McGready's preaching, the sermons of Gilbert Tennent exhibit an even fuller use of the language of love, sexuality, and marriage to describe the relationship between Christ and his beloved.

FROM THE FRONTIER TO PHILADELPHIA:
TENNENT'S EDUCATION AND MINISTRY

Gilbert Tennent was born into a family of Scots living in Ulster, in the northeast of Ireland. By the close of the seventeenth century, Ulster had become an enclave of dissenting Presbyterians, rebels against both the English crown and the Anglican Church, who were forced by the government to settle there.

These dissenters kept alive the Scottish Presbyterian tradition of field communions, or sacramental occasions, a distinctive practice that helped to maintain ties to their heritage.[1]

When Gilbert was fifteen years old, his family moved to America, eventually settling in Bucks County, Pennsylvania. His father, William Tennent, served as a Presbyterian minister there and in time established what became known as the "Log College" (so dubbed because it met in a building constructed with logs), a grassroots theological school for young men unable to travel the long distances to New England or Scotland for their ministerial training.[2] The first student to be schooled in William Tennent's theological and homiletical program was his oldest son, Gilbert.[3]

In the Middle Colonies in the early eighteenth century, obtaining a theological education was no easy task. There were no local colleges or universities, and most young men were unable to afford the cost of attending schools in Europe or the Northern Colonies. As a result, many studied privately with a local pastor or at a home-based school such as William Tennent's. This method was controversial; many Presbyterian pastors who had been educated at theological institutions criticized the lack of consistency in training among those ministers who were schooled privately and bemoaned the absence of established standards for ordination. Most agreed that Tennent's students showed competence in biblical languages, for instance, but some cast aspersions on what they considered to be the teacher's lack of expertise in theology and philosophy.[4] Tennent's Log College clearly met a need, however. During the 1730s large numbers of Scots left Ulster for America, and by the end of the decade fully one-third of Presbyterian ministers had been educated at the University of Edinburgh or by William Tennent.[5]

The elder Tennent insisted that the spiritual experience of the heart is as important as the spiritual instruction of the mind.[6] As Coalter explains, he also "stressed spiritual over external participation in church rites," such as the Lord's Supper. A formal reception of the sacrament was inadequate, but a spiritual reception was the mark of a lively and conscientious piety.[7] Gilbert Tennent, along with the other ministers who were products of the Log College, echoed the same themes in their own revivalist activities. They derided

1. Janet F. Fishburn, "Gilbert Tennent, Established 'Dissenter,'" *Church History* 63 (1994): 31.

2. Milton J. Coalter Jr., *Gilbert Tennent, Son of Thunder* (Westport, CT: Greenwood Press, 1986), 4–5. This is the only published full-length biography of Gilbert Tennent.

3. Ibid., 9.

4. Ibid., 49–50.

5. Fishburn, "Established 'Dissenter,'" 34.

6. Coalter, *Gilbert Tennent*, 8.

7. Ibid., 6–7.

"the emptiness of contemporary ritual and mere rational assent to theological tenets," and asserted that "conviction was the first step to salvation and practical piety the unavoidable culmination of a true experience of divine grace in the human heart."[8] This concern with striving for a balance between learning and piety placed William Tennent and the Log College fellows squarely in the camp of New Side Presbyterians, who were much more interested in revivalism than their more sedate Old Side (antirevivalist) colleagues.[9]

If Presbyterian clergy were divided on questions of education and enthusiasm, they were united in viewing preaching as being of the utmost importance. As Hughes Oliphant Old points out, it was common for eighteenth-century clergy to express their theological ideas through sermons rather than treatises.[10] Leonard J. Trinterud, in his now-classic study of American Presbyterianism, further explains that "one of the striking aspects of the preaching of the Log College men was its heavy dogmatical approach and content." Even in the context of revivalism, they were less interested in popular or topical preaching and more concerned with faithfully and rigorously laying out the Federal theology, then standing "between it and their people to reason and plead."[11]

This characteristic can be observed in the eucharistic sermons of Gilbert Tennent as well as in the body of his preaching as a whole. It is especially apparent in the sermons of preparation for Communion that Tennent is concerned with his hearers' right understanding of the process by which they are saved by grace. For him, a solid grasp of doctrine is every bit as important as an enlivened experience of grace. It will be clear from the analysis of the sermons below that the sermons preached just before the celebration of the sacrament take on a more poetic, more persuasive tone, but sermons preached in the days before Communion are focused on giving clear theological explications. Like other Federal theologians, Tennent consistently speaks of two

---

8. Ibid., 9.

9. Fishburn, "Established 'Dissenter,'" 34.

10. Hughes Oliphant Old, "Gilbert Tennent and the Preaching of Piety in Colonial America: Newly Discovered Manuscripts in Speer Library," *Princeton Seminary Bulletin* 10, no. 2, new series (1989): 133–34.

11. Leonard J. Trinterud, *The Forming of an American Tradition: A Re-examination of Colonial Presbyterianism* (Philadelphia: Westminster Press, 1949), 177. Federal theology was built on the idea that God is in covenant with God's people (beginning with Adam, the "federal" head of humankind, and continuing with Jesus Christ) and was systematized in the Westminster documents. "Though typically Puritan, and carried to its clearest development by Puritanism," Trinterud explains, "the Federal, or Covenant, theology was to take its deepest roots in Scottish Presbyterianism. The 'Covenanter' movement in Scotland, together with the adoption of the Westminster symbols by the Scottish Church, settled this theology deep in the hearts of the Scottish people" (171).

types of religious knowledge: the doctrinal, or speculative; and the subjective, or experimental (experiential, in contemporary parlance); his concern with balancing both is apparent throughout his preaching.[12]

In his early days on the frontier, Tennent was known as a fiery preacher. In 1740, when George Whitefield conducted one of his evangelistic tours through New York and New England, he invited Tennent to accompany him. The experience led Whitefield to call his companion "a son of thunder [who] does not fear the faces of men."[13] Within a few years of itinerating with White-field, however, Tennent found himself in a rather different environment when Second Presbyterian Church in Philadelphia, a new congregation founded as a result of Whitefield's preaching, called him to be their pastor. (Philadelphia was well-populated with Scots-Irish immigrants and was a natural place for Presbyterian churches to achieve a strong foothold.[14]) Not surprisingly, this more-sophisticated urban environment required something of a stylistic shift in Tennent's preaching, yet his theological and spiritual convictions and his "covenanting spirit" remained unchanged.[15]

Janet Fishburn explains that although Tennent's focus may have shifted somewhat during his ministry in Philadelphia, he never cut his ties with the New Side pastors and churches on the frontier.[16] Her point is borne out in the case of the Communion sermons, which show a remarkable consistency in style and content throughout Tennent's ministry. Even as Second Pres-byterian became "more self-consciously Presbyterian" in its polity and its worship under Tennent's leadership,[17] and while the patterns associated with sacramental occasions—usually rural affairs—gave way to more sedate and regularly scheduled observances, Tennent continued to adapt the spirituality he inherited from his Scots-Irish ancestors.[18] Although the external trappings of that spirituality may have altered over the years, the internal convictions did not change. Whether in the fields of New Jersey or the streets of Phila-delphia, Gilbert Tennent always maintained that the celebration of the Lord's

12. Ibid., 187.

13. George Whitefield, *George Whitefield's Journals*, ed. William Wale, reprint ed. (Gainesville, FL: Scholar's Facsimiles and Reprints, 1969), 344; quoted in Coalter, *Gilbert Tennent*, 72–73.

14. Janet F. Fishburn, "Pennsylvania 'Awakenings,' Sacramental Seasons, and Ministry," in *Scholarship, Sacraments, and Service: Historical Studies in Protestant Tradition; Essays in Honor of Bard Thompson*, ed. Daniel B. Clendenin and W. David Buschart (Lewiston, NY: Edwin Mellen Press, 1990), 63. Fishburn quotes one source as estimating that during a 20-year period ending in 1750, between 6,000 and 12,000 Scots-Irish persons emigrated from Ulster to America each year.

15. Fishburn, "Established 'Dissenter,'" 35.

16. Ibid., 36.

17. Coalter, *Gilbert Tennent*, 139–40.

18. Fishburn, "Established 'Dissenter,'" 38–39.

Supper was crucial to the life of faith, that proper preparation was necessary for participation in the sacrament, and that unparalleled comfort and joy are found when the believer meets Christ in communion.

TENNENT'S EUCHARISTIC SERMONS

Gilbert Tennent was a prolific preacher and author. His ministry spanned nearly forty years; eighty of his sermons were published during his lifetime, in addition to essays on both political and ecclesial matters.[19] He was best known for his sermon "The Danger of an Unconverted Ministry," preached at Nottingham, Pennsylvania, in 1740, in which he delivered a scathing indictment against ministers whose sermons (and lives) were doctrinally orthodox but lacking in the conviction that comes from spiritual awakening.[20] "Unconverted Ministry" was reprinted numerous times, and Tennent was chagrined that it became his trademark sermon. As Hughes Oliphant Old says, "It made him look like a firebrand, and he really was not anything of the sort."[21] What Tennent was, rather, was a Presbyterian minister steeped in Reformed theology and convinced of the necessity of both doctrinal understanding and fervent piety. He also believed that preaching was for both sinners and saints. Tennent was known for preaching the "terrors"—the demands of the law that would convict sinners into recognizing their need for salvation. The terrors, as Leonard Trinterud explains, were not only for those outside the church, but also for "the smug, the self-righteous, the secret hypocrite, and the presumptuous Church member who expects God to take him as he is and for what he is. . . . This preaching of the terrors of the law was not, therefore, an emotional orgy, but a vehement attack on all forms of self-righteousness."[22] Yet Tennent also preached the comforts of the gospel to those who had already been convicted, "supplying the gospel balsam to sin's deep wound."[23]

It was not unusual for those hearing Tennent's preaching to respond demonstratively. His critics accused him of stirring up the crowds who came to hear his revivalistic preaching, but Tennent maintained that emotional reactions were to be expected when people came face-to-face with their own

---

19. Old, "Gilbert Tennent," 134; see also the bibliography of sermons provided in Coalter, *Gilbert Tennent*, 203–10.

20. Gilbert Tennent, *The Danger of An Unconverted Ministry, Considered in a Sermon on Mark VI.34. Preached at Nottingham, in Pennsylvania, March 8. Anno 1739*, 40. 2nd ed. (Philadelphia: Benjamin Franklin, 1740).

21. Old, "Gilbert Tennent," 134.

22. Trinterud, *Forming of an American Tradition*, 183.

23. Coalter, *Gilbert Tennent*, 45.

"damnable state."[24] The revivals, in fact, were highly emotional events. William Tennent Jr. described a revival at the Freehold church where his brother John was pastor:

> I have seen both Minister and People wet their tears as with a bedewing Rain. It was no uncommon Thing to see Persons in the time of Hearing, sobbing as if their Hearts would break, but without any public Out-cry; and some have been carry'd out of the Assembly (being overcome) as if they had been dead.[25]

As seen in McGready's preaching, the goal of the preacher during Communion seasons was not only to convince the unconverted of their sinful state, but also to urge believers to come to the Table. In a sermon that focuses on preaching, ordinances, and the public worship of the people, Tennent asserts that "the preached word which is a part of public worship is not only appointed as the ordinary mean of the conversion of sinners, but likewise as the stated mean of the edification and establishment of the saints."[26]

PREPARATION FOR COMMUNION

Although Trinterud asserts that the Log College men "strove to bring every man and woman present at the service to communion with God and each other in the sacrament," and that they never required evidence of conversion for admission to the Table,[27] it is clear that Tennent and others did indeed have expectations about proper preparation for the sacrament. Six months of preparation, in the form of doctrinal preaching and guidance from the clergy, preceded the revivals at Freehold, New Jersey, where Gilbert Tennent's brother, John Tennent, was pastor from 1730 to 1732.[28] Not long after that time, in 1735, Gilbert Tennent introduced an overture to the Philadelphia Synod, urging ministers to attend to their parishioners' preparation for Communion, and to "make it their awful, constant, and diligent care, to approve themselves to God, to their own consciences, and to their hearers, [as] serious faithful

---

24. Ibid., 105.

25. Maurice W. Armstrong, Lefferts A. Loetscher, and Charles A. Anderson, eds., *The Presbyterian Enterprise: Sources of American Presbyterian History* (Philadelphia: Westminster Press, 1956), 36.

26. Gilbert Tennent, sermon manuscript, AMs, n.d., The Gilbert Tennent manuscript collection, Henry Luce III Library, Princeton Theological Seminary, Princeton, NJ. See the transcription of this manuscript (12) in Appendix D, below.

27. Trinterud, *Forming of an American Tradition*, 181.

28. Armstrong, Loetscher, and Anderson, *The Presbyterian Enterprise*, 36.

stewards of the mysteries of God, and of holy exemplary conversions."[29] Furthermore, Tennent believed that children should receive catechetical training from their parents, and that adults ought "to be regularly visited for close examinations of their behavior and, during private precommunion conferences, tested in their experimental knowledge of grace."[30]

Clearly, then, Tennent took preparation for Communion quite seriously and expected the members of his congregation to do the same. While his preaching was, to be sure, evangelistic in character, the sacrament was for faithful Christians and did not operate as a "converting ordinance" (in the sense that non-Christians might be converted to the faith in or by the sacrament) for unbelievers. In his sermon "Brotherly Love Recommended," preached at a sacramental observance in 1748, Tennent makes it clear that among those listening are people who will not commune, as well as people who are preparing for that event: "But let me speak a few Words to the Communicants, and then conclude," he says, addressing the remainder of his sermon to those who would come to the Table.[31]

Tennent's communion sermons reflect his desire that the people not only prepare for Communion, but also seek it, long for it, and delight in it. To that end he preached two types of sermons in the context of the sacramental occasion: preparatory sermons, which urged people toward self-examination and repentance; and invitation (or action) sermons, which sought to woo believers to communion with Christ at the Supper. Over the course of the days preceding the celebration of the sacrament, he cautions listeners that those who come to the table unworthily are guilty of "profaning a sacred Institution"; it is as if they "put a new Spear into his blessed Side, and Thorns into his holy Head." He goes on to add, however, that Paul's admonition against eating and drinking judgment "was never intended by the blessed God, to frighten humble and sincere Persons from their Duty; but only to deter the Wicked and Secure (that is, those who did not intend to prepare themselves for the sacrament and those who imagined that they did not need to do so)."[32] To those who might hesitate to come to the table because of their sense of

---

29. *Minutes of the Presbyterian Church in America, 1706–1788*, ed. Guy S. Klett (Philadelphia: Presbyterian Historical Society, 1976), 122–23; quoted in Coalter, *Gilbert Tennent*, 41.

30. Coalter, *Gilbert Tennent*, 41–42.

31. Gilbert Tennent, *Brotherly Love recommended, by the Argument of the Love of Christ: A Sermon, Preached at Philadelphia, January 1747–8. Before the Sacramental Solemnity. With some Enlargement* (Philadelphia: Benjamin Franklin and David Hall, 1748), 33.

32. Gilbert Tennent, "The Duty of Self-Examination, considered in a Sermon, On I Cor. 11.28. Preached at Maiden-Head in New-Jersey, October 22, 1737. Before the Celebration of the Lord's-Supper," in *Sermons on Sacramental Occasions by Divers Ministers* (Boston: J. Draper, for D. Henchman in Cornhill, 1739), 132.

unworthiness, Tennent echoes Calvin by answering that the only proof of worthiness required by Jesus Christ "is an afflictive Sense of our Unworthiness, and an earnest Hunger after his Righteousness."[33]

The fullest explication of what is expected of those who seek to meet the Lord at his Table is seen in his sermon "The Duty of Self-Examination," preached in October of 1737 at Maidenhead, New Jersey. Using as his text 1 Corinthians 11:28 ("But let a man examine himself, and so let him eat of that bread, and drink of that cup"), he lays out what is necessary preparation for Communion. Beginning with Question 97 of the Westminster (Shorter) Catechism, "What is required of them who come to the Lord's Supper?" he proceeds immediately to his paraphrased answer: "To examine themselves whether they repent them truly of their former Sins; stedfastly purposing to lead a new Life; having a lively Faith in God's Mercy through Christ, with a thankful Remembrance of his Death, and be in Charity with all Men." Commenting further, Tennent continues, "These I take to be a sufficient Explication of the Matter of the Duty enjoyn'd."[34] In the pages that follow, he provides several reasons why believers should examine themselves before the sacrament: because God commands it; because guilt is contracted by one who participates unworthily, thereby subjecting that person to judgment; because it is necessary for a sense of comfort and hope in approaching the Table; and because "it is necessary in order to know our Sins, Mercies, and Wants; that we may mourn over the first, be thankful for the second and seek a Supply of the third."[35] Not only does Tennent supply the reasons for examining oneself before Communion, but he also provides a guide for how to go about such a process. Self-examination, he instructs, should be done solemnly, speedily (without delay), impartially, decisively, and regularly.[36]

This rigorous exercise is not for the purpose of reducing believers to groveling repentants, but to transform them into joyful communicants. At the end of his long sermon concerning the duty of self-examination, Tennent holds up a felicitous image, to which he calls believers:

---

33. Gilbert Tennent, "The Unsearchable Riches of Christ. Considered, in Two Sermons on Ephes. iii.8. Preached at New-Brunswick in New-Jersey, before the Celebration of the Lord's-Supper; which was the first Sabbath in August, 1737," in *Sermons on Sacramental Occasions by Divers Ministers* (Boston: J. Draper, for D. Henchman in Cornhill, 1739), 21–22. Calvin expressed this conviction in his *Short Treatise on the Lord's Supper* (152): "Therefore, when we feel our faith to be imperfect, and our conscience not so pure as not to accuse us of many vices, this must not hinder us presenting ourselves at the Holy Table of our Lord; provided that amid this infirmity we feel in our hearts that, without hypocrisy and deceit, we hope for salvation in Christ, and desire to live according to the rule of the gospel."

34. Tennent, "Duty of Self-Examination," 134.

35. Ibid., 136.

36. Ibid., 136–37.

> In the last place, be exhorted to put in Practice the Apostle's Direction in our Text. Let us conscientiously compare ourselves with what has been offered; and if upon Examination we find the Characters of the aforesaid Graces of Knowledge, Faith, Love, Repentance, and new Obedience in us, with some Measure of the Exercise of them, then should we come to the Lord's Table as to the Banquet of a Friend, eat that Bread, and drink that Cup.

He cannot resist adding one final sentence: "But if otherwise, stand off upon your Peril, till ye get your Hearts changed by divine Grace."[37] In spite of this final warning, it is the blessing of the Table to which he beckons the faithful.

Preparation for Communion does not only involve repenting from sin, but also achieving an awareness of the graces that Christ offers to believers. In "The Unsearchable Riches of Christ (II)," Tennent explains that those who seek communion with Christ not only know their own sin, but also have caught a glimpse of the all-sufficiency of Christ as well as their own inability to come to him by their own volition. Those who would come to the table "desire after Christ" (here Tennent cites, without quoting, verses from the second and fifth chapters of the Canticles, as well as Psalms 84 and 73). Believers seek after Christ as the Spouse sought after her lover (Canticles 3); they have "clos'd with Christ," accepting his offer of grace, rejoiced "at their finding of this Treasure," have "thoughts and affections" for Christ, and "labour to preserve and increase" the riches they have found in him.[38] Such is the process that one experiences who is truly prepared for the sacrament.

WOOING BELIEVERS TO THE TABLE

The path to the Table is stringent, and the process of preparation, which begins months before, culminates in the days just before celebrating the sacrament with preaching that urges the faithful to engage in thorough self-examination. When the day of Communion comes, however, the preaching takes on a radically different tone. In the sermon delivered just before the sacrament—what is sometimes called the "action sermon," when the invitation to the Table is given—the preacher acts as an advocate for Jesus, the lover who would woo his beloved to union in the sacrament. Occasionally Tennent compares himself to the servant of Abraham, who was dispatched to Laban's

---

37. Ibid., 143.
38. Gilbert Tennent, "The Unsearchable Riches of Christ: Sermon II," in *Sermons on Sacramental Occasions by Divers Ministers* (Boston: J. Draper, for D. Henchman in Cornhill, 1739), 52.

household in order to find a wife for Isaac. After calling the biblical story to mind, he exclaims:

> Even so we say unto you, the Great God who sent us is a mighty king, . . . and he has but one eternal son; to him hath he given all he hath, and this son of his is fallen in love with you. Will you accept his offer, if you will deal truly and kindly with our master [today]?[39]

He is even more direct in a sermon aptly titled "The Espousals, or a Passionate Perswasive to a Marriage with the Lamb of God," in which he begins by stating his purpose:

> Christian friends and dear Brethren, my Errand to you this Day from the Great God the Father of Jesus, resembles that of Eliezer of Damascus, Abraham's Servant, who was sent to wooe a Wife for his Masters Son: Brethren I come a wooing in the Name and Behalf of Christ my great Master the King's Son. My Business with you to day is to persuade you to be speedily and sincerely espoused to the Lamb of God, the Lord Jesus Christ. . . . Abraham's Servant had good Success, the God of his Master propser'd his Way; Rebeca, readily consented and said I will go, [Gen. 24] ver. 58. O that there may be found here some Rebeca, Lydia, or Zacheus, who is willing to consent to Day to a Marriage with the Lord Jesus.[40]

The theme of betrothal, or espousal, is prominent in Tennent's preaching at the sacrament. "De nuptiis cum Christo" ("On Marriage with Christ") draws on the parable of the wedding banquet from Matthew 22 and uses marital imagery, as well as numerous citations from the Song of Songs, to describe the nature of the believer's relationship to Jesus. Again Tennent states his purpose up front: "I shall at this tyme propose arguments to excite the sinners' compliance with the invitation to this marriage by showing that it is their true interest to do so."[41] He proceeds to describe the properties of the love of Jesus, who "designed to redeem and espouse us to himself forever." "O who would not espouse such a prince who sympathizes with his people in all their

---

39. Gilbert Tennent, "De nuptiis cum Christo," sermon manuscript, AMs, [17]53, The Gilbert Tennent manuscript collection, Henry Luce III Library, Princeton Theological Seminary, Princeton, NJ. See the transcription of this manuscript (1) in Appendix B, below.

40. Gilbert Tennent, *The Espousals, or, A Passionate Perswasive to a Marriage with the Lamb of God, wherein The Sinners Misery and The Redeemers Glory is Unvailed in. A Sermon upon Gen. 24.49. Preach'd at N. Brunswyck, June the 22d, 1735* (New York: Printed by J. Peter Zenger, 1735), 4–6.

41. Tennent, "De nuptiis"; see Appendix B, below.

sorrows," cries Tennent, "who puts his left hand of power under their heads and with his right hand of love and mercy embraces them?"[42] Unlike that of mortal men, the preacher argues, Christ's love is abiding:

> It is not hot and cold, as it is among men. What heat of love will some men show to those they espouse at first, but they soon cool in their affections. . . . Christ betroths forever. Is not this consideration enough to engage you to embrace the redeemer and return love for love?[43]

As the title implies, Tennent's sermon "The Espousals" relies heavily on images of marriage and love. After listing the qualities of Jesus that would make him a desirable husband, the preacher queries, "Will you not then, poor Sinners, give your Consent to be espoused to this beautiful Jesus?"[44] In case the listeners do not find Christ's charms persuasive enough, Tennent reminds them that marriage to Christ is necessary for salvation. "An absolute necessity should constrain you to be espoused to Christ," he warns, "for unless you be divorced from your Lusts, and Married to him, you'll be Damned to all Eternity."[45]

This harsh tone of warning is not the norm in these sermons, but the exception. Much more emphasis is placed on persuading the believer to come to the Table and to enjoy communion with Christ. "Consider how Christ woos you," Tennent cajoles. "Christ Jesus not only sends his Servants to woo and warn you, but he comes himself to invite you." Jesus is a patient lover, for "he bears with many Afronts, Delays, Refusals, and yet repeats his Love adresses; which considering his Majesty and our meanness is very admirable!" Furthermore, Christ is passionate, wooing "by the most endearing Compellations." (Here Tennent cites Canticles 5:2 and 4:8.)[46]

As the "Servant," Tennent gives much attention to trumpeting the charm and beauty of Jesus, often drawing on images from the Song of Songs. Jesus "is the perfection of beauty, the chiefest among ten thousand" (cf. Song 5:10);[47]

---

42. Ibid.; cf. Song 2:6; 8:3.

43. Tennent, "De nuptiis"; see Appendix B, below.

44. Tennent, *The Espousals*, 23.

45. Ibid., 34.

46. Ibid., 30.

47. Gilbert Tennent, "1. De unquentis ti, 2. De amore [Chris]to," sermon manuscript, AMs, Ag. [17]57, The Gilbert Tennent manuscript collection, Henry Luce III Library, Princeton Theological Seminary, Princeton, NJ. This manuscript has been transcribed and published in James B. Bennett, "'Love to Christ'—Gilbert Tennent, Presbyterian Reunion, and a Sacramental Sermon," *American Presbyterians* 71 (Summer 1993): 77–89; in notes below, page numbers refer to this publication; for this particular reference, see 83.

he is "the Beauty and Delight of the Heavens, the Darling of the blessed God, the inestimable Pearl of Price, the Rose of Sharon, the Lilly of the Vallies [2:1]. . . . All Nature faints before this transcendent Beauty, and yields nothing to represent his Excellency fully."[48] Tennent often alludes to Canticles 5:10 to describe the loveliness of Jesus, sometimes continuing to incorporate the next two verses as well, as in "The Espousals": "His Head is as the most fine Gold, his Locks are bushy and black as a Raven, his Eyes are as the Eyes of Doves, by the rivers of Waters washed with Milk, and fitly set."[49] Elsewhere Tennent evokes the whole of chapter 5 to illustrate how

> Christ is inexpressibly precious to Believers: the Spouse, in the 5th Chapter of the Song, after she had said what she could in Praise of her Lord's Excellency, by comparing him to the most amiable Things in nature, perceiving the Subject of her Discourse to swell beyond all Expression, she concludes abruptly, by saying, that he was alto-gether lovely; which was as much as to say, that his Loveliness was inexpressible.[50]

THE RAVISHING LOVE OF CHRIST

In the Song of Songs, the male lover speaks of being "ravished" by his com-panion. In the Communion sermons of Gilbert Tennent, it is most often the believer—the one in the role of the female lover of the Song—who finds oneself ravished by Christ. "O the ravishing Beauty, and surprising Glory of this blessed Love. . . . No wonder the Saints of the Church Militant are melted into Love and Ravishment, while they behold, by an Eye of Faith, the ami-able Glory and burning Radiancy, of this immerited, incomprehensible, and effectual Affection!"[51] Tennent extols the "ravishing Charms of his Grace"[52] and declares that "the love of Christ is sweet and soul-ravishing," then quotes Canticles 1:2 ("Let him kiss me with the kisses of his mouth: for thy love is better than wine") and 4:9 ("Thou hast ravished my heart, my sister, my spouse; thou hast ravished my heart with one of thine eyes, with one chain of

---

48. Tennent, "Unsearchable Riches (II)," 41.

49. Tennent, *The Espousals*, 24.

50. Gilbert Tennent, "The Preciousness of Christ to Believers, Consider'd in a Sermon on I Pet. ii. 7. Preach'd at New-Brunswick in New-Jersey. The first Sabbath in August, before the Celebration of the Lord's-Supper, Anno Domini, 1738," in *Sermons on Sacramental Occasions by Divers Ministers* (Boston: J. Draper, for D. Henchman in Cornhill, 1739), 263.

51. Tennent, "Unsearchable Riches (II)," 42–43.

52. Tennent, "Unsearchable Riches [I]," 12.

thy neck").[53] When the saints recognize "the depth of the riches both of the wisdom and knowledge of God" (Rom. 11:33) in the person of Jesus Christ, they "cry out with ravishment."[54]

In *The Espousals*, Tennent seeks to convince his hearers that Christ, as husband, is to be espoused. "All the Perfections of His Nature are engag'd to advance their eternal Interest, his Wisdom is theirs to guide them, his Power to guard them, his faithfulness to support them, his Love to ravish them, and his fullness to supply them," he proclaims.[55] Believers are not only delighted with Christ's love, but also changed by it, since "their Wills shall be ravished with embracing the supreme Good."[56]

Tennent's most exuberant recital is heard in "The Preciousness of Christ to Believers," another sermon preached just before the celebration of the sacrament. Just as "the Spouse in the Song was much enamour'd with the personal Beauty and Glory of Christ, . . . none can believingly behold the blessed Jesus, without being pleased and ravish'd with his Beauty."[57] And how does the believer apprehend this ravishing beauty? By faith.

> Thro faith they behold the ravishing Beauty and charming Glory of Christ, which makes them deem him the chief among ten thousand; the Rose of Sharon, the Lillies of the Valleys. Through Faith they sit under the Shadow of this blessed Apple Tree, and taste his pleasant Fruits. O! How infinitely amiable is the Person of Christ to the enlightened Understanding![58]

Being ravished by Christ is not only a matter of understanding, however; it is an experience as well. As Tennent puts it, "The Child of God has Soul-ravishing Discoveries of Christ at Times by Faith; and he does feel in himself a great Difference between his present and former Views of the Redeemer: Formerly he did but hear of Christ by the hearing of the Ear, but now his Eye sees him."[59] To be ravished by the love of Christ, then, is a matter of both mind and heart.

If the alluring love of Jesus captures the soul of the believer, so too do his sufferings. "Christ is precious to Believers," Tennent says,

---

53. Tennent, "De nuptiis"; see Appendix B, below.
54. Tennent, manuscript 12; see Appendix D, below.
55. Tennent, *The Espousals*, 26–27.
56. Ibid., 39.
57. Tennent, "Preciousness of Christ," 252.
58. Ibid., 259.
59. Ibid., 266.

on the Account of his Sufferings in their Stead: O how do their Hearts beat and burn with Love, and melt with Grief, when they behold him in the Garden of Gethsemane sweating a shower of blood; treading the Wine Press of his Father's Wrath alone, and meekly suffering all other Indignities that inhuman Wretches laid upon the innocent Lamb of God. O! how is their Admiration rais'd . . . and their Joy increas'd by considering the Fruits of his Sufferings and his Love in them. And how precious is our Saviour in the Ordinance of the Supper? by which he design'd to represent to his People his Sufferings for them.[60]

The table is the place where believers "behold the dreadful Agonies of his Soul," and consider that his sufferings were for their own sake, "which should stir up in us, my dear Brethren, the strongest Affection. O methinks! the holy Jesus looks exceedingly lovely as he comes with died Garments from Bozrah and Edom."[61]

Indeed, by urging contemplation of the sufferings of Christ, Tennent leads worshipers to an impassioned celebration of the sacrament. In "Brotherly Love Recommended," preached just before the sacrament in 1748 in Philadelphia, one hears echoes of earlier sermons as he leads his listeners from consideration of Christ's sufferings to passionate urgings toward union. Tennent engages in an extended exposition of the anguish of Jesus, again speaking of agony, sweat, and wrath; he holds up before his congregation's gaze the physical and emotional torture inflicted on the Christ, ending with Jesus' cry of abandonment from Psalm 22. He exhorts his listeners to gratitude, to acceptance of the love of Christ, and to penitence, and then turns his attention to the communicants, urging them to come with sorrow for sin and resolve to live for Christ. In language from Revelation, Psalms, and the Song of Songs, he urges them on to embrace their Lord:

Behold my dear Brethren! the blessed Bridegroom cometh, clothed with Majesty, as with a Robe, with Light, as with a Garment; with Zeal, as with a Cloak. See he is girt with a golden Girdle, his Head and Hairs are white as Snow, and his Eyes are as a Flame of Fire, his Feet like unto fine Brass, as if they burned in a Furnace, and his Voice as the Sound of many Waters! [cf. Rev. 1:13b–15] See the unrivall'd Beauty of his Person, and the inexpressible Riches of his Love! Our adorable Jesus, Is white and ruddy, the chiefest among Ten thousand! He is white in Regard of his unsullied Innocence, and red in Regard of his severe sufferings for us! See he comes from Bozra and Edom,

60. Ibid., 264–65.

61. Gilbert Tennent, *A Sermon Upon Justification: Preached at New-Brunswick, on the Saturday before the Dispensing of the Holy Sacrament, which was the first Sabbath in August, Anno 1740* (Philadelphia: Printed and sold by Benjamin Franklin in Market Street, 1741), 28; cf. Isa. 63:1.

with his Garments died red! his Vesture is discoloured, or rather adorned with his Heart's-Blood; O amazing Sight! See those Wounds, Believer, he patiently and willingly bore for thee! Wounds which are Scars of Honour, Signatures of Victory, and Arguments of Love and Endearment! Surely his Garments smell of Myrrh, Aloes, and Cassia, out of the Ivory Palaces: Now let the everlasting Doors of your Souls open to embrace your Lord; now let your Bowels move for him: now let your Hands drop with Myrrh, with sweet-smelling Myrrh, upon the Handles of the Lock! [cf. Song 5:4–5] While the King sits at his Table, let your Spikenard send forth the Smell thereof; seeing the Marriage of the Lamb is come, O let the Spouse make herself ready to embrace him. Amen. Even so come Lord Jesus. Amen. Amen.[62]

The goal is clear. After the months of preparation and the days of intense self-examination, the faithful communicant longs for union with Christ in the Lord's Supper. This yearning and seeking is a prominent theme in Tennent's eucharistic preaching, and he draws from the story of the lovers in the Song of Songs as well as from the Psalms in describing this facet of the life of faith. It is God that the pious soul seeks; the Divine is found in the person of Jesus Christ. The believer desires Christ, and that desire is voiced with the words of the Canticles and the Psalms. Tennent waxes eloquent in his sermon "The Unsearchable Riches of Christ (II)" when he explains that Jesus is the desire of all nations:

With what pious Passion does the Psalmist's Soul pant after this blessed God, in the 42d, 63d, and 84th Psalms? Even as the pursued Hart after the Water Brooks, or the parched Earth after the Rain; yea, his very Heart and Flesh cry'd out after God, even after the living God, and followed hard after him! With what holy Vehemence does the poor Church long for this Redeemer? Isai. 26.9 With my Soul have I desired thee in the Night, yea with my Spirit within me, will I seek thee early. Cant. 2.5. Stay me with Flagons, comfort me with Apples, for I am sick of Love. Cant. 5.4, 5, 6. My Beloved put in his Hand by the Hole of the Door, and my Bowels were moved for him. I rose up to open to my Beloved, and my Hands dropped with Myrrh, and my Fingers with sweet smelling Myrrh, upon the handles of the lock. —But my Beloved had withdrawn himself, and was gone, my Soul failed when he Spake; I sought him, but I could not find him. O! that the compassionate Jesus wou'd bless our poor Souls with such a Sickness this Day! O! that the rich and good Saviour, would set us as a Seal upon his Heart, as a Seal upon his Arm, and give us Desires stronger than Death![63]

62. Tennent, *Brotherly Love*, 35–36.
63. Tennent, "Unsearchable Riches (II)," 32; for a similar passage, cf. "Preciousness of Christ," 260–61.

Tennent often uses this heightened language to describe the soul that is "sick with Longing,"[64] the "insatiable desires" of the bride who prepares to meet her Bridegroom in the sacrament,[65] and the "unwearied Endeavour after his Presence . . . and sweet Delight in it when obtain'd."[66]

That "sweet Delight" is found in Communion; the table is the place where the marriage between Bridegroom and bride is consummated. Tennent often announces the coming of the Bridegroom as he calls people to spiritual marriage.[67] Jesus is the husband that supplies all wants[68] and whose riches can fulfill the wife's every desire.[69] Not only is Christ an all-sufficient husband, but also all-knowing, all-powerful, and ever-present; he is beautiful, prudent, loving, indulgent, beneficent, and ever-faithful.[70] Yet it not just the virtues of Christ that attract the believer, but also the promise of blissful intimacies. An invitation to the table is an invitation to the very embrace of Christ, where the believer may "enjoy the kisses of [his] marriage love."[71]

Tennent even makes bold use of sexual metaphor to describe what awaits the believer: "It is conjugal love," he exclaims. "Nothing will satisfy him but the nearest relation. It is the espousing of the soul to himself that he aims at, that he may manifest the dearest embraces, the sweetest intimacy."[72] The invitation to communion with Christ is the invitation to the table:

> What say you now? Will you come to this wedding and eat of the king's supper? [Will you] accept of Christ? He does but ask your consent. Will you embrace him, accept of him for your all? What do you say? What answer shall I return to the great king that sent me to you?[73]

Although marriage is a prominent metaphor in Tennent's vocabulary for discussing union with Christ, his understanding of this union is multivalent. Faith is akin to union with Christ;[74] it is "the Bond of our Union to Christ."[75] At times Tennent asserts that God calls people to worship so that they might

---

64. Tennent, "Unsearchable Riches (II)," 38; cf. "Preciousness of Christ," 260.
65. Tennent, "Unsearchable Riches (II)," 58; cf. "Preciousness of Christ," 260.
66. Tennent, "Duty of Self-Examination," 139; cf. "Preciousness of Christ," 261.
67. Tennent, "Unsearchable Riches [I]," 21.
68. Tennent, "Unsearchable Riches (II)," 53.
69. Tennent, "De nuptiis"; see Appendix B, below.
70. Tennent, *The Espousals*, 20–27.
71. Ibid., 32.
72. Tennent, "De nuptiis"; see Appendix B, below.
73. Ibid.
74. Tennent, *Sermon Upon Justification*, 16, 23.
75. Tennent, "Preciousness of Christ," 259.

have "communion in [God's] love."[76] It is not surprising, then, that he also understands communion with Christ in the context of the Word and the experience of love it can arouse:

> Have you had Communion with Christ by his Word and Spirit? This is a Natural and necessary Consequence of a vital Union, can you say with the Apostle, I John, 1:3, And truly our Fellowship is with the Father, and with his Son Jesus Christ? Know ye what it is by Experience to have the kisses of the King, his Love spread abroad in your Hearts, so that you could say with the Spouse, my beloved is mine, and I am his, he feedeth among the Lilies?[77]

Tennent reaches the height of his descriptive powers, however, when he speaks in almost mystical terms in describing this union, as in "The Preciousness of Christ to Believers":

> As the Countenance of Moses shone by conversing with God on the Mount, with such Brightness that the People of Israel could not behold it. So the Soul by beholding of, and having Communion with the blessed Jesus, through Faith, is transformed into the divine Image, and derives such Beauty, from the eternal Fountain of it, that she is all glorious within: Divine Light is shed into the Mind, and divine Love and Holiness into the heart, so that all the Powers are chang'd and turn'd in their free and general Drift towards the precious Lord Jesus as their Center.[78]

He sounds a similar tone in "Love to Christ" as he expounds on the manifestation of Christ's love to believers' souls. "How can we but love him when we view him in the relation of a father, a husband, a Brother, a Friend?" Tennent cries.

> And indeed this love is more and more increased by enjoying communion with him. The more intimate a believer is with Christ, the oftner he sees him and receives visits from him. And the more familiar fellowship he has with him, the more he loves him, every new glimpse of him, every fresh enjoyment of him adds fire and fervor to love.[79]

It is in this sort of mystical-sounding language that the line between spiritual and physical metaphor is blurred; here one can catch a glimpse of the

---

76. Tennent, sermon manuscript 12; see Appendix D, below.
77. Tennent, *The Espousals*, 12–13.
78. Tennent, "Preciousness of Christ," 256.
79. Tennent, "Love to Christ," 88.

enthusiasm that marked the Scots-Irish sacramental occasions in America. Tennent alludes to this enthusiasm in one sermon when he criticizes the spiritual state of his detractors. Only believers "receive the Communications of Christ's Love, which very much endear Christ to the Soul," he insists. Unbelievers see religion only as "a circle of dead duties, issuing from a presumptuous Hope, and mercenary, slavish Principles: They are such Strangers to the Power of Piety, and to Communion with the divine Majesty in Duty, that some of them brand it with the odious Names of Enthusiasm, Melancholy, Phrenzie."[80]

It is not difficult to imagine how sacramental occasions, under the leadership of a minister who insists that the Lord's Supper was instituted to "enflame hearts"[81] and who incites people to enjoy the marriage embraces of Jesus, might erupt with emotional, even ecstatic, energy. The metaphors of wooing and espousal, the description of union with Christ that uses physical as well as spiritual images, and the rhetoric of a preacher who exhorts worshipers to "let your Spikenard incessantly diffuse to all around you, its aromatic, delightful, and useful Fragrance, and your hearts glow with unremitting, pious, and noble Ardors"[82]—all combine to create a picture of sacramental occasions full of emotion, spiritual fervor, and demonstrative celebrations of the Supper. Yet these celebrations were not simply frenzied ordeals, but truly exercises of obedient believers whose theology and piety were solidly Reformed. Tennent expresses this balance in the call to the table that ends his sermon "The Preciousness of Christ":

> Attend upon the Word and Ordinances of Christ: for that which begets Faith will also nourish it. The Lord has not only given his Word or Promise and Oath to confirm our Faith, but he has also instituted holy Ordinances as Seals to strengthen it; and with this View we ought to partake of them. In that sacred Supper which we purpose through Grace to partake of, we may, in the Ministers giving the Elements to the People, believingly, behold God the Father giving his only begotten Son with all the Purchase of his Blood to us: And in our receiving them, we shou'd labour to receive Christ with them in our Hearts. We shou'd give Diligence, by a sincere, regular, and steady performance of all the Duties of Religion, to make our Calling and Election sure.

---

80. Tennent, "Preciousness of Christ," 266–67.

81. Tennent, "Duty of Self-Examination," 132.

82. Gilbert Tennent, *A Persuasive to the Right Use of the Passions in Religion, Or, The Nature of religious Zeal Explain'd, its Excellency and Importance Open'd and Urg'd, in a Sermon on Revelations iii.19. Preached at Philadelphia, January 26th, 1760* (Philadelphia: Printed and Sold by W. Dunlap, 1760), 7.

But more particularly, I exhort those who have experienc'd the aforesaid Work of Faith in themselves, and none but such to come to the holy Table of the Lord. And that ye may come profitably, endeavour by solemn calling upon God to get your Faith in Exercise, O let your Spikenard send forth the smell thereof, while the King sits at his Table; for by this alone ye can discern your blessed Lord, and have Communion with him: O! this will make him precious in your Esteem indeed, incomprehensible, inexpressibly, incomparably, and everlastingly.[83]

OTHER THEMES

While betrothal and marital images are prevalent in Tennent's preaching on the Lord's Supper, other themes are also present, many of which echo common Reformed concerns. In "The Duty of Self-Examination," Tennent explains how and why the sacrament was instituted, drawing on the biblical witness, describing the actions of the Supper as derived from those undertaken by Christ with his disciples, and emphasizing the love expressed by Jesus for his people. He refutes the Roman Church's understanding of transubstantiation in the process, explaining that the elements signify his body and blood and drawing on the principles of metonymical and figurative speech to make his point. In his sermon "Brotherly Love Recommended," Tennent expounds on the meaning of the Supper in terms that are clearly Reformed. Believers take part in the Lord's Supper to "shew forth his Death till he come again." The sacrament "is design'd not only as a Sign to represent the Strength of the Redeemer's Affection," he explains, "but as a Seal to confirm our Interest in it."[84] He continues in a rhapsody of language from the Song of Songs, then, before going on to speak of the sufferings of Christ and the memorial aspect of the Communion meal.

Tennent often lifts up the sacrament as the source of comfort, nourishment, and strength for Christ's people. The Lord's Supper, he says, was instituted for the weak, and not only for the strong,[85] and for the encouragement of faith. "Tho' you don't find such Degrees of Vehemence in your Affections towards Christ as you do desire, or as you have felt," he encourages, "yet may you come to have your smoking Flax inflam'd [cf. Isa. 42:3], your faint Desires

---

83. Tennent, "Preciousness of Christ," 273–74.
84. Tennent, *Brotherly Love*, 26.
85. Tennent, "Duty of Self-Examination," 142.

encreas'd."[86] Christ's love provides strengthening and nourishment, and Tennent's rhetoric implies that the sacraments are the locus for the giving of that love. In "The Unsearchable Riches of Christ (II)," he assures his listeners that

> the Riches of Christ's Love can satisfy all the Wants of our Souls, and fill us with marrow and fatness: These can cloath us with the Robes of Righteousness, nourish us with the Bread of Life, revive us with the Wine of divine Consolation, and satisfy us with the crystal Waters of eternal Salvation.[87]

In urging believers to the Table—the marriage covenant—the preacher reminds them of Christ's promises to give rest to the weary and comfort to mourners "with the oil of joy and garment of praise."[88] Jesus himself is "bread for the hungry, Waters for the thirsty, Rayment for the Naked, Eye-salve for the Blind, a Balsom for the Wounded, Liberty for the Captive, and Rest for the Weary."[89]

The balance between doctrinal and experimental (or experiential) knowledge is a prominent theme throughout Gilbert Tennent's preaching ministry. This theme is evident in his eucharistic sermons as well. One of the most direct treatments is in "A Persuasive, to the right Use of the Passions in Religion; or, the Nature of religious Zeal Explain'd, its Excellency and Importance Open'd and Urg'd." Although this was not a eucharistic sermon, it was preached to his congregation in Philadelphia in 1760 (near the end of his life and ministry) and serves to explain in a forthright manner the issue that continually emerges in all of his preaching, sacramental and otherwise. In "A Persuasive," Tennent spells out the proper uses—and the misuses—of both zeal and knowledge. The first paragraph, at once forthright and poetic, sets the issue before the congregation with vigor:

> Light and Heat are inseparable Companions in true Religion, without the latter, the former is cold Formality; and without the former, the latter is wild Enthusiasm: Tho' the Passions be bad Guides, they are notwithstanding good Servants, and therefore should neither be neglected nor destroyed, but excited, and duly regulated in their Tendencies, by Reason and Revelation, according to the Nature and Importance of their Objects. . . . If therefore you have any gratitude to God, or regard to your own Interest, Be Zealous! Ardent Love is termed Zeal (Num. xi. 29. Psalm lxix. 9.). By this Word, our Lord

---

86. Tennent, "Unsearchable Riches [I]," 22. "Smoaking flax" is a biblical allusion.
87. Tennent, "Unsearchable Riches (II)," 33.
88. Ibid., 51.
89. Tennent, "Preciousness of Christ," 265.

enjoins a laudable Emulation of Piety and Virtue, and an ardent strong affection in religious Worship: Be Zealous, shake off your Sloth and Lukewarmness, and Labour earnestly in the Use of all appointed Means to recover your first Love, your former Warmth, Spirit, and Savour; that so you may be such burning and shining Lights, such savory Salt, in a dark and degenerate World. . . . Let your Spikenard incessantly diffuse to all around you, its aromatic, delightful, and useful Fragrance, and your Hearts glow with unremitting, pious, and noble Ardors![90]

As the sermon progresses, Tennent urges his listeners to be knowledgeable as well as zealous, seeking to achieve a balance between understanding and fervor, doctrine and experience, in their lives of faith.

This sentiment is repeated again and again in the eucharistic sermons. The clearest treatment is in "The Duty of Self-Examination," preached at a sacramental occasion in New Brunswick, New Jersey, in 1737, in which Tennent distinguishes between "doctrinal and speculative knowledge of divine Truth" and "spiritual and experimental Knowledge." Doctrinal knowledge, he says, is preparation for experience. For a person to be prepared for the Lord's Supper, one must understand the nature of sin and the remedy offered by Christ, as well as have knowledge of the sacrament as a seal of the covenant of grace. Furthermore, he explains, spiritual experience attends the sacrament; "the almighty Spirit of God opens the Mind to receive the Truth by the Shines of a supernatural Light, and sets them home upon the Heart by an almighty Power."[91] Knowledge, then, arouses emotion in the context of the sacrament; both head and heart are engaged in the Supper.

Tennent can be scathing in his attacks on those who would value only right doctrine and fail to give evidence of spiritual zeal. The forcefulness of his view is unmistakable in "The Divinity of the Sacred Scriptures":

Whatever notional, dead, dry Knowledge, you may have attained of some divine Things by the Force of Education, yet you have no clear, experimental Knowledge of them; otherwise you could no more live contentedly in the State you are in, than you could lye contentedly in a burning Fire: You only speak by Rote and Hearsay of divine Things, like Parrots.[92]

90. Tennent, *Persuasive to the Right Use of the Passions*, 5–7.

91. Tennent, "Duty of Self-Examination," 137.

92. Gilbert Tennent, "The Divinity of the Sacred Scriptures Considered; And the Dangers of Covetousness Detected: In a Sermon, On Jeremiah 22.29. Preach'd at New-Brunswick in New-Jersey, April ult. 1738," in *Sermons on Sacramental Occasions by Divers Ministers* (Boston: J. Draper, for D. Henchman in Cornhill, 1739), 157.

At other moments, however, he seeks to persuade calmly:

> Another reason why a child of God desires to dwell in God's house
> is to enquire in his temple, respecting his duty to God and God's
> dealings toward him; he wants not only to be conformed to God's
> nature and to have communion in his love, but he wants to be further
> instructed in the mind of God, respecting what is required of him.[93]

In his preaching and his essays, both sacramental and nonsacramental, Tennent consistently urges believers to tend not only to the life of the mind, but also to the fires of the heart.

Although the style and content of Tennent's preaching changed considerably after he moved from the frontier lands of New Jersey to an established congregation in the city of Philadelphia, his preaching on the sacraments remained remarkably consistent. The sermon that is extant from 1748, "Brotherly Love Recommended," and the sermon that exists in manuscript form from 1753, "De nuptiis cum Christo," both exhibit the same passionate urgings to the marriage covenant that are seen in the sermons from the 1730s. Throughout his entire ministry, Gilbert Tennent exhorted his hearers to repentance and zeal, persuaded them of the charms of their Bridegroom, and wooed them with words of love, leading them to union with Christ at the Lord's Table.

Not only can one see the consistencies in Tennent's corpus of sermons; one can also notice numerous connections between Tennent's preaching and Calvin's theology. Both men see union with Christ as multivalent, occurring not only in the sacrament but also in the Word. For both, union is a state of faith as well as something that grows and is nourished over a lifetime of participation in the Lord's Supper. Furthermore, Calvin's concern with piety is akin to Tennent's insistence that the life of faith involves both heart and mind, knowledge and emotion, understanding and fervor. Although Tennent's heightened language bears more resemblance to that of some mystical writers than to Calvin's careful prose, the theological inheritance is unmistakable.

The chapter that follows will further demonstrate that Gilbert Tennent, and James McGready after him, were not only the heirs of Calvin's theology, but also of a rich Scots-Irish liturgical, homiletical, and devotional tradition. A survey of the work of John Willison, a minister in Scotland and a prolific writer, will show that the American holy fairs exhibited the same Reformed theology, evangelical fervor, eucharistic vitality, and spiritual mysticism of the Scots-Irish sacramental occasions of the seventeenth and eighteenth centuries.

---

93. Tennent, sermon manuscript 12; see Appendix D, below.

6

The Scots-Irish Inheritance

It seems, on such occasions, as if the voice of the Bridegroom were heard, saying to the church at large, "Rise up, my love, my fair one, and come away; for, lo, the winter is past, the rain is over and gone: the flowers appear on the earth; the time of the singing of the birds is come, and the voice of the turtle is heard in our land; the fig tree putteth forth her green figs, and the vines with the tender grape give a good smell. Arise, my love, my fair one, and come away." (Cant. ii. 10–13)[1]

So begins an account of the sacramental revival held at Cambuslang in 1742, an event unparalleled in Scottish history, which some have compared to the gathering in Cane Ridge.

Sacramental occasions were celebrated in Scotland since at least the 1620s; they became more and more central to religious life once Presbyterianism was firmly established at the end of the seventeenth century.[2] As communion seasons increased in importance, so did the amount of devotional material written to prepare communicants for worthy and faithful participation in the sacrament. Although they had long appreciated the devotional literature of

---

1. Duncan MacFarlan, *The Revivals of the Eighteenth Century Particularly at Cambuslang, with three Sermons by the Rev. George Whitefield, taken in shorthand, compiled from original manuscripts and contemporary publications by D. MacFarlan* (London and Edinburgh: John Johnston, 1847; reprint, Glasgow: Free Presbyterian Publications, 1988), 9.

2. Schmidt, *Holy Fairs*, 44–46; J. H. S. Burleigh, *A Church History of Scotland* (London: Oxford University Press, 1960), 254–55.

the Puritans,[3] Scottish Presbyterians began to develop their own tradition at the end of the seventeenth century, one that reflected both the theological inheritance of John Calvin as well as elements of the medieval mysticism in which the Reformers had been steeped. It is this Scottish devotional material—in the form of sermons, catechisms, meditations, and songs—that provided the rich soil in which American Presbyterian sacramental piety grew.

The most prolific and influential author of this devotional literature was John Willison (1680–1750). Although there were certainly other figures who made significant contributions through the publishing of sermons and devotional aids, it was Willison whose work was most widely known. Ordained in 1703, he became the pastor of the church in Brechin, where he stayed until he was called to Dundee in 1716. Willison remained there until his death; during his long pastorate he was beloved as a spiritual leader and caregiver, respected as a mediating force in the turbulent political and ecclesial climate of eighteenth-century Scotland, and renowned as the author of what would be popular and enduring devotional works.

Most significant were Willison's sacramental writings, which continued to be published for a century after his death in both Scotland and America. His *Sacramental Directory*, in which he provides a thorough guide to preparing for and participating in communion, was first published in 1716 in Edinburgh and reprinted in both Scotland and America until the middle of the nineteenth century. *Sacramental Meditations and Advices*, a collection of short readings and prayers, first appeared in 1747 in Dundee and went on to multiple editions in Scotland, Ireland, and America; the latest editions were published in New Jersey in the 1970s. Willison's several catechisms, prepared for mothers, young people, and adult communicants, were also printed and reprinted on both sides of the Atlantic. His *Sacramental Catechism*, written in 1720, was published in Scotland until the late eighteenth century, then appeared in America in 1830 and 1867; Soli Deo Gloria Publications (Morgan, PA) issued a reprint in 2000.

Willison's sermons, hymns, and songs were widely published as well, sometimes bound together in one volume. *The Balm of Gilead*, a collection of sermons first issued in London in 1742, included five that were preached on sacramental occasions. Subsequent editions (some of which were published

---

3. Schmidt, *Holy Fairs*, 45–46. Schmidt names William Perkins, Thomas Shepard, and Lewis Bayly as Puritan influences. As noted in chap. 2 (above), Puritan preaching sometimes reflected the themes under examination in this study. Thomas Shepard's "Behold the Happiness of those Espoused to Christ," included in his *Parable of the ten virgins*, uses language echoed in Tennent when he refers to the love of Christ as "conjugal love." Thomas Watson's "Mystic Union Between Christ and the Saints" is based on Song 2:16 ("My beloved is mine, and I am his"); he, too, asserts that "there is a conjugal union between Christ and believers."

along with other devotional materials) were released in Scotland, England, and the United States until 1830, indicating that worshipers read and reread these sermons for a century after they were preached, and that Willison's explanations of eucharistic doctrine, as well as his guides for spiritual preparation for the sacrament of the Lord's Supper, remained in use for decades after his death. His works, as Leigh Schmidt observes, "are crucial to the study of Scottish sacramentalism and revivalism."[4]

Noted historian of the Scottish church, J. H. S. Burleigh, describes John Willison's writings as "the favourite religious literature among the people of Scotland."[5] Willison was concerned with teaching right doctrine to laypeople, using biblical sources as well as denominational standards to make accessible a Reformed understanding of the sacraments. He was equally committed to providing devotional materials that would aid people in preparing for the celebration of the Lord's Supper; his meditations led people through a process of self-examination and repentance, as they recalled the sufferings of Christ, reviewed the state of their lives, and prayed in earnest for forgiveness and renewal. In his sermons and meditations, Willison sought not only to remind people of Christ's sacrificial death and their need for repentance, but also to woo them to the Table and the union with Christ that awaited them in the sacrament.

Willison's works likely found a ready audience among Scottish Presbyterians, given their long tradition of family worship. As Stanley Hall notes, in 1647 the Scottish General Assembly first published the Directory for Family Worship, which provided guidelines for personal and family prayer. "Family worship was to be held at morning and evening, under the leadership of the male head of the household," Hall explains, and was to include the reading of Scripture, psalm singing, prayer, and instruction.[6]

In addition to penning some of Scotland's most significant Christian literature, John Willison was witness to, and participant in, some of the country's most notable religious events. In 1742 he traveled to the town of Cambuslang, where he served as one of several preachers at what would become one of the largest and most infamous sacramental revivals in Scottish history. William McCulloch was the minister at Cambuslang, and in response to his parishioners' requests for midweek teaching and worship, he began to hold additional services. These meetings grew in size and in enthusiasm until they culminated in the gathering of thousands of people whose mourning of their sins and

---

4. Schmidt, *Holy Fairs*, 46.
5. Burleigh, *Church History of Scotland*, 291.
6. S. R. Hall, "American Presbyterian 'Directory for Worship,'" 82–83.

anticipation of Communion evoked great emotion. Willison was there, along with evangelist George Whitefield, whose sermon drew a crowd that some estimated at thirty thousand.[7] McCulloch preached the action sermon on the day of the Communion, using as his text Song of Songs 5:16: "His mouth is most sweet; yea, he is altogether lovely. This is my beloved, and this is my friend, O daughters of Jerusalem." On Sunday evening, Whitefield preached a sermon based on Isaiah 54:5: "Thy Maker is thy husband; the LORD of hosts is his name."[8]

Writing about the "work at Cambuslang," Willison recalled:

> I had occasion to converse with many who had been awakened and under conviction there; I found several in darkness and great distress about their soul's condition, and with many tears bewailing their sins and original corruption, and especially the sin of unbelief, and slighting of precious Christ. Others I found in a most desirable frame, overcome with a sense of the wonderful love and loveliness of Jesus Christ, even sick of love, and inviting all about them to help them to praise Him.[9]

As though defending the events of the revival against detractors, he wrote of the many people with whom he had spoken:

> I could observe nothing visionary or enthusiastic about them for their discourses were solid, and experiences Scriptural. . . . Upon the whole, I look upon the work at Cambuslang, to be a most singular and marvelous outpouring of the Holy Spirit, which Christ has promised; and I pray it may be a happy forerunner of a general reviving of the work of God in this poor decayed Church, and a blessed means of union among all the lovers of our dear Jesus.[10]

A review of John Willison's voluminous output paints a picture of the eucharistic theology and practice of these Scottish Presbyterians and provides

---

7. Burleigh, *Church History of Scotland*, 292–93.

8. MacFarlan, *Revivals of the Eighteenth Century*, 65. MacFarlan writes that Whitefield's sermon "has more references to it, as having been blessed to individuals, than any other of all that great man's addresses. It is printed in the first edition of his works, and in the more recent collections of his sermons. But no one can obtain from these publications a correct impression of the sermon as delivered. We have been able to trace the same discourse as delivered in four or five places of the west, not very distant from one another, during the same season."

9. Richard Owen Roberts, ed., *Scotland Saw His Glory: A History of Revivals in Scotland*, by W. J. Couper, James Burns, Mary Duncan, et al. (Wheaton, IL: International Awakening Press, 1995), 135.

10. Ibid., 136.

insight into that of American Presbyterians of Scots-Irish descent. Cambuslang may have been the largest sacramental revival of the eighteenth century, but it was certainly not the last; annual communions persisted in Scotland and remained the centerpiece of Presbyterian sacramental piety for years to come. When one traces the streams of tradition that flowed from Scotland to America among those who gathered at sacramental occasions on both sides of the Atlantic, John Willison emerges as the theological and spiritual forerunner of American frontier preachers of Scottish descent. Firmly grounded in a Reformed understanding of Word and sacrament, Willison, like his American counterparts, makes rich use of spousal imagery and language from the Song of Songs to express the eucharistic piety of Scots-Irish Presbyterians.

WAITING FOR REVIVAL

In the preface to his *Sacramental Directory*, John Willison bemoans how infrequently communion is celebrated in Scotland; this problem is one of his motivations for writing a devotional guide. It seems that some ministers, caught between the laity's fears surrounding the sacrament (a holdover from the pre-Reformation church) and the desire to avoid eliminating celebrations of the Lord's Supper altogether, had resorted to administering the sacrament only once in two or three years. Although the General Assembly passed four acts between 1710 and 1724 urging more frequent celebration, only a portion of Presbyterian ministers were holding the sacrament annually.

Willison argues for more frequent observances, harkening back to the early church's practice of weekly communion, and recalls John Calvin's desire for celebration of the sacrament every Lord's Day. Quoting Calvin, whose views "hath very great weight with me," he refers to a lengthy passage in book 4 of the *Institutes* in which Calvin discusses the patterns of the early church.[11] Though he wishes to restore the practice of weekly celebration so that the people would be spiritually fed each week, Willison recognizes that change happens slowly and argues for communion four times a year. A chief motivation is to "avoid the superstitious approach to the table that was part of the

---

11. John Willison, *A Sacramental Directory: Or, a Treatise concerning the Sanctification of a communion Sabbath. Containing Many proper directions, in order to our Preparing for, Receiving of, and right Behaving after, the Sacrament of the Lord's Supper.* Sixth Edition, corrected and inlarged (Glasgow: Robert Duncan, 1769), xi. The first edition of this book was published in 1716 in Edinburgh; a copy of this edition was not available to this author. The preface of the 1769 volume is dated 1740 and refers to a second edition, which appeared in 1726.

Easter communion mass," and so he advises that the sacrament be observed on the first Sundays of March, June, September, and December, dates that were not associated with any particular liturgical festival.[12]

Willison is equally concerned with the quality of preaching in the Church of Scotland. He refers to the Westminster Directory's instruction on the significance and nature of preaching, and he exhorts ministers to emphasize Reformed themes.[13] Willison then explains what sermons should seek to do; among their many purposes, preachers should lead their listeners "to the true and only source of all grace and holiness, viz. Union with Christ, by the holy Spirit's working faith in us, and renewing us more and more after the image of God."[14] Both the Lord's Supper and preaching are to "exalt Christ," and ministers are to preach new birth, justification by faith, and the workings of the Holy Spirit, which allow for Christians to live redeemed and sanctified lives.[15]

As the preface comes to a close, readers hear the reason for Willison's impassioned exhortations on celebrating the sacrament and engaging in faithful preaching. He has heard of great revivals in other parts of the world—close to home in England, Wales, and Germany, and on the other side of the Atlantic in New England, Georgia, New Jersey, Pennsylvania, and New York. He has heard of the ministries of Whitefield and Edwards, and he longs for revival in Scotland:

> May not *Scotland* look for a visit from him among the rest, and even plead that ancient kindness may revive toward it? . . . O for grace to pray in hope, mourn in hope, labour in hope, and wait in hope, seeing our dearest Lord and Saviour Jesus Christ, which is our hope, is gone up, and sits at the helm! O when shall the power of this great Lord be present to heal us! Come, Lord Jesus, come quickly, *Amen.*[16]

Willison wrote those words in 1740; his prayers were soon answered. The wave of revival that included the remarkable gatherings at Cambuslang and Kilsyth in 1742 was on its way, and this devotional guide that Willison first penned in 1716 would be used by communicants in both the Old and New Worlds for more than 150 years.

---

12. Ibid., iv–v, viii.
13. Ibid., xxviii.
14. Ibid., xxx.
15. Ibid., xxxi–xxxii.
16. Ibid., xxxix, xliii.

JOHN WILLISON'S
"SACRAMENTAL DIRECTORY"

In his *Sacramental Directory*, John Willison provides would-be communicants with a complete guide to preparing for sacramental occasions. He explains that the *Directory* is designed to be used along with his *Sacramental Catechism*, which covers questions regarding right doctrine and proper conduct. In the *Directory*, however, he seeks "to give practical directions for the right improvement of communion sabbaths."[17] While it is clear that Willison is thoroughly schooled in church history and Reformed theology and well-informed about the concerns and challenges facing his church, this is a work whose chief aim is to give practical, pastoral advice. The book is pocket-sized, making it handy for devotional use, and presents a complete and measured approach for communion preparation in three parts:

> I. Directions how to prepare for a communion-sabbath before it come.
> II. How to spend it when it come.
> III. How to behave ourselves when it is over.[18]

Preparation for communion is vitally important for Willison and his Scottish colleagues, just as it would be for his American counterparts. Why? "This holy table is . . . the solemn trysting-place of the great God, where he used to meet with men, and to entertain converse and communion with them." Believers are to come to the Table out of obedience to Christ's command, to remember Jesus with thanks, "and also to receive and embrace him as their bleeding high priest into the arms of their faith, apply his benefits, rest upon his merits, seal a covenant with him."[19] Willison carefully enumerates the steps involved in preparation for the sacrament, each of which he thoroughly expounds:

> 1. Sequestrating ourselves from the world. 2. Self-examination. 3. Humiliation for sin. 4. Renewing our personal covenant with God in Christ. 5. Reformation of what is amiss. 6. Exciting of all the graces to a lively exercise. 7. Meditation on the death and sufferings of Jesus Christ. 8. Earnest prayer to God for preparation and assistance in the work.

17. Ibid., 2.
18. Ibid.
19. Ibid., 42, 3–4.

All of these steps are necessary, he explains, "if you would have a joyful meeting with thy lovely bridegroom in the sacrament."[20]

True to the heritage of his Reformed forebears, Willison explains the hazards of unworthy communicating. He gives painstaking instructions so that the would-be communicant might go through a thorough process of self-examination, offering questions to ask oneself and biblical passages upon which to meditate. The focus is on recognizing one's own sin and the need for grace and reconciliation with God, not in order to be shamed, but to prepare for union with Christ. Using vivid language that reflects the Psalms and the Song of Songs, Willison suggests the sort of questions a would-be communicant might pose:

> Have I been brought to see my absolute need of Christ to save me from sin and wrath? . . . Have I seen such beauty, and tasted such sweetness in Christ, that he is truly precious to me, and altogether lovely in my esteem, so that I would gladly part with all things for him? . . . Are my desires his, to long and pant for his presence? My love his, to embrace him?

The believer is to reflect on what "discoveries" have been made of Christ, to say in the words of the Canticles, "'Once I saw little beauty in Christ, but now I see him to be the chiefest among ten thousands, nay, among all the thousands in the world.'"[21]

Willison commends other disciplines as well, including fasting, reflecting carefully on one's adherence (or lack thereof) to each of the Ten Commandments, and meditating on the sufferings and death of Christ. He provides prayers of confession and prayers for mercy and instructs communicants on how to pray before approaching the Table. "I know not how to pray, or to prepare myself; how to receive Christ, or behave myself at his table," begins one prayer. "Behold the bridegroom cometh, but I am not ready; I want the wedding garment; O what shall I do for clothing to my naked soul? *My beloved hath spoke, saying, Rise up, my love, my fair one, and come away*."[22] The goal of proper preparation, then, is to achieve nearness with God in the sacrament. Using language that will be echoed more than a century later in McGready's sermons, Willison speaks in the voice of the communicant: "I go not there for bread and wine, but to see Jesus."[23]

---

20. Ibid., 47–48.
21. Ibid., 70–71; cf. Song 5:16; Ps. 42:1; Song 5:10.
22. Willison, *Sacramental Directory*, 156; cf. Song 2:10.
23. Ibid., 162–63.

It is in the second chapter of the *Directory*, in which Willison gives directions on how to conduct oneself on the day of communion, where the fullest use of language from the Song of Songs and other spousal imagery appears. Here he suggests what the communicant ought to think about, gives instructions for prayer, and provides further meditations on Christ's sacrifice and love. In the *Directory*, as in his sermons, Willison's use of marital imagery is most pronounced just before the sacrament. As one prepares to approach the Table, one prays:

> O give me a heart to consent willingly to the bargain, and say, My beloved is mine, and I am his. Lord, help me cheerfully to say *Amen* to the covenant, and all the articles of it, that I was reviewing and renewing yesternight: O let the marriage-knot this day be cast, that sin or Satan, death or hell, may never be able to loose again: let him this day *Kiss me with the kisses of his mouth*: O for sweet communion and fellowship with him at his own table: Lord, shew me a token for good, set me as a seal upon thine arm; manifest thy self to me, as thou dost not to the world.[24]

"Come with burning love and affection to Christ," Willison urges the would-be communicant.

> Come with much hunger and thirst to this full feast. . . . When the desire opens the heart widest, then he opens his hand largest to fill it, Psalm lxxxi. 10. . . . The spouse cries, Cant. ii.4 [5]. *Stay me with flagons*; as if she had said, "My thirst is so great, it is not a drop or a little cup that will quench it, I would have whole flagons."[25]

The one who comes faithfully to the Table is the one who comes longingly, hungrily.

Willison is fastidious in prescribing the proper attitude of one who would come to Communion. The communicant approaches the church building with reverence, praying with every step. One advances to the table fearfully, for "as communion love is the sweetest, so communion wrath is the sorest." When one nears the Table, one does so expectantly and fervently. "When you are going to the table, labour to stir up your souls, and all your faculties and affections," Willison exhorts; "excite all your graces and desires to attend Christ; O see that your souls be lively, and your hearts fix'd, when you are about to draw near and seal a marriage covenant with Christ." If such fervor

---

24. Ibid., 175; cf. Song 2:16; 1:2; 7:6.
25. Willison, *Directory*, 178–79.

is lacking, exclaims Willison, "dispatch presently a swift messenger to heaven, an earnest ejaculation and prayer, to call for the help of God's Spirit, as Cant. iv. 16. Intreat him to breathe upon your dry bones with a fresh gale and take a coal from his own altar to inflame your affections."[26]

In case the communicant requires still more guidance, Willison provides themes on which one is to meditate while at the Communion table: the suffering and death of Christ, the evil of sin that brought on that suffering, the holiness and justice of God, how the "lower table" represents "the communion-feast above." After offering a careful and reasoned exposition upon each of these themes, Willison then launches into near-ecstatic speech:

> "O the unfathomable love of Jesus! His name is love, his nature is love, his words were love, and his actions were love. He preached love, he practised love, he lived in love, he was sick of love, nay, he died for love." The apostle might well call it, an unknown love, Eph. iii. 19. We may feel it, but O we cannot fathom it.

He then compares the love of Christ with that of another biblical lover. "Jacob shewed great love to Rachel, in his enduring the heat by day and the frosts by night for her: But our lovely bridegroom shewed far greater love to his spouse in undergoing the cursed, painful and shameful death of the cross for her."[27] The thought of this kind of love will surely melt hearts, Willison exclaims; like "wax hot within you, . . . the flame of love to God should break out in the most lively and active manner: Now your spikenard should send forth the smell thereof; now the sweet odour of your graces should fill all the house."[28] Filled with desire to see Christ, the soul looks to him and says, in the words of the Canticle, "Make haste, my beloved, be thou like a Roe, or a young Hart on the mountains of spices. Make no tarrying, O my God; O when wilt thou come to me?"[29]

The themes of Christ's loveliness and his passion become intertwined as Willison instructs the communicant on how to excite one's love to Christ by extolling the beauty of the Savior's wounds. Even the apostle was "ravished with the love of Christ," he proclaims; indeed, believers love Christ with their all, seeking to please him, to love his commandments, his people, and his cross, for this Christ is "altogether lovely."[30]

---

26. Ibid., 183–86.
27. Ibid., 207–8.
28. Ibid., 209; cf. Song 4:13–14.
29. Willison, *Directory*, 214; cf. Song 2:8–9, 17.
30. Willison, *Directory*, 219–20.

After supplying further meditations for each moment of the sacramental act—the taking, blessing, and breaking of bread, and the giving of the bread and the cup—Willison tells the believer how to pray, offering language from the Song of Songs as a model:

> When the bread and wine are offered to you, and you hear Christ saying, Take, eat, drink: O then cast open all the doors and gates of your soul, that the King of glory may enter in. . . . Stretch out faith's arms as far and wide as you may, to welcome, embrace and clasp about our Saviour, and say, My beloved is mine, and I am his: Now may the marriage be sealed and ratified, and the knot cast which shall never be loosed again.[31]

Scripture is a worthy basis for prayer, he says, especially the Psalms and the Canticles. "You may put some of the Spouse's petitions at this time," he instructs.

> *Draw me, we will run after thee*, Cant. i. 4. "Awake, O north-wind, come thou south, blow upon my garden, that the spices thereof may flow out. Let my beloved come into his garden, and eat his pleasant fruits, Cant. iv. 16. Make haste, my beloved, and be thou like to a Roe or young Hart upon the mountains of spices." Cant. viii.14.[32]

Not only thus does Willison—the consummate devotionalist, catechist, and preacher—use the language from the Song of Songs to teach and inspire; he also urges communicants to adopt this speech, full of the sensual imagery of love, as the very language of prayer.

In the final chapter of the *Directory*, Willison advises the communicant on how to behave after the sacrament is over. Awe, thanksgiving, and rejoicing are invited, as well as a sense of renewed devotion. We also hear the pastor comforting those who doubt that they have had an experience of Christ in the sacrament; even here, Willison draws on the Song of Songs to describe the more subtle ways that Jesus sometimes brings people into his banqueting house to kiss them with the kisses of his mouth. If there are some who do not "feel any benefit or change," he reassures them with the analogy of the absent lover from the third chapter of the Canticles.[33]

The *Sacramental Directory* comes to a climactic close as Willison describes the eschatological nature of the sacrament. Although throughout the work

---

31. Ibid., 231.
32. Ibid., 232.
33. Ibid., 237, 254, 256.

there are references to the lower and upper tables, as well as allusions to language from Revelation, it is in the final lines of the *Directory* that Willison virtually sings of the consummation that is to come. Those who have met Christ at the Lord's Table long for more and sweeter meetings, he says, and they ask when the next communion shall be, that they might "taste his love and goodness again in the sacrament." And well they should; but even more, believers should anticipate the feast that will come in eternal glory. For then the bridegroom will come "and marry you to himself forever." Then the joys of the lower table will be usurped by the delights of the higher table, and "you shall have not a sacramental but a beatific vision; where you shall . . . see him without a vail; where all your sorrows shall be turned into joys." The love poetry of the Canticles combines with the plea of Revelation as the believers anticipate that final consummation: "Make haste, my beloved, let the day break, and shadows flee away. Even so, Lord Jesus, come quickly." With a final burst of rhapsody, the sacramentalist prays for every communicant who awaits that glorious day:

> Take me to that place where mysteries shall be turned into revelations, faith into vision, hope into fruition, espousals into embraces, sorrowful sighs into nuptial songs, drops of tears into rivers of pleasures, transient glances into the radiant and direct beams of the sun of righteousness, short tastes into everlasting feasting and fulness. How small are the comforts of the lower table, if compared with these of the higher table? How dark are the discoveries believers have here, if compared with these bright manifestations above. But because I have insisted on this head formerly, I shall add no more here upon it; but wish that we may come at length experimentally to know the difference, to our everlasting comfort.[34]

WILLISON'S SACRAMENTAL SERMONS

Although Willison's *Sacramental Directory* was his most systematic treatment of the doctrinal and devotional concerns related to the Lord's Supper, it was but one of an array of devotional tools that the Scots-Irish Presbyterians used to prepare themselves for Communion. In addition to the *Directory*, a number of Willison's sacramental sermons appeared in print. Certainly the sermons were preached, but it is clear that they were published in order that communicants would be able to study them over and over again; he self-consciously writes that churches in other parts of the world might be interested in what

34. Ibid., 286.

he has to say.[35] Five sacramental sermons appear in a volume titled *The Balm of Gilead*. Like the *Sacramental Directory*, the sermons make use of themes and images that were later used by Gilbert Tennent and James McGready in their own preaching, raising the possibility that these American preachers were formed in their sacramental thinking and expression by the same tradition that shaped John Willison, and perhaps even by Willison himself.

The first of the five sacramental sermons was preached on a fast day before the celebration of the Lord's Supper. Like his American counterparts, Willison understands the preaching task to include persuading unbelievers as well as calling to repentance practicing (and backsliding) Christians. He draws on the Psalms as well as the Song of Songs to point to the need for both conversion and renewal, exhorting "two sorts of persons, . . . those who are strangers to God, and know nothing of his presence, [and] . . . those who have known it, but he is become a stranger to them."[36] The consummate pastor, Willison describes the various ways that people become estranged from God. "When we turn slothful and formal in duty, and do not stir up ourselves to seek God's face," he explains, God withdraws, like the beloved in the Canticles, and the believer, like the spouse, experiences "much travail and sorrow." The one who seeks God, counsels Willison, counts "all worldly things but loss and dung," and with the psalmist asserts, "'Whom have I in heaven but thee? and there is none upon earth that I desire besides thee.'"[37] In the preparation for and celebration of the sacrament, Willison instructs, the seeking soul should "follow hard after him, and pursue him closely (as it were) from one ordinance to another."[38] The sermon then enumerates the ways that communicants must prepare for the "solemn tryst" that is the sacrament, "so as to get distance removed and breaches made up, that God may not be a stranger to us on the feast-day."[39]

Two preparation sermons follow, "The Happiness of Being in Covenant with God" and "The Right Improvement of the Day of Grace," in which images of Christ as husband and lover abound. Although Willison explains that numerous metaphors may be used to describe the relationship between God and believer, his use of spousal imagery is vivid. "Doth not a chaste wife long for the return of her husband?" he asks in reference to the coming of the

---

35. John Willison, *Balm of Gilead, consisting of Sermons Preached on Various Occasions. Likewise Sacramental Meditations and Advices. By the Reverend John Willison of Dundee* (Edinburgh: Printed by J. Pillans & Sons for John Bourne, 8 Greenside Street, 1819), iii.

36. Willison, "Of God's Withdrawings from his People, and Their Exercise Under Them," in *Balm of Gilead*, 125.

37. Willison, *Balm of Gilead*, 118–19; cf. Song 3:1–7, Ps. 73:25.

38. Willison, *Balm of Gilead*, 120; cf. Ps. 63:1.

39. Willison, *Balm of Gilead*, 126.

day of judgment. "And will not a believing soul, betrothed to Christ, long for the glorious bridegroom's return to consummate the happy marriage?"[40] This covenant relationship is revealed to the believer in both Word and sacrament; it moves the soul to rapture.

> It sweetens the thoughts of Christ to a believer. . . . When the word brings the news of his glory to your ears, or the sacrament sets him forth as crucified before your eyes, your hearts may presently warm to him, and cry . . . with the spouse, "My beloved is mine, and I am his."

Indeed, the covenanted soul reads the word "as a love-letter" that in turn "will make the Lord's Supper sweet."[41]

Willison emphasizes the mutual character of the soul's relationship to God in Christ. The believer must strive to rid oneself from all other loyalties, resolving to say with the spouse, "I am my beloved's, and my beloved is mine." Christ seeks the believer, too, and like the lover in the Canticles, he begs entrance to the believer's heart: "'Rise up, my love, my fair one, and come away.' Why do you weary my patience, and let me stand so long neglected, 'till my head is wet with the dew and my locks with the drops of the night?'"[42] Conversely, the believer is urged to pray frequently, asking for God to be at work in one's soul. "Cry with the spouse, 'Awake, O north wind, and come, thou south, blow upon my garden, that the spices thereof may flow out,'" exhorts Willison. "Let the north winds of the law come, and convince and awaken; and the south winds of the gospel come, and refresh and comfort."[43]

Anticipating the sacrament is a joyful thing, and Communion itself is "a foretaste of heaven."[44] It is the very presence of Christ that makes it so—there the believer goes "to see Jesus." "O let Christ appear and be made known to me in the breaking of the bread!" Willison exclaims, echoing the language of Luke 24.

> Let me meet with my Saviour there, see his face, and hear his voice; and let me come from his table with my pardon sealed, my corruptions subdued, my graces quickened, my heart enlarged, and my soul refreshed and encouraged to run in the ways of thy commandments, and so inseparably united to thee, that no temptation may be ever able to dissolve the union.[45]

---

40. Ibid., 139.
41. Ibid.; cf. Song 2:16.
42. Willison, *Balm of Gilead*, 154; cf. Song 2:10, 13; 5:2.
43. Willison, *Balm of Gilead*, 155; cf. Song 4:16.
44. Willison, *Balm of Gilead*, 140.
45. Ibid., 128.

The final two sacramental sermons included in *Balm of Gilead* were preached after the celebration of the Lord's Supper. Here, too, Willison uses spousal imagery to describe the bond that has been forged between Christ and the believer. The communicant has become an heir of glory "by closing with Christ in a marriage-covenant." The believer has married "the heir of all things" and is thereby rendered "freed from bondage," with "heaven [as] . . . your dowry." The whole process of preparation and celebration is summed up in Willison's exuberant prose:

> The glorious Bridegroom courted and espoused you to himself on the day in which you might have been led forth to execution! He took off your prison-garment, and clothed you with robes of righteousness and garments of salvation! He took the chains from off your arms, the rope from about your neck, and put his own comeliness on you, that you might be fit for the King's table![46]

In supping, the believer has been strengthened by the sacrament for the living of the Christian life,[47] having experienced union with the lover-husband-Christ and a foretaste of the consummation to come.

SACRAMENTAL MEDITATIONS AND ADVICES

Some editions of *The Balm of Gilead* appeared with additional devotional material, including Willison's *Sacramental Meditations and Advices*, originally published in 1747.[48] The meditations are short, usually two to three pages in length, and focus primarily on the suffering of Christ and the need for repentance. The "advices" that follow the meditations are brief reflections in question-and-answer format. Also included are a lecture on the institution of the Lord's Supper as put forth in 1 Corinthians 11, a preparation sermon based on Joshua 3:5, an action sermon on Canticles 2:4, and songs based on Scripture. In one volume, then, the faithful communicant is equipped with a complete guide to preparing for the sacrament and a full complement of devotional aids.

In the meditations, as in the sermons, language from the Song of Songs and other spousal imagery is pervasive. As the product of his maturity, the

---

46. Ibid., 179–80.
47. Ibid., 192.
48. John Willison, *Sacramental Meditations and Advices, Grounded upon Scripture-Texts, proper for Communicants, to Prepare their Hearts, Excite their Affections, quicken their graces, and enliven their devotions, on sacramental occasions*. The edition referenced here is included in *Balm of Gilead*.

meditations and advices are perhaps the most poetic and exuberant of Willison's writings. In this series of short reflections, all of the chief themes of his eucharistic piety are expressed, and the attentive reader notices numerous antecedents to the writings of James McGready and Gilbert Tennent. The preface to the meditations makes clear that a cycle of spiritual renewal is necessary for the faithful believer, and that sacramental occasions are the opportunities "for renewing covenant, and entertaining fellowship and communion" with God. Willison urges the communicant to enter into the preparation process with fervor, so that the sacrament may not be treated as a perfunctory matter in which Christ is not really present. "Formality," Willison insists, "will provoke the Master of our solemn feasts to withdraw from them, and then what poor, dry, melancholy, and lifeless things will they be? What are sacraments without Christ's presence in them? O let us never be satisfied with communion-sabbaths, without communion with Christ in them!"[49] He closes his preface by praying the words of the spouse: "'Awake, O northwind, and come, thou south; blow upon my garden, that the spices thereof may flow out.'"[50]

In Willison's meditations and advices, as in Tennent's sermons, the minister is often presented as an advocate for Christ, the lover. "The Bridegroom is come again to court a bride, and has sent his friends in his name to demand her consent, saying, as they did to Rebekah, Gen. xxiv.58. 'Wilt thou go with this man?'" After courting the believer for a long time, Christ desires one's consent to the marriage, and the Communion table is the place where the contract is spread before them. To consent to go with Christ is to say with the spouse, "My Beloved is mine, and I am his," and to be ever ready for the husband-Christ's coming at the last day.[51]

Like the American preachers who followed him, Willison depicts Christ in the language of the Canticles, as "white and ruddy, . . . the chiefest among ten thousand." The believer cannot help but be "ravished" by his love, filled with affection as well as with repentance.[52] Willison is rhapsodic on this point as he sings along with the author of the Song of Songs:

> Come, take another view of this beautiful Bridegroom that is in your offer. Behold how delicate his complexion is! "He is white and ruddy"; *white* in regard of his innocence, and *ruddy* in his bloody passion. O how peerless is his person! how ravishing his beauty! how charming his voice! how stately his goings! How fragrant are his garments! they

49. Ibid., 205.
50. Ibid., 206.
51. Ibid., 280, 326, 328–29.
52. Ibid., 215, 285.

smell of aloes, myrrh, and cassia. Search all the world, you cannot find his equal; one glimpse of him is enough to ravish men and angels. His locks are black and bushy as the raven, his lips are like lilies dropping sweet-smelling myrrh, his legs as pillars of marble set upon sockets of fine gold; his countenance is as Lebanon, excellent as the cedars; yea, he is altogether lovely![53]

Another line of continuity between the Scots-Irish and American preachers can be seen when Willison speaks of Communion as a tryst. The believer who would test one's own readiness for the sacrament must examine oneself to see if affection for Christ is growing. "Are you drawn to duty with a view of enjoying his presence therein?" Willison queries. "Are you drawn off from resting on duties, or putting any attainments in Christ's room? Then you may conclude your heart is effectually drawn by a lift-up Saviour; and so may, with holy confidence and joy, draw near to him in the sacramental trysting-place, and hold communion with him there."[54] The believer goes to the Table, then, "to remember [Christ's] dying love, and renew my marriage vows."[55] In voicing the sentiment of the believer who chooses to seal the marriage contract, Willison speaks words that can be heard as nothing less than wedding vows:

Therefore I do, with all my heart, accept of him as my Lord and Husband: Lord, I make choice of thee, and all that is thine; for richer, for poorer; for better, for worse; for well, for woe; for prosperity, for adversity: I make choice of thee for all times and conditions, to love, honour, and obey thee, above all. I renounce all other lords of lovers, and will have none but Christ: I renounce my own will, and take thy will for my law. . . . I take thy Spirit for my guide, thy word for my rule, thy glory for my scope, thy testimonies for my counsellors, thy promises for my encouragement, thy Sabbaths for my delight, thy people for my companions: Lord Jesus, I take thee for my life, holiness for my way, and heaven for my home. And as I accept of thee, and all that is thine; so I give up myself to thee, and all that is mine, soul and body, with all my faculties and affections, senses, and members, to be thy agents and instruments; with all my enjoyments to be employed for thy use and service.[56]

One might say that the marriage bed is a metaphor for the Communion table, for the believer who meets Christ in the sacrament experiences union with him there.

---

53. Ibid., 327.
54. Ibid., 347.
55. Ibid., 281–82.
56. Ibid., 281.

The day of Communion, then, is not only a memorial of Christ's death, but also a remembrance of the marriage-day, when the believer renews the marriage-covenant with Christ. Furthermore, it is "a memorial of the consummation of your marriage with Christ at the great day, when he will come to receive home his espoused bride, and conduct her to the King's palace with joy and triumph."[57] The sacrament is an expression of eschatological hope, where past actions and future promises converge in present celebration. And so the believer takes part in the Communion Sabbath here on earth in anticipation of that above:

> Here we are oft put to mix our praises with mourning and tears, because of sin prevailing, or the Spirit withdrawing. Here Judases, and unworthy guests, thrust in among the disciples; but at the higher table there is no such mixture, all is pure and holy, and there is nought to allay their joy. Here our communion Sabbaths are soon over, and have nights, week-days, and trials to succeed them; but the communion Sabbath above, the feast, music, and assembly, are everlasting, without interruption or uneasiness of any sort. O then improve these short Sabbaths, as memorials and means to prepare you for this everlasting Sabbath; and, in all ordinances here, keep your eye upon the heavenly festival.[58]

THE FINAL WOOING

Included as an appendix to *Balm of Gilead* is an action sermon, based on Canticles 2:4 ("He brought me to the banqueting house, and his banner over me was love"). This sermon would have been preached on Sunday morning, just before the celebration of the sacrament. As with the sermons of Tennent and McGready, it is here in the action sermon where the preacher labors most fervently to woo the believer to the Table on behalf of Christ.

Willison begins this sermon by explaining that the Song of Songs "is an allegorical description of the mysterious union and communion betwixt Christ and his Church." He identifies the banqueting house as the Lord's Supper and the one who brings the spouse into this house as Christ.[59] As he spins out the metaphor, Willison identifies the various "dishes and delicacies" to be found at the sacramental feast, and in doing so lays out a doctrine of salvation, explaining the concepts of pardon, reconciliation, adoption, and

---

57. Ibid., 368–69.
58. Ibid., 371.
59. Willison, "Action Sermon," in *Balm of Gilead*, 425.

the comforts and graces that follow. Here again, the Table is presented as the place of union: "It is here Christ trysts with his people, here he walks with them, and is held by them in the galleries; here he visits them, and holds communion with them, intimates his love, and kisses them with the kisses of his mouth."[60] Here, too, the preacher reinforces the idea of the sacrament as a covenant, and the place where believers experience the overwhelming love of Christ. "O but many a poor soul has been ravished with Christ's love here, and with the wine of his consolation"; Willison exclaims, "he hath made rare discoveries of his love to them!"[61]

The sermon comes to a climax with the final wooing to the marriage-Supper, as Willison issues a litany of invitations to come to the Table "with holy awe and reverence," "with a holy fear," "with a broken and bleeding heart." The believer is to come wearing the wedding garment, and to come with love, since "Christ's heart is burning and bleeding with love to you." The communicant is to "come with panting and thirsting desires to see and meet with Christ," giving oneself over to him with adoration and praise. "If ye come in such a frame," the preacher promises, "you will be taken into the banqueting-house, and his banner over you will be love."[62] Once again, the believer is wooed to the Table as to the marriage bed, that the heart may be ravished and the soul might enjoy union with Christ, in anticipation of the final consummation at the heavenly marriage feast.

A SACRAMENTAL CATECHISM

In addition to his sermons and meditations, John Willison also published several catechisms designed to educate young or new believers that they might be prepared for proper celebration of the Lord's Supper. Like the devotional writings, the catechisms were published in Scotland, England, and America for well over a century. *A Sacramental Catechism* first appeared in Edinburgh in 1720 and was printed in New York as late as 1867. As the title page explains, this catechism intended to provide both doctrinal and practical instruction regarding baptism and the Lord's Supper, and included an appendix of meditations and prayers to be used before and after communion.[63] Willison is concerned that young people be properly prepared to participate in the

---

60. Ibid., 428.
61. Ibid., 431.
62. Ibid., 434–35.
63. John Willison, *A Sacramental Catechism, or, a Familiar Instructor for Young Communicants* (Glasgow: Printed by David Niven, 1794).

sacrament of the Lord's Supper, since it is there that they ratify their own baptismal covenants. Communicants come to the table for the first time, then, only after sufficient study.

The material in the catechism is similar to that found in Willison's other writings, though it is presented in the usual question-and-answer format. Characteristically loyal to the Reformed tradition, the author explains that his sacramental catechism relies heavily on the Larger Catechism, as well as other sources used throughout the Church of Scotland. Nevertheless, since the Shorter and Larger Catechisms must cover a broad range of topics, he explains, he is compelled to provide a catechism that focuses on the sacraments. Willison is addressing youth in this material, and he makes significantly less use of marital metaphors; he does, however, exhort his readers to be espoused to Jesus and to accept him as their husband, and he emphasizes the covenantal nature of the sacrament. References to the Song of Songs are less frequent in the catechism than in Willison's other writings, although the familiar language of the Canticles breaks forth in the meditations and prayers that are appended to the catechetical material. The following excerpts may be designed for young people, but they lack none of the color of Willison's other devotional materials. "O come put in thy hand by the hold of the door, and let heaven's sweet smelling myrrh drop upon the handles of the lock, that I may awake from my drowsiness, and open all my doors to the King of glory," reads one prayer. In another meditation, one prays for "a heart-ravishing sight of Christ's beauty" at the table. Elsewhere, one exclaims, "Can my heart be but ravished with his love?"[64]

In the preface to the catechism, Willison urges his young readers not simply to learn right doctrine, but also to seek an inward experience of the Spirit, "that light in your heads might be joined with heat in your hearts."[65] The very structure of his *Sacramental Catechism* undergirds his urging; for after the faithful students have acquired the proper understanding of the sacrament, the teacher puts in their mouths the words of the Canticles, that their prayers might be vivid, fervent, and passionate.

WILLISON'S HYMNS AND SONGS

Like his theological ancestor John Calvin and his contemporary Isaac Watts, John Willison recognized the value of the sung word as a tool for teaching doctrine, inspiring fervor, and preparing would-be communicants to approach

---

64. Ibid., 254, 259, 277.
65. Ibid., v.

the Table. To complement his various writings, Willison composed song collections devoted to putting the words of Scripture and Reformed doctrine on the lips of believers. In his *One Hundred Gospel-Hymns* he offers a rationale for why Christians should sing. Beginning with scriptural warrant, Willison argues that songs were meant for the praising of God, and that not only psalms, but also hymns and spiritual songs as well are appropriate for Christian worship. His hymns are primarily concerned with the suffering of Christ and sacramental themes. Singing them, he believes, would prevent praise from becoming perfunctory, encourage "delight and cheerfulness," and serve as "a kind of apprenticeship" for singing the songs of heaven. Furthermore, he sees singing as "not only a praising Ordinance, but also a teaching Ordinance," and a means for enlivening the spirit. By singing, he claims, people "find their Hearts melted for Sin, and warmed with Love." For all of these reasons (and because, he says, hymnbooks are scarce in Scotland), he makes his own offering of spiritual songs.[66]

The issue of whether or not Presbyterians could rightly sing songs other than psalms is apparently still pertinent, for Willison appeals to Pliny and Tertullian, as well as to the apostle Paul, in making his case. He is also concerned that he be perceived as expressing a Trinitarian theology; while he states that his main objective is to provide hymns that allow Christians to sing of Christ, he assures his readers that this is not to the neglect of praising God. Regarding his sacramental songs (which account for 19 of the 51 hymns in the collection), he declares, "Seeing [that] the great Design of the Sacrament is to keep up the Remembrance of Christ's Death, surely Sacramental Songs should be full of his Love and Sufferings, without indeed forgetting the other two Glorious Persons of the Trinity."[67] Clearly, then, singing is an important expression for Willison, but only understood in the context of Reformed sensibilities. Although he takes his cue from Watts in crafting songs and Scripture paraphrases, Willison continues to uphold the Psalms as a centerpiece of worship; his goal is to expand the singing repertoire for worship.

Another interesting portion of Willison's corpus is the collection of thirty-two "Scripture Songs" that appear in *Balm of Gilead*. Among these songs are eight paraphrases of the Song of Songs; together they express the entire content of the biblical book. Most songs are cast in the form of dialogues between Christ and the spouse, and in the manner of Watts's psalm paraphrases, remain

---

66. John Willison, *One Hundred Gospel-Hymns, In Memory of Redeeming Love, and of the Death and Sufferings of the Lord Jesus Christ, for Perishing Sinners, Much adapted to Sacramental Occasions* (Dundee: H. Galbraith, 1767), iii–ix. This volume was apparently published posthumously and reissued in 1791. Despite the title, the collection includes only 51 hymns.

67. Ibid., xv.

true to the text while interspersing direct references to the saving work of Jesus. One reads, for example, "Dear Jesus, as a bunch of myrrh / Shall in my bosom lie; / To lodge with me he'll not demur, / While nightly shades do stay"; and "Bring strength'ning flaggons unto me, / with cordials from above; / Fetch me sweet apples from the tree, / For I am sick of love." Sacramental undertones are apparent in Song 14: "On honey, wine, and milk I feast; / All friends, come eat with me, / And drink my wine of heav'nly taste, / Yea, drink abundantly." The covenantal relationship and the sensual delights of marriage are implied in Song 16: "To my beloved I belong, / And my belov'd to me; / To feed among the lily flow'rs, / Great pleasure taketh he."[68]

Despite Willison's apology for singing his songs in worship, it is unlikely that they were ever used that way. The resistance to singing in public worship remained strong in Scotland, even through the nineteenth century. So even though Willison's hymns and paraphrases are singable—composed in common meter (8.6.8.6)—they were probably used only devotionally.[69] Even if they were never sung, these songs would have served as a means of remembering Scripture, learning doctrine, inspiring affection, and meditating on Christ and his relationship to his spouse, the believer, whom he met with joy in the sacrament.

THE LEGACY OF JOHN WILLISON

John Willison was arguably the most prolific and influential pastor-author of his time, although the themes and concerns expressed in his writings can be observed in several of his contemporaries as well. Although a thorough exposition of their works is beyond the scope of this inquiry, we recognize that the sacramental sermons of Ralph Erskine (1685–1752) and, to a lesser extent, his brother Ebenezer Erskine (1680–1754) reveal the same doctrinal and thematic material. Language from the Song of Songs, rhapsodies on the loveliness of Christ, use of the metaphor of sight, the wooing of the believer to the Table, and reflections on the eschatological nature of the sacrament—all these are present. (A passage from Ralph Erskine's sermon "The main Question of the Gospel-Catechism, What think ye of Christ?" sounds remarkably like the portion of James McGready's sermon "The Saving Sight," which is quoted in chap. 4.) Both Ralph and Ebenezer Erskine make extensive use of the language of "leaning upon her beloved" (Song 8:5).

68. Willison, "Scripture Songs," in *Balm of Gilead*, 440–42.
69. Robin A. Leaver, personal correspondence.

Other figures of Willison's era made significant contributions as well. Robert Craighead's *Advice to Communicants* (1695) was published in several editions on both sides of the Atlantic. As mentioned above, Isaac Watts composed his own paraphrases of the Song of Songs. Nevertheless, it is John Willison who stands out as "the consummate Scottish catechist and spiritual writer" of his time. As Leigh Eric Schmidt explains, no other Scot "wrote more on the Lord's Supper; no one gave fuller expression to the piety connected with the festal communions. Through catechisms, meditations, devotional directions, sermons, and songs, . . . Willison articulated the range, scope, and power of the Scottish sacraments. His works . . . were by turns systematic and fervent, didactic and visionary," and his work served to instruct and inspire generations of Scots-Irish and American Presbyterians.[70]

70. Schmidt, *Holy Fairs*, 46.

PART 3

Analysis and Conclusions

The Song of Songs and American Sacramental Revivals

SUMMARY

The course of this inquiry has demonstrated that Presbyterians on the American frontier and their Scottish ancestors shared not only a liturgical practice but also a vocabulary of faith in the celebration of the sacramental occasions. Most notably, the use of the Song of Songs and other biblical marital imagery has been explored as a primary way of describing the understanding and experience of union with Christ in Communion. In private devotion and in public worship, believers longed for, prepared for, and finally consented to union with Christ, whose fervent invitation evoked their heartfelt response.

In the sermons of American preachers James McGready and Gilbert Tennent, and in the writings of their theological and liturgical ancestor John Willison, one sees evidence of a four-stage movement inherent in the celebration of the Communion season. First, believers actively participate in a process of preparation through a prescribed pattern of prayer, meditation, and public worship. Devotional reading is key, as communicants contemplate the state of their moral and spiritual lives, review their understanding of doctrine, submit themselves to the examination of church elders and/or clergy, and devote themselves to prayer. Through this process they also listen to preaching that accompanies them through each phase. As a result of this rigorous program of public and private worship, they are ready to approach the Table.

In the second stage, ministers play the part of advocate in their preaching, urging believers to the Table on behalf of Christ. They woo them with the language of love, promising union, faithfulness, and the fulfillment of longing. In doing so, the preachers make use of biblical marital imagery, particularly the poetry of the Song of Songs, comparing believers to the lover/spouse/bride and Christ to the lover/spouse/bridegroom. The desire of believers for Christ is matched only by the desire of Christ for the believers; in fact, his desire is even greater, for the Bridegroom who is lovely, and chief among ten thousand, waits for, cajoles, and offers an unbreakable covenant to the bride, who is stained, unfaithful, and unworthy. The wooing is fervent, the love language is heightened, the passionate yearning of both bride and bridegroom is strong.

Third, there is the anticipation of union with Christ at the Table. In their sermons, the preachers point to the Table as the locus of that union; the eucharistic Table is the marriage bed for the bride, who seeks to be joined with the Bridegroom in the sacrament. This union is experienced in part at the earthly table and in full at the heavenly wedding banquet. This means, then, that union with Christ in Communion is understood not only as the culmination of a spiritual journey of repentance and renewal, but also as the foretaste of the final consummation, which will be enjoyed in heaven.

The fourth stage is that of thanksgiving. After Communion has been celebrated, there is grateful response in worship, in acts of charity, and in a renewed corporate life. Although mention has been made of this pattern of worship in the sacramental season—where believers gathered for a final day of preaching and worship on the Monday following the Communion service—these sermons have not been considered since they do not usually employ the marital imagery that is the focus of this inquiry. Nevertheless, the experience of union with Christ in Communion was not understood as an individualized mystical experience, but as a communal sacramental encounter that resulted in the expression of gratitude liturgically, morally, and ecclesially.

In examining the sermons and devotional writings of representative Scots-Irish and American Presbyterian preachers, the prevalence and passion of language from the Song of Songs, other biblical marital imagery that represents Christ as a bridegroom or a husband, and psalms expressing the yearning or longing of a person for God—all these are unavoidable. This study set out to answer two basic questions: (1) What does the use of this biblical love poetry and the accompanying marital images mean in the eucharistic theology of the American holy fairs? (2) Where did this language come from? While this author cannot pretend to have exhausted all possible roads of inquiry into these questions, some conclusions may be drawn regarding them both.

THE LANGUAGE OF THE
SONG OF SONGS AND ITS MEANING
FOR THE EUCHARISTIC THEOLOGY
OF THE AMERICAN HOLY FAIRS

The two questions are surely related. It has been frequently recognized that the romantic, even erotic, language from the Song of Songs is employed to describe union with Christ. Use of this language to explain the soul's union with Christ, or the union of Christ with the church, and the tradition of interpreting the Song of Songs allegorically—these stretch back to the early days of the church. The Middle Ages saw an explosion of commentaries and sermons on the Canticles, as well as various devotional writings that used the imagery of spiritual marriage to describe the soul's union with the divine. This rich body of literature inspired theologians and preachers in a wide array of ecclesial traditions for centuries to come. For the Scots and their American descendants, however, this language is most closely associated with the Eucharist; the language of the Song of Songs is used again and again to express union with Christ *in the context of the Lord's Supper*.

In the Reformed tradition, union with Christ is something that one understands and gives assent to; yet it is not only a concept, but also an experience, a mystery that evokes awe. The same might be said for the believer's approach to Communion: one understands eucharistic doctrine, but in the end understanding must fall down before mystery. Perhaps for this reason these Presbyterian preachers at sacramental revivals resorted to highly poetic and pictorial language—metaphor that goes beyond theological formulations—in order to reflect both the intellectual and the spiritual apprehensions of union with Christ in Communion. Also, the emotive, passionate language of the Canticles lends itself well to the rhythms of meditation and fervor that are part of the sacramental occasions. The sermons and devotional material designed to carry a communicant through self-examination and repentance did not shy away from highly pictorial language describing the sufferings and passion of Christ; in the same way, the writings that aimed to woo the believer to the Table used the most vivid biblical language available to achieve that end.

This language is also useful for expressing the eschatological emphasis that is apparent in the sermons and devotional materials read by American Presbyterians involved in sacramental revivals. As Denys Turner explains, "The Song is a poem charged with a sense of sexual fulfilment *anticipated*." He points to "the tensions of interplay between 'presence' and 'absence,' between 'now,' but 'not yet,' between the 'possession' of the beloved and his 'elusiveness,' of 'oneness with' and 'otherness than.'"[1] This characteristic of the Song of Songs is useful for expressing the partial, temporal nature of union with Christ in the earthly sacrament of Communion, in comparison to the full and final consummation that will take place at the marriage supper of the Lamb. The already/not yet nature of the union that believers enjoy with Christ is a chief component of the Reformed understanding, one that can be seen in Calvin and is reflected later in the preaching of both Scottish and American ministers who spoke of the "lower" and "upper" tables.

What, then, does this language mean? In short, for American Presbyterians of Scots-Irish descent, the eucharistic Table is the marriage bed for Christ the Bridegroom and the believer who is bride. It is the goal of spiritual desire, the locus of union, and the foretaste of heavenly consummation. On earth the believer is espoused to Christ in a marriage covenant; in the sacrament the marriage contract is sealed; in heaven the marriage will be fully and joyfully consummated, and the covenant eternally unbroken.

Union with Christ, as Calvin said, is the goal of the Christian life. This is not, however, a solitary enterprise. The rhythms of piety practiced at sacramental occasions place the striving for this union in the context of corporate worship rather than individual contemplation. Furthermore, this corporate ecclesial context has moral and ethical implications. The emphasis on worthiness to come to the Table is not only about personal sanctification; it is also about the health and strength and faithfulness—the discipline, to use Calvin's term—of the church. Preparation for Communion is not only necessary for the purging and cleansing of the individual soul, but also for the reconciliation and purification of the corporate body.

CONTINUITY AND CHANGE

Chapter 3 argued that Calvin's understanding and experience of union with Christ might be described as "mystical," yet only if one relies on a definition of mysticism such as that proposed by Gerson. This definition does not focus on ecstatic experience or solitary contemplation, but involves both intellectual and experiential components. Like Gerson, Calvin places the believer in the context of a worshiping community rather than alone in a cloistered room; he thus is less interested in medieval expressions of mysticism than he is in Christians' spirituality, or piety. The sermons considered here show an interest in balancing matters of head and heart, and it is reasonable to assert that

---

1. Denys Turner, *Eros and Allegory: Medieval Exegesis of the Song of Songs* (Kalamazoo, MI: Cistercian Publications, 1995), 84–85.

the sacramental occasions in both Scotland and America reflected Reformed theology and piety. One might also argue, however, that these sermons reveal a continuity with the more mystical strain seen in certain medieval writings. The insights of Heiko Oberman are instructive here. In his study of the beginnings of the Reformation era, Oberman quotes the work of three theologians writing at the cusp of the late medieval and early Reformation eras, theologians for whom spiritual marriage is a significant metaphor: Gerson's *Mystical Theology* (1407), John von Staupitz's *Libellus* (1517), and Luther's *Freedom of a Christian* (1520). All three of these works treat the subject of the relationship between Christ and the believer by using the symbolism of love and marriage. He explains:

> Each is mystical in tone, but not necessarily mystical in the sense of describing an unusual experience of union with God. On the contrary, what all three have in common is that this mystical experience is no longer regarded as the privilege of a few elect aristocrats of the Spirit; in accordance with the late medieval phenomenon of democratisation of mysticism, the bridal kiss and the intimate union of God and man now mark the life of every true believer.[2]

Oberman refers to a section of Gerson's work where "he emphasizes experience more than reason" in describing the soul's (and the church's) process of repentance and purging before becoming one with the Divine. Noting that Gerson's view is "thoroughly traditional, and is found in the same form in St. Bernard, Ficino and Cusanus," he quotes Gerson:

> But when it has finally come so far that one is sufficiently pure, that is that one has a clear conscience so that one no longer . . . looks at God as a judge who metes out punishment, but as completely desirable, and lovable, . . . then fly with a feeling of security into the arms of the bridegroom, embrace and kiss him with the kiss of peace which surpasses all understanding [Phil. 4:7], so that you can say with grateful and loving devotion: "My beloved is mine and I am his" [Song 2:16].[3]

Here one can clearly hear the similarity between Gerson's description of preparation for union and the Scottish/American Presbyterian emphasis on preparation and repentance that culminates in a joyful and loving embrace with the Divine. This is not to say that Gerson had a direct influence upon the

---

2. Heiko Oberman, *The Dawn of the Reformation: Essays in Late Medieval and Early Reformation Thought* (Edinburgh: T&T Clark, 1986; reprint, Grand Rapids: Wm. B. Eerdmans Publishing Co., 1992), 32–33.

3. Ibid., 33.

figures who are the subject of this inquiry. It is to say, however, that it is possible to identify what one might call "continuities" between certain medieval mystics and post-Reformation theologians and preachers.

While Oberman is more interested in the relationship between Scholasticism and the Reformation theology that followed, it is useful for this study to note that he argues for continuity between the medieval and Reformation traditions.[4] As observed earlier in this work, even a cursory sampling of medieval writings suggests that the boundary between the theology and practice of medieval Christians and that of their Reformation-era counterparts was far from impenetrable. It follows, then, that the Scottish Presbyterians, while treading firmly in the footsteps of Calvin, could at the same time speak in tones that echoed their medieval spiritual forebears, applying the imagery of love and marriage to their revivalist, eucharistic context. Certainly Calvin and his heirs were careful to distinguish particular characteristics of Reformed eucharistic theology from that of the Roman church, especially with regard to the doctrines of transubstantiation and real presence. Nevertheless, it is possible to see that while Reformation and post-Reformation figures worked hard for change in matters of theology and church discipline, they also claimed spiritual and theological continuities as well.

Specifically, one can point to the use of language from the Song of Songs and other biblical marital imagery and make the case for continuity between pre- and post-Reformation views of mystical union. McGready, Tennent, and Willison held fast to their Reformed conviction that union with Christ is effected in both Word and sacrament; that union with Christ is connected with both justification and sanctification; that the life of faith in general, and participation in Eucharist in particular, is a matter of both understanding and experience. In doing so, they expressed Calvin's own convictions. In their use of vivid sexual and marital metaphors, however, they echoed the colorful and evocative language of Calvin's medieval ancestors. The eucharistic theology of the Scots-Irish and American holy fairs, then, exhibits both continuity and change. Or to put it another way, one can see continuities with both medieval mysticism and the Reformed theological tradition.[5]

---

4. Ibid., 37.

5. Stanley Hall argues that any discussion of "continuity" implies causation, which is exceedingly difficult to prove. It might be more accurate, he suggests, to note a "reappearance" or "similarity." Hall further proposes that one might speak of the sacramental seasons as expressions of catholicity involving "norms of communal preparation for sacramental communion." Again, this study does not seek to prove causal relationships between medieval and post-Reformation practices, but rather to point out similar expressions of piety and practice. Hall's comments, therefore, are instructive and invite further reflection. Stanley R. Hall, personal correspondence.

A somewhat surprising example of continuity with the medieval tradition can be seen in John Willison's works, in which Christ is characterized as a nursing mother. Caroline Walker Bynum has observed that "seeing Christ or God or the Holy Spirit as female is thus part of a later medieval devotional tradition that is characterized by increasing preference for analogies taken from human relationships."[6] This is evident in Bernard's writings on the Song of Songs, which include references to Christ as a nursing mother.[7] It is fascinating, then, to discover in one of John Willison's *Sacramental Meditations* a similar allusion, used in conjunction with language from the Canticles: "'Awake, O north wind! Come then south! Blow upon my garden'; bring faith to life, that I may suck honey from Christ in the sacrament. Christ's breasts are now full; O let not faith be wanting!"[8] A related maternal image, well-documented in medieval sources, is found in Willison's *Sacramental Directory*—that of the pelican. After meditating on the sacrificial love of Christ, which he compares to that of Jacob for Rachel, he writes, "But our lovely bridegroom shewed far greater love to his spouse in undergoing the cursed, painful and shameful death of the cross for her." He follows this marital image with a maternal one:

> It is reported of the Pelican, that when her young ones are stung with some poisonous serpent, she beats her breast with her beek, till the warm blood gushes out, which they suck and recover: We were all stung mortally by the old serpent the devil; but behold the love of our heavenly Pelican, he lets out his heart's blood to recover us.[9]

One must be judicious in claiming direct influence. Nevertheless, given the Reformers' acquaintance with medieval writers, and the stress on theological education and knowledge of the Christian tradition among Presbyterians, it is not unlikely that the Scots, like the Puritans, were versed in the writings of medieval mystics.

OTHER CONTINUITIES
WITH MEDIEVAL PRACTICE

Devotional reading. The importance of devotional reading among the Scots-Irish Presbyterians in both the Old World and the New has been demonstrated, and the widespread publication of sermons and devotional literature

---

6. Bynum, *Jesus as Mother*, 129.
7. Ibid., 145, 147.
8. Willison, "Sacramental Meditation VI," in *Balm of Gilead*, 224.
9. Willison, *Sacramental Directory*, 191.

observed. In her study *Women, Reading, and Piety in Late Medieval England*, Mary C. Erler makes the case that devotional books were of great social importance in the medieval world, and that "reading with a spiritual intention was more widespread than we find it easy to realize." In the course of her study of diaries, wills, and book ownership, she discovers that at the end of the fifteenth century "devotional works constitute the largest subject category in the surviving output of English printers." Her study leads her to the claim that "a literature of spiritual formation" was central to medieval culture.[10]

Richard Kieckhefer similarly argues that "the flourishing of mystical literature in the late Middle Ages was largely the product of shifting boundaries within the Church: the formation of a lay reading public and an audience for contemplative literature outside the cloister."[11] This, too, is a topic that invites more attention than can be devoted to it here. The point to be made, however, is that devotional reading, which is a well-documented practice in the medieval era, continued for centuries to be a significant activity for Protestant and Catholic Christians alike, and central to the rhythms of piety of the sacramental revivals in Scotland and America.

Liturgical time. Although it may not seem so at first glance, the understanding of liturgical time also signals continuity between medieval, Reformation, and post-Reformation Christian practices. The Reformers saw the festivals of the Roman church as superstitious and idolatrous, and therefore they set about expunging all holy days from the calendar. Sunday was to be the only holy day, and the sacrament was to be celebrated frequently. Particularly important to the Reformers was the need to break the cycle of observing Communion only on Easter and to erode the belief that there was anything particularly special about that festival day.[12] Furthermore, they were intent on eliminating any sort of adoration or procession of the host, such as that carried out during the feast of Corpus Christi. By the seventeenth century, Scottish reformers had established a new pattern (at least officially): every Sunday was to be a time of celebration, when worshipers would enjoy communion with God and one another, and the old community festivals, feasts, and processions were no longer observed.[13]

10. Mary C. Erler, *Women, Reading, and Piety in Late Medieval England* (Cambridge: Cambridge University Press, 2002), 4.

11. Richard Kieckhefer, "Convention and Conversion: Patterns in Late Medieval Piety," *Church History* 67, no. 1 (March 1998): 33–34.

12. W. McMillan, "Festivals and Saint Days in Scotland After the Reformation," in *Records of the Scottish Church History Society*, ed. W. J. Couper and Robert McKinlay, vol. 3 (Edinburgh: Scottish Church History Society, 1929), 2.

13. Schmidt, *Holy Fairs*, 17.

As Leigh Schmidt notes, those old patterns did not disappear altogether; they resurfaced in the Presbyterian sacramental occasions. He explains that these Presbyterians would never have acknowledged any resemblance of their practices to Catholic tradition; they were loyal to the theological and liturgical programs of Calvin and Knox. "Yet paradoxically these evangelical Presbyterians, in originating the sacramental occasion, were successful as much because of Catholic legacies as Protestant innovations," Schmidt asserts. "The rise of festal communions early in the next century suggested that the old rhythm that went along with the popular festivals of late medieval Catholicism was not as easily eradicated as the early reformers had hoped."[14]

Stanley Hall observes that these annual sacramental occasions stood in significant contrast to the official model put forth in the Westminster Directory and the liturgical practices prescribed by the Church of Scotland.[15] Yet the 1645 Act of the General Assembly of the Kirk of Scotland did put some restrictions on the sacramental occasions, limiting the number of clergy involved to one or two, stipulating the number of sermons to be preached (only one on each day), and advising that the setting be in a usual place of worship (indoors) that offered overflow seating.[16] These specifications reflect the Presbyterian concern with order and point to a measure of disagreement—and accommodation—within the church around the appropriateness of the Communion festivals.

Ironically the steadily declining lack of Communion observances in Scotland contributed to the rise of the sacramental occasions. In spite of official prescriptions of monthly or quarterly observances, Scottish Presbyterians celebrated the sacrament less frequently, even to the extent of lapsing for several years. This failure was due to a variety of factors: political disruption, poverty so severe that bread was scarce, a dearth of clergy, negligence on the part of ministers, and the logistical challenge of bringing together people who were spread over far-ranging parishes.[17] As celebrations grew less frequent, and annual sacraments became more common, the festival quality reemerged. From May to October, worshipers and revelers from around the Scottish countryside would make their way from kirk to kirk, celebrating the harvest and renewing ties with family and friends. Some would regard this as their annual time of spiritual renewal; others would attend as many holy fairs as they could, seeking social delights more than spiritual ones.

---

14. Ibid., 18–19.

15. S. R. Hall, "The American Presbyterian 'Directory for Worship,'" 78.

16. Ibid., 79.

17. D. E. Meek, "Communion Seasons," *Dictionary of Scottish Church History and Theology* (Edinburgh: T&T Clark, 1993), 200.

The 1650s brought significant developments in the Communions. More ministers took part, and more sermons were preached. A fast day was often observed in the middle of the week. By the end of the seventeenth century, sacramental occasions were so popular and so numerous that summer and fall were each essentially one long sacramental season. "In an ironic twist," Schmidt observes, "the evangelical Presbyterians, the most Puritan group in Scotland, wound up recovering much of the eucharistic festivity of late medieval Catholicism in their own sacramental occasions."[18]

It would be facile to suggest that these usages and practices continued from medieval to post-Reformation times without alteration. Nevertheless, it is possible to see that patterns of the pre-Reformation church regarding language, devotion, and time did not come to an abrupt halt in the Protestant traditions but continued or resurfaced, taking on new shapes and nuances.

THE CHALLENGE OF INTERPRETING SEXUAL LANGUAGE

Among the numerous questions that lie beyond the scope of this study is that of how previous generations understood sexual language. Contemporary responses to erotic, sexual, or physical language differ greatly from those of medieval readers. Bynum is instructive here:

> Medieval authors do not seem to have drawn as sharp a line as we do between sexual responses and affective responses or between male and female. Throughout the Middle Ages, authors found it far easier than we seem to find it to apply characteristics stereotyped as male or female to the opposite sex. Moreover, they were clearly not embarrassed to speak of all kinds of ecstasy in language *we* find physical and sexual and therefore inappropriate for God.[19]

Ann E. Matter further illuminates the subject when she acknowledges that use of passionate, sexual language to convey a message of "purity, chastity, and transcendence" might seem paradoxical to modern readers. Yet she reminds those readers that (as Bynum has shown in previous works) medieval writers understood Christ's blood as spiritual food, connected not only to the Eucharist but "also to milk from the breast of mother Jesus, or even to the milk of the Virgin Mary which fed God incarnate in human form. The body of Christ and the human body shared the ability to bleed, feed, die, and give

---

18. Schmidt, *Holy Fairs*, 33, 20.
19. Bynum, *Jesus as Mother*, 162.

life." Echoing Foucault, she asserts that "since the 'sexual enlightenment' of the sixteenth and seventeenth centuries," contemporary people have found it difficult to apply "bodily language" to "spiritual states." This, she bluntly states, "is our problem, not a medieval one."[20]

This topic is obviously a deep one and invites further study beyond the confines of the present project. Yet it is useful to recognize differences in the way medieval and contemporary ears hear the language of love and marriage as it is applied to spiritual matters. In considering the writings of Scots-Irish Presbyterians in Scotland and in America, then, one must observe the similar use of this language to that of medieval writers. The believer, whether male or female, is cast in the role of the bride. Similarly, the preachers considered here did not balk at using sexual or marital images in describing the believer's union with Christ.

In relating how Scottish ministers collected the remembrances of worshipers at the Cambuslang revival, Leigh Schmidt observes that they left the worshipers' own language intact, language that reflected the sexual and marital metaphors the preachers themselves used. The editors of these collections, however, deleted some of the more vivid descriptions. Schmidt observes that

> the ministerial editors usually left such expressions unadulterated; for they themselves understood their eucharistic experiences in much the same terms. In sermon after sermon and meditation after meditation, they too recalled the intimate love between Christ and his fair one. "Let him there kiss me with the Kisses of his Lips," Willison prayed in one of his sacramental meditations, "and enable me to embrace him in the Arms of my Faith, saying, *This is my Beloved, and this is my Friend*." Pastors and people shared passionate longings for the Bridegroom.[21]

In other words, Scottish ministers in the sixteenth and seventeenth centuries saw this language as not only expressive but also appropriate; the echo of that language in the American preachers considered here implies the same.

CONCLUSIONS

It is quite a distance from Kentucky in 1800 to Geneva in 1560, let alone twelfth-century Bernard of Clairvaux. Having traversed that span of time and, in the process, covered a rather broad range of topics, it remains to focus on the task at hand: How might American Presbyterian sacramental revivals of

---

20. Matter, *Voice of My Beloved*, 138–39.
21. Schmidt, *Holy Fairs*, 163–64.

the First and Second Great Awakenings be characterized? And what is there to say about the use of biblical love poetry and images of marriage in the context of those revivals?

First, it must be said that this is not your grandmother's revival. Before the days of Charles Finney or Billy Graham, there were the Presbyterian sacramental occasions that were theologically Reformed, sacramentally centered, evangelical in nature, concerned with the conversion of unbelievers as well as the repentance and renewal of believers, and eschatologically oriented, reflecting the belief that union with Christ in the earthly sacrament is a foretaste of the final consummation in heaven.

It must be acknowledged that just as the Scottish context reflected a division between those who approved of revivals and those who did not, so too did the American context. While the proponents of sacramental occasions defended them as times of spiritual awakening and renewal, detractors pointed to the excesses and indiscretions that accompanied the large public occasions. Nevertheless, in spite of some of the objectionable behaviors that surrounded the communions and the enthusiastic forms of worship that some found distasteful, the sacramental occasions played a central role in the piety of the New Side, or revivalist, school of American Presbyterians.[22] American Presbyterians who were involved with revivals held to their Reformed theological convictions, and their interest in revivalism was tempered, to be sure, with the Reformed concerns for intellectual integrity, biblical scholarship, and proper education for clergy. They valued, too, the personal and ecclesial discipline that had been a part of the Reformed tradition since the days of Calvin, particularly as it pertained to preparation for, and worthy participation in, the sacrament. At the same time, however, they were equally concerned with the spiritual vigor of their churches, and they drew on biblical sexual and marital imagery to express that vitality. There is a sense in which this heightened language of the Song of Songs was a fitting complement to the high energy and emotion of the revival context. As has been observed in the sermons that were preached just before believers gathered at the Table, the wooing and cajoling often came to a climactic finish as the preacher/advocate whipped listeners up into a state of expectation and desire. At the end of a long and arduous

22. An interesting question that lies beyond the scope of this study is if, or how, the rhetoric of New Side Presbyterians may have affected their Old Side opponents. Gilbert Tennent eventually became part of the established church, leaving behind the frontier when he moved to Philadelphia. James McGready, for his part, remained true to his Presbyterian roots when pushed to side with Arminian-leaning ministers involved in the Kentucky revivals. And at least one author has made the case that Old Side stalwarts Archibald Alexander, Charles Hodge, and Benjamin Warfield were as concerned with piety as with orthodoxy. See W. Andrew Hoffecker, *Piety and the Princeton Theologians* (Phillipsburg, NJ: Presbyterian & Reformed Publishing Co., 1981).

period of preparation was joyful blessing—forgiveness, union, and a taste of the sweetness of divine love.

The claim being made is this. In the sermons of American Presbyterian preachers involved in sacramental revivals, one observes theological expressions inherited from their Scottish forebears. These expressions are rooted in a solid Reformed theological heritage and are flavored with a strain of mysticism seen in medieval writers, one that is appreciated and in some ways reflected (if not imitated) in the works of John Calvin. Using language from the Song of Songs as well as other marital imagery, these preachers bring a Reformed mystical eucharistic theology to a frontier revivalism that was at once evangelical and sacramental. For American Presbyterians of Scots-Irish descent, the eucharistic Table was a marriage bed, where union with Christ was experienced in anticipation of the final consummation in heaven, and believers who sought to meet their Bridegroom were ravished with the love of Christ.

IMPLICATIONS FOR TWENTY-FIRST-CENTURY REFORMED WORSHIP

Outlining a program for the renewal of Reformed worship is clearly beyond the parameters of this study. Yet this inquiry into the nature of the American sacramental occasions leads one to imagine how the conclusions herein might inform those who serve the church today. It surely is not a new thought that the Presbyterian church in America would be well-served by reclaiming the centrality of the sacraments. While the issue of frequency of communion has been alluded to here and continues to be a matter of debate, it cannot be denied that in spite of the infrequency of celebration in the Scots-Irish revival tradition, the Lord's Supper was a central element of Presbyterian piety. As modern-day Presbyterians move toward more frequent celebrations, a new embracing of the power of the sacraments is in order. Although the church need not return to the practices of the American frontier, it must consider how sacramental celebrations might be enriched so that communicants might experience spiritual vitality, intellectual understanding, emotional fervor, and physical engagement.

A second contribution to present-day worshipers might be the recognition that Presbyterian theology and practice has, from the very start, included a mystical strain. One does not have to attend many Presbyterian services in the United States to see how worship has been drained of any palpable sense of mystery. The tradition's strong grounding in intellectual understanding has been a gift to the church; but the gift has come at a dear price. An ongoing conversation between those involved in liturgical matters and those who are engaged in the study of spirituality could yield great rewards for the renewal of Presbyterian worship. As Dennis Tamburello remarks, "Spirituality is not Catholic or Protestant—it is simply, as von Hügel would say, an essential element in religious life."[23]

Finally, looking back at the holy fairs provides a reminder that passion is an integral part of vital worship. In her recent study of youth and the church, Kenda Creasy Dean makes the point that "a passionless church will never address passionate youth. It is highly questionable whether a passionless church addresses anybody, or if it even is the church in the first place."[24] Dean's provocative remark serves as yet another reminder that the health and faithfulness of the church, present and future, depends in no small part on a rediscovery of passion. Perhaps if there is one thing that can be learned from the holy fairs, it is that in the sacraments we are made part of the mystery and passion that is at the heart of the faith—and that union with Christ is not only something to be understood, but also to be experienced, a union of minds, hearts, and wills that leads to the passionate living out of divine love in the world.

23. Tamburello, *Union with Christ*, 109.
24. Kenda Creasy Dean, *Practicing Passion: Youth and the Quest for a Passionate Church* (Grand Rapids: Wm. B. Eerdmans Publishing Co., 2004), 69.

Appendixes

Notes on the Appendixes

Appendix A is a facsimile of the first page in the manuscript of Gilbert Tennent's sermon "De nuptiis cum Christo"; a transcription of this whole sermon is included in Appendix B. Two additional transcriptions appear in Appendixes C and D. The Tennent manuscripts are located in the Luce Library of Princeton Theological Seminary in Princeton, New Jersey. The three represented here are from a set of thirteen sermons of Gilbert Tennent that are previously unpublished. Of the entire set of manuscripts, these three are pertinent to this study.

The quality of the manuscripts varies; some corners are torn, and in some places the handwriting is indecipherable. In these instances blanks appear in the transcription. The transcripts included here are virtually complete, although occasionally words or phrases are missing or supplied. All biblical citations are shown in the original positions in the text. Quotation marks are used when a text is (nearly) identical to the King James Version; otherwise they are treated as paraphrases. Punctuation and spelling have been generally preserved.

Paragraph indentations have been inserted in order to facilitate reading of the transcriptions, and spellings have been updated and corrected. Occasionally information is provided in brackets or footnotes to assist the reader in understanding the meaning of language that is unclear or archaic to the twenty-first-century ear.

Appendix A

Facsimile Page from Gilbert Tennent's
Sermon Manuscript 1

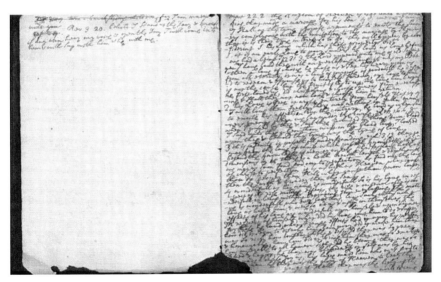

(*continued on next page*)

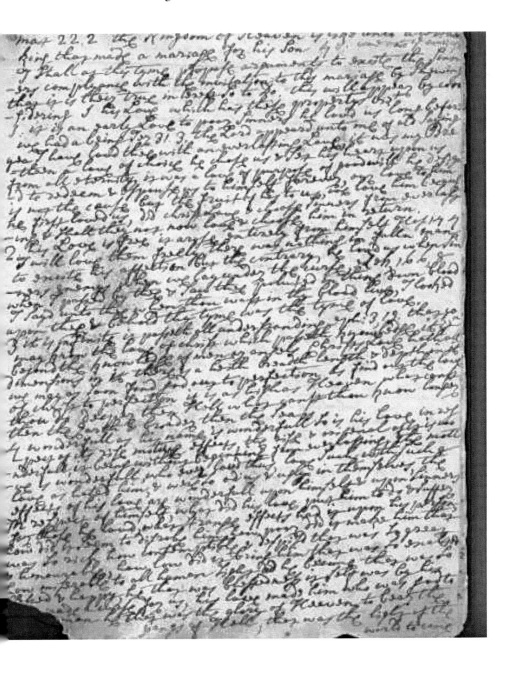

Appendix B

Transcription of Gilbert Tennent's
Sermon Manuscript 1

De nuptiis cum Christo

February [17]53

Rev. 3:20. "Behold I stand at the door and knock. If any man hears my voice and open the door, I will come in to him and will sup with him and he with me."

Matt. 22:2. The kingdom of heaven is like unto a certain king that made a marriage for his son. 4th v.: come unto the marriage. I shall at this tyme propose arguments to excite the sinners' compliance with the invitation to this marriage by showing that it is their true interest so to do. This will appear by considering 1. His love which has these properties, viz.

1. It is an early love to poor sinners. He loved us long before we had a being. (Jer. 31:3) "The LORD appeared unto me of old saying, Yea, I have loved thee with an everlasting love." It was, my brethren, a love of choice. He chose us and set his heart upon us from all eternity. It was a love of purpose, of good will; he designed to redeem and espouse us to himself forever. Our love to him is not the cause but the fruit of his to us. We love him because he first loved us. Did Christ love and choose sinners from everlasting and shall they not now love and choose him in return?

2. His love is free, it arose entirely from himself. (Hos. 14:4) "I will love them freely." There was nothing in fallen man to invite his affection but the contrary, he loved us when sinners, enemies, when we lay under the curse. (Ezek. 16:6, 8) "When I passed by thee and saw thee polluted in thine own

blood[,] I said unto thee when thou was in thy blood, 'Live!' I looked upon thee, and behold thy time was the time of love."

3. It is infinite, it passeth all understanding. (Eph. 3:19) "That you may know the love of Christ which passeth knowledge." It is beyond the knowledge of men or angels. Christ's love hath all dimensions in it. There is a height, breadth, length and depth in it. We may as soon find God out to perfection as find out the love of Christ to perfection. It is as high as Heaven. What canst thou do deeper than Hell? What canst thou know longer than the earth and broader than the sea?

4. [It is] Wonderful. As his name is wonderful, so is his love in respect of its rife [i.e., widespread] motive effects [i.e., moving to action]. The rife and original[1] [effect] of it is wonderful, it being without beginning. From everlasting the motive is wonderful. Whoever loved thus, love[d] such with such a love as hated him, and were so odious and ugly in themselves. The effects of his love are wonderful upon himself and upon sinners. In respect of [to] himself, what did his love put him to do and suffer for whose he loved! What strange effects had it upon his person! How did it seem to disrobe—how poor did it make him that was so rich—how contemptible and despised that was so great and honourable! How low did it bring him that was so exalted—how miserable to all human sight did he become, that was so blessed and happy! He that was blessedness itself was by his _____[2] made accursed for us. His love made him who was God to [become] man. He that was the glory of Heaven to bear the pangs of Hell—that was the light of the world to come under the greatest darkness—that was the life of all creatures to come under the power of death.

Besides the effects of his love on sinners are also wonderful for

1. It causeth them that hated him to love him above father and mother, son or daughter, house or land, yea or life itself.

2. It causeth poor sinners to love him after this manner whom they never saw. And is this not wonderful and amazing! (I Pet. 1:8) "Whom having not seen, ye love; in whom, though now ye see him not, yet believing, ye rejoice with joy unspeakable."

3. It hath a like wonderful effect upon the souls of sinners, as Elijah's garment had when cast on Elisha. (I Kings 19:19, 20) "So he departed hence and found Elisha the Son of Shaphat plowing with twelve yoke of oxen and Elijah passed by him and cast his mantle upon him. And he left the oxen and ran after Elijah, and said, "Let me, I pray thee, kiss my father and my mother, and then I will follow thee." No sooner doth Christ cast the mantle of his love on poor sinners but immediately they leave all and follow him.

---

1. Initial, constituting what will be reproduced.
2. Corner is torn: perhaps "crucifixion."

4. It makes a marvelous change on the souls of sinners. (I [II] Cor. 3:18) "But we all, with open face beholding as in a glass the glory of the Lord, are changed into the same image from glory to glory, even as by the Spirit of the Lord."

5. The love of Christ is sweet and soul-ravishing. (Cant. 1:2) "Let him kiss me with the kisses of his mouth, for thy love is better than wine." (Cant. 2:5) "Stay me with flagons, comfort me with apples, for I am sick of love." Nothing on earth tastes so sweet as the redeemer's love.

6. It is conjugal love. Nothing will satisfy him but the nearest relation. It is the espousing of the soul to himself that he aims at, that he may manifest the dearest embraces, the sweetest intimacy. (Hos. 2:19[–20]) "I will betroth thee unto me for ever in righteousness, in judgment, in lovingkindness, and in mercy, and thou shalt know the Lord."

7. [It is] complacential[3] love. He delights in the soul that believeth in him. (Is. 62:5) "As the bridegroom rejoiceth over the bride, so shall thy God rejoice over thee." (Cant. 4:9) "Thou hast ravished my heart, my sister, my spouse. Thou hast ravished my heart with one of thine eyes, with one chain of the neck." Christ is delighted with the eye of faith by which the soul came to behold him, and was induced to love him, and delight in him.

8. [It is] compassionate. It is a love of sympathy. (Is. 63:9) "In all their afflictions he was afflicted and in his love and pity he redeemed them and carried them all the days of old." (Heb. 4:15) "We have not a high priest that cannot be touched with the feeling of our infirmities; but was in all points tempted like as we are, yet without sin." O who would not espouse such a prince who sympathizes with his people in all their sorrows, who puts his left hand of power under their heads and with his right hand of love and mercy embraces them? Who bears them in his arms and carries them in his bosom and gives them cordials to revive their fainting spirits, (Heb 5:2:) "Who can have compassion on the ignorant, and [on] them that are out of the way," afflicted and compassed with our infirmity, which by sympathy he made his own, for he bore our sicknesses.

9. [It is] abiding love. It is not hot and cold, as it is among men. What heat of love will some men show to those they espouse at first, but they soon cool in their affections, and alas, so doth our love to Jesus Christ, which is for a lamentation. We are too subject with the church of Ephesus to leave our first love. Christ may say to us, as to his people of old, I remember the kindness of thy youth, the love of thine espousals, when thou wentest after me into the wilderness, to a land that was not sown. But Christ's love to us doth never decay. (John 13:1): "Having loved his own that were in the world, he loved

3. Amiable, wanting to please.

them unto the end." Much water cannot quench his love, nor can the floods drown it.

10. [It is] inseparable love. No enemy, no infirmity in his people can separate his love from them. Ill men sometimes cause some men to withdraw their love from their wives—a small thing may separate their love from their dearest friends—but nothing can separate Christ's love from believers. (Rom. 8:[38–]39): "I am persuaded that neither death nor life nor angels nor principalities nor powers nor things present, nor things to come, nor height nor depth, nor any other creature can separate us from the love of God which is in Jesus Christ our Lord."

11. [It is] eternal love. It is like himself—as he is eternal, so is his love. He is the same yesterday, today, and forever, and so is his love to his people. (Is. 54:10): "For the mountains shall depart, and the hills be removed; but my kindness shall not depart from thee, neither shall the covenant of my peace be removed, saith the LORD that hath mercy on thee." Christ betroths forever. Is not this consideration enough to engage to you embrace the redeemer and return love for love? His love makes every bitter thing sweet and hard thing easy.

A second argument that would offer shall be drawn from the riches of Christ. Riches and honor are with him, yea, durable riches and righteousness (Prov. 8:18). The Lord Jesus must needs be very rich, because he is the Father's heir, yea, heir of all things. All that the Father hath the Son hath considered as he is God and father of all things are given to him as he is mediator, whether things in heaven or things on earth. He is the father's first born whom he hath appointed heir of all things (Heb. 1:2) and therefore the inheritance must needs be his. (John 13:3): "Jesus knowing that the Father hath given all things into his hands."

Abram's servant, who was sent to Laban's house to espouse a wife for his master with design to recommend him, said "I am Abram's servant. The Lord hath blessed my master greatly, and he is become great and hath given him flocks and herds and silver and gold, manservants, maidservants and camels and to my master's son he hath given all that he hath (Gen. 24 [quoting from vv. 34–36]). Even so we say unto you, the great God who sent us is a mighty king; the world is his and the fullness thereof, all things in heaven and earth. The cattle upon one thousand hills are his, and he has but one eternal son; to him hath he given all he hath, and this son of his is fallen in love with you. Will you accept his offer, if you will deal truly and kindly with our master today?

2. But to evince[4] farther that Christ is rich, consider that he hath all the kingdoms of the earth given to him to dispose of as he sees good; the father

---

4. Show clearly.

hath given him the heathen for his inheritance and the uttermost parts of the earth for his possession (Ps. 2:8). For a time for wise reasons he has suffered his enemies to triumph, but by and by every knee shall bow before him, and every tongue confess that Jesus is Lord to the glory of God the father. God will overturn, overturn, overturn until he comes whose right it is, and he will give it unto him. The kingdoms of this world shall become the kingdoms of the Lord and of his Christ. The kingdom and the greatest of the kingdoms under the whole heavens shall be given to the people of the saints of the most high, whose kingdom is an everlasting kingdom, and all nations shall serve and obey him (Dan. 7:27).

3. Christ must needs be very rich, considering the greatness of his family, which he feeds and clothes at his own charge. The whole world is his family, all the _____ of it, the power as well for, the silver and the gold is his, as well as the wool and flax.

Yea, not only all the riches of the earth are his, but [also] the riches of heaven. Likewise, O what a crown and throne hath[5] Christ that communicates all[6] the grace to his people. He is the only begotten of the father, full of grace and truth, of whose fullness we have all received and grace for grace.

But what is Christ rich in, and what are the quality of his riches?

1. He is rich in wisdom. He is not only wise, but [also] hath great abundance thereof. In him are hid all the treasures of wisdom and knowledge. (Col. 2:3) He communicates of his own wisdom to make others wise. No person that needs of him but he imparts his wisdom to.

2. [He is rich] in goodness. (Rom 2:4): "Or despisest thou the riches of his goodness." The earth is full of the goodness of the Lord. Brethren, greatness and goodness meet in Jesus Christ. It is rare to find them met in men. The sea is not so full of water or the sun of light as he is of goodness, yea all the drops of goodness that are in creatures are derived from the immense ocean thereof that is in him. Goodness in men too often proves like the morning cloud and early dew, but the goodness of the Lord endures forever. All of various kinds of goodness are in him in the highest perfection.

He is of a sympathizing, gentle, and loving disposition, and ever so, he is not good by fitts like some men who often fail in goodness; all their goodness is soon darkened and eclipsed by a disordered frame of heart. But the goodness of Christ remains invariable.

3. [He is rich] in grace. (Phil. 4:19): My God shall supply all your need according to the riches of his grace by Jesus Christ. (John 1:14): We beheld his glory as the glory of the only begotten of the father, full of grace and truth.

---

5. Page is torn.
6. Page is torn.

4. [He is rich] in mercy. All kinds of mercy are in him. Goodness may be shown to all sorts of persons, but mercy is vouchsafed to the miserable. Had man never fallen, God's goodness had been manifested to him but his mercy only respects men fallen, which is alone made known in Jesus Christ. In mercy he pitied, as in mercy he redeemed us and in abundant mercy he renewed, sanctified, and pardoned us. Yea, he is merciful to all that call upon and embrace him.

5. [He is rich] in glory. (Eph. 1:18): That ye may know what is the hope of his calling, and what is the riches of the glory of his inheritance—those our minds cannot comprehend or our tongues express, for it does not yet appear what we shall be.

Now the riches of Christ have the following qualities.

1. They are spiritual, such as enrich the soul. He gives part of his outward riches to those that hate him, to those that have their portion in this life. But their souls _____thed[7] with roses in respect of their better part. _____[8] are poor, miserable, blind and naked, but such a[s][9] are united to Christ are adorned with the beauty of holiness, which to an enlightened mind surpasses the sun in his brightness.

2. The riches of Christ are incorruptible. Earthly riches are of a low, base, and corruptible nature. (Matt. 6:19): Lay up for yourselves treasures in heaven, whose moth and rust cannot corrupt, nor thieves break through and steal. The apostle James bids wicked, rich men to weep and howl for the misery that shall come upon them. Your gold and silver is cankered, and the rust of it shall be a witness against you. You have heaped up treasure against the last day [Jas. 5:3]. But Christ's spiritual riches are of a better nature; they will never canker or corrupt or be spoiled with moth.

3. [The riches of Christ are] incomparable. No earthly thing can be compared with it. What Solomon speaks of, wisdom may be applied to it. The merchandise of it is better than the merchandise of silver and the gain thereof than fine gold. She is more precious than rubies, and all things thou canst desire are not to be compared unto it (Prov. 3:14, 15).

4. [The riches of Christ are] inexhaustible. They cannot be spent! His treasures can never be drawn dry. It is like a well that hath a mighty spring in the bottom of it, but it is the very reverse with earthly treasure—the greatest mass of it may be wasted and spent.

5. [The riches of Christ are] soul-satisfying. He that coveteth silver, saith Solomon, shall not be satisfied with silver. Earthly riches and honours are

7. Page is torn.
8. Page is torn.
9. Page is torn.

unsatisfying! Alexander the Great, who conquered all the eastern world, was as much unsatisfied after all his victories as he was before. So it is in respect of the riches of this world; they satisfy not. This is a curse and plague that attend the rich men of the earth: the more they have, the more they covet. But the riches of Christ are of a satisfying nature. (John 4:14): He that drinketh of the water that I shall give him shall never thirst again, but the water that I shall give him shall be in him as a well of water springing up to eternal life. Thirsting not again denotes full satisfaction and soul content. This is to be found in the riches of grace, and nowhere else. Solomon saith that a good man shall be satisfied from himself—not from any self-sufficiency he finds, but from that true peace and content he has received from Jesus Christ.

6. [The riches of Christ are] unsearchable. (Eph. 3:8): "Unto me who am less than the least"—There is, my brethren, no bottom of Christ's treasure. As no man can find out God's perfection, so no man or angel can find out Christ's riches. They pass for current coin in the court of heaven and not only satisfy the soul of man but [also] the justice of God. No riches but these can pay the millions we owe to the law and justice of God and save us from the infernal prison.

7. The riches of Christ are harmless riches. They will not ensnare or hurt any soul that obtains them. Earthly riches oftentimes poison and destroy the possessors of them; many one day will lament that they had so much of them, so much gold and silver, because they captivated and ensnared their souls. Riches in the hand do no man hurt, but they often get into the heart. They set their hearts upon them and love them more than Jesus Christ. What was it that made the young man sorrowful and reject Christ? Was it not his great possessions, i.e. his immoderate love to them, and therefore our Savior observed that a rich man shall hardly enter into the kingdom of God, nay that a camel may as easily go through the eye of a needle as a rich man into the kingdom of God? Was it not love to the riches of this world that made demons turn away from Christ or apostatize from the truth? On this account Paul gave that counsel to Timothy (I Tim. 6:17): Charge them that are rich in this world that they trust not in uncertain riches, but in the living God. And in the same chapter he saith but they that will be rich fall into temptations and a snare which draws men into destruction and perdition [6:9]. If men have wealth and no heart to do good with it, [it] is certainly a snare and a curse to them. But in spiritual riches there is no snare, no danger.

8. The riches of Christ are certain riches. Others are uncertain—they make to themselves wings and fly away. A man may with Job be rich today and poor tomorrow, but what saith our Savior?—with me are durable riches and righteousness; no man can carry any of the riches of this world—any of it—with him. (I Tim. 6:7): We bring nothing into this world and it is certain we shall

carry nothing out. But if we have the riches of Christ, we shall carry them out of the world with us. We shall carry pardon of sin, holiness, grace and joy with us, and although faith will be turned into vision, and hope into surety,[10] yet love[,] that blessed grace[,] will abide with [us for] ever. Nay, sirs, at death we shall partake of greater riches than we had here. We shall then possess the riches of glory which far exceed the riches of grace.

Neither men or devils can rob us of those riches. Fire can't consume them, nor rust corrupt them. They lie in a safe hand. Christ is our trustee; in him all our spiritual riches are laid up. He is Lord treasurer. Could the devil pluck Christ out of Heaven[,] we might lose our riches, but that is impossible! And as impossible it is for the devil to deprive us of our soul riches. For as our life is hid with Christ in God, so also are our riches. God entrusted the first Adam with all his riches in his own hand, and he soon run out of all. Therefore he hath made a better covenant with the second Adam, and in him with all that believe in him. Christ is our surety; he hath engaged to the father for all that are given to him, and therefore keeps all our riches in his own hand, and gives us out of his fullness according to our present wants—and this secures all our riches. Can the wife want anything whilst all fullness, all inconceivable riches[,] are in her husband's possession forever?

9. The riches of Christ are eternal. They are everlasting riches, once spiritually rich and forever rich. The crown of glory is an everlasting crown. It is a crown that fadeth not away. Also it's called an incorruptible crown, and a crown of eternal life. The saints' riches shall continue to the day of eternity; they shall last as long as God himself endures. God is their portion, and Christ their riches, and therefore their riches are eternal.

From [hearing] I infer that it must needs be the true and only interest of poor sinners to espouse Jesus Christ. What mortal but would accept of such an offer, considering how rich he is! Poverty hinders many a match; the person is liked, but the portion is not sufficient. But here is no room for such an objection.

Sinners, if you marry him, all is yours. All his riches are yours and yours forever. Christ requires nothing with you—no, though you are much in debt and owe ten thousand talents, he hath enough to pay all. Nay, that very moment you believe in him he will discharge all your debts and enrich you with inconceivable riches. What say you now? Will you come to this wedding and eat of the king's supper? [Will you] accept of Christ? He does but ask your consent. Will you embrace him, accept of him for your all? What do you say? What answer shall I return to the great king that sent me to you?

---

10. Page is torn.

Appendix C

*Transcription of Gilbert Tennent's
Sermon Manuscript 4*

[no title; no date]

> Canticles 4:16. "Awake, O north wind and come, thou south; blow
> upon my garden that the [spices] thereof may flow out."

1. A garden is a piece of ground distinguished and separated from others for
the owner's use. So the church oft is distinguished and separated from others
by electing and redeeming grace. By effectual calling they do also differ from
others, and by their lives and conversations they distinguish themselves; and
being set apart for God's use, service, and glory they are a peculiar people to
him. The garden is taken out of common or waste ground. So the church and
every believer or member thereof is taken out of the common mass of mankind, to be a chosen and select people to Christ.

2. The ground of a garden before it be planted is as barren and unprofitable
as the rest out of which it is taken, and thus the people of God are naturally
barren, blind, sinful always to God and every way as vile and rebellious as any
other sinners in the world, and were by nature children of wrath—who has
made thee to differ from another[?]—

3. In a garden nothing choice or rare comes up naturally of itself until it is
sown or planted therein; so no spiritual good thing can spring up in any hearts
'til the seed of grace is sown in us, or a divine principle implanted. By nature
we are dead in sins—and in us there dwells no good thing. We can't will any
good.

4. A garden must be walled or fenced for its security from danger, that its
fruits be not trodden down and devoured. So the church of God and every
Christian is hedged off, walled in. It is said of Job that the almighty had made

a hedge about him on every side; and is not Jehovah a wall of fire about Jerusalem (Zech. 2:5)[?]

5. A garden before it be sown or planted must be dug and enabled to bring forth fruit to God. The fallow ground of our hearts must be dug up by the spade of the Law in the hand of the Holy Spirit, and hence the people of Israel were enjoined to plow up the fallow ground of their hearts and not to sow among thorns (Jer. 4:3).

6. In a garden is a variety of flowers, herbs, and plants. So in the church of Christ are many members who have gifts differing from each other, and grace also. Some have greater gifts and larger measures of grace than others, but among them are many precious plants and flowers of great worth and value. The men of Israel are called his pleasant plants (Jer. 5:8).[1]

7. A garden must often be watered or else it will soon fade, the fruit thereby wither away and flowers hang down their heads; thus God's people must be often watered in spiritual rain with the dew of Hermon, or else their growth and greenness will fail and they wither as a leaf.

8. A garden must be often weeded, otherwise the fruit will be hurt in their growth and suppressed by the weeds that grow naturally in it. The church is also hurt by corrupt members in which, after due admonition, should be cast out, else the whole lump is in danger of being leavened. And do not weeds spring up in the hearts of the best Christians from that root of bitterness which is in everyone, which unless they are pulled up will hinder their growth in grace? We should therefore through the Spirit mortify—watch the leaven left in.[2]

9. A garden must have the door carefully kept and looked after lest thieves and beasts of prey get in and spoil it. So the door of the Church should be carefully kept by those that have the charge of it, viz. the ministers, that none be admitted but such as the almighty orders them to admit, and indeed we must watch over ourselves.

10. A garden flourishes best that hath the warm beams of the Sun shining on it. Thus it is with our Church, when the Sun of righteousness arises with healing under his wings upon them, then they grow up as calves of the stall. [Mal. 4:2]

11. A garden is attended with several seasons, winter as well as summer, and though in the winter many flowers seem decayed and their glory gone, yet the sharp frosts and cold winds of the winter are necessary in their place and time, as well as the warmth of the summer. I say they are necessary for the killing of weeds and worms which would otherwise abound; thus the nipping frost

---

1. The correct citation is Isa. 5:7.
2. This line is unclear.

and north wind of affliction and temptation are as necessary to the saints as the summer of peace and comfort and prosperity. For God seeth need of the one as well as the other to destroy those weeds of corruption that are in us.[3]

12. In a garden whatsoever choice flower the owners sees is fully ripe, if he has a mind to it, he crops it off and takes it to himself. So in the Church these flowers or saints that Christ sees are ripe for heaven, he crops off by death and takes to himself. A godly man dies when he is ready and ripe for death. When a holy man dies it is harvest time with him, though in a natural capacity he may be cut down while he is green or cropped in the bud or blossom, yet in his spiritual capacity he never dies before he is ripe. God ripens his speedily when he intends to take them out of the world.

13. The owner of a garden loves to walk in it to see how the plants and fruits do thrive and flourish. So the Lord Jesus, who is the owner and proprietor of his Church, loves to take his walks in it. (Cant. 5:1) "I am come into my garden, my sister, my spouse," and Cant. 7:12, Let us get up early to the vineyards, let us see whether the vine flourish and the pomegranates bud forth. There will I give thee my love. And elsewhere he is said to walk in the midst of the seven golden candlesticks.

14. A choice and fruitful garden is valued highly by the owner. He esteems it above one hundred times as much barren land. So the Church of God, though it be comparatively a little spot, is highly prized by Jesus Christ. He esteems his own people above all the people of the Earth, hence he calleth them his inheritance, his jewels. (Is. 43:3, 4) "I gave Egypt for thy ransom, Ethiopia and Seba for thee. Since thou wast precious in my sight, thou hast been honourable, and I have loved thee: therefore will I give men for thee, and people for thy life." Wicked men are like barren mountains; they are the king's waste such whom he little esteems.

15. A garden is usually a small piece of ground, and so is Christ's Church in comparison of the wilderness and waste places of the world, but a little flock, a small remnant, a few that shall be saved. Broad is the gate and—[4]

16. A garden is a pleasant and fruitful place and so is the Church when compared with the world that liveth in wickedness and is overrun with the briars and thorns of sin.

17. A rare and fruitful garden will afford fruit to plant others; on this account many gardens have sprung out of one. So from the Church of God that was first planted in Judea, many churches proceeded in a little time, by means of the fruitfulness of that one spiritual garden. Seven gardens more were planted

---

3. An unreadable fragment follows.

4. The sentence stops here. The author may have intended to finish quoting Scripture. This may be an allusion to Matt. 7:13–14.

in Asia, viz., Ephesus, Smyrna, Pergamum, Thyatira, Sardis, Philadelphia, and Laodicea, besides many others.

18. In a garden worms do much hurt when they get to the roots of plants and flowers. They seem green and flourishing, when there are some devouring worms gnawing at their roots by which means in a little time they die, are pulled up, and cast away. So in the Church sin [is] predominant, which may be compared to a worm or hurtful vermin, doth great injury. A professor seems very green, amiable, and fair to the eye, like some plants full of leaves, but there is some worm at the root of many—some secret lust indulged which makes them in a little time wither and die, so that they are fit for nothing but to be plucked up and cast away. Many for a time run well but are hindered; by and by they are offended, and go no more with God's people. They grow weary of well-doing. Of such the almighty complains, O Ephraim, what shall I do unto thee.—Some begin in the Spirit, but if any man draw back—many return with the dog to the vomit [2 Pet. 2:22]. Now the spices in this garden which the spouse is desirous should flow out are pomegranates, camphire, with spikenard, saffron, calamus and cinnamon, with all trees of frankincense, myrrh and aloe (Sol. 4:13, 14). Of this chapter by which may be meant the several graces of the Spirit that are to be found in the members of the Church of Christ, which are compared to those spices[.]

1. Because the graces of the Spirit are many, and therefore many herbs and spices are mentioned (See Gal. 5:22).

2. Because they are various of different sorts. The variety of plants and herbs and flowers of different species adds to the pleasantness of a garden or orchard. If they were all of one sort it would not be so delightful; thus there is a beauty in the variety of the Christians' graces. Faith, hope, love have their different but harmonious charms.

3. Because they are rare and excellent. The herbs and spices here mentioned such as spikenard, camphire, and cinnamon are not to be found everywhere. No, they are rarely to be met with, and thus the graces of the Spirit are rare jewels, they are but few that have them. All men have not faith.

4. The spices before mentioned are all of them of a sweet smell, and so the graces of the Spirit of Christ are of a sweet perfume to him, and to all which are wise and good. The smell of these ointments is preferred by him to all spices (Sol. 4:10).

5. Some of these herbs and plants cheer the heart and revive the spirits, such as saffron, cinnamon, and camphire, and thus the Spirit of God by the exercise of grace greatly comforts the hearts and revives the spirits of his people. Hereby they are kept from fainting under their pressures in the multitude of our thoughts. Within us his comforts delight our souls.

6. Some of them preserve from putrefaction as myrrh and aloes, and

therefore were used in embalming dead bodies (John 19:39). And is it not by the graces of the Spirit that our dead souls are revived and kept from putrefaction and spiritual death?

7. Some of them are green in winter time, as saffron and aloes. Thus the grace of God keeps alive and is green in winter storms and tempests, for it is an immortal seed.

8. Some grow higher and taller than others, such as the calamus; cinnamon and myrrh exceed in height the spikenard and saffron. Now the farmer may extend the graces of faith, hope and love which rise upwards in their actings on the Lord Jesus Christ, and the latter the graces of humility and meekness, both which are in their places admirable and useful.

9. All these emit the most fragrant odor when they are cut, bruised, or burnt, and thus do the graces of the Spirit when they are exercised and tried in the furnace of affliction.

10. They are all one way or other more or less medicinal and healthful to the body of men, and so are the graces of the Spirit to our souls. But why and how should the church pray for the blowing of the north and south wind that those spices may flow out?

1. Because without the Spirit's influence, grace will not be exercised. It is God that worketh in us.

2. By the exercise of grace it is increased and hereby God is glorified, our souls comforted, and others edified.

3. Hereby we are prepared for services and sufferings. We need not in this situation be slavishly afraid of any event, for it will certainly be well with us, and everything we meet with shall work together for our good.

4. Without it we have little comfort in ourselves and are of little use to others—dead, as it were, while we are alive.

5. Without this we are in danger of falling to the reproach of God's name and to the shame and grief of his people, which is a very affecting thought. Without this we shall abuse prosperity to pride and luxury, and shrink in the day of adversity from Christ's standard, or faint under the weight of our woes.

6. The example in this text should excite us as well as the dreadful storm that is now gathering fast upon the church and nation.

But how should we pray for the Spirit's influences? _____ [5]

1. Frequently. Night and day, my brethren, we should be crying to our God for the influences of the Holy Spirit upon ourselves and others for a divine effusion upon the whole community, without which we are like to be a ruined enslaved people, without which we are like to cease to be a nation anymore, and be trampled under the feet of our popish enemies.

---

5. A single illegible word follows that may be a heading for the next section.

2. Fervently. It is fervent prayers of the righteous that avail much. It is then and then only when we seek God with our whole hearts, that we are like to find him. When Jacob wrassled with the angel he prevailed, for he wept and made sup[plication].

3. Believing.[6] Let us still maintain honourable thoughts of God's p____.[7] He can if he pleases command deliverances for Jacob, even when reduced to the greatest extremity, and all appearance of deliverance fails, and no door of escape opens. In the mount God has been seen and doubtless will be. For those things were written for our learning upon whom the ends of the world are come, nor has God said to the house of Jacob to seek his face in vain. Jehovah loves to act like himself, like a god, and surprise his people with sudden salvations. When prepared for them, our sins and stupidity are more to be dreaded than all of policy and power of our other enemies.

4. Perseveringly and importunately. Let us continue constant in prayer that we be answered and plead with arguments drawn from perfections of God's nature and promises of his word, as well as from the instances of his goodness to his people of old, from his honour, truth, and our covenant relation to his majesty.

Has God a Church in the world that may excite

1. Our admiration at the pains the almighty has taken to separate this garden from the wastes [?] of the world, to plant precious spices in it and hedge it by his providence from the intrusions of the beasts of prey. It has been preserved; for many ages it is not yet rained. The burning bush is not yet consumed.

2. Our hope that it will be preserved in time coming

1. Because of God's promise he hath said that the gate of Hell shall not prevail against it and that no weapon formed against it shall prosper.

2. Because it is his property. The blessed Jesus has bought the ground at the price of his most precious blood, to make a garden of it. He hath planted and sown it at his own charge. He keeps and waters it and watches over it night and day, and they that touch it touch the apple of his eye. Now is not property the source of care?

3. Let the saints of God take care to be fruitful, seeing that Christ hath been at so much cost and pains about them. To this end, see that you are plants of his planting; otherwise you will be rooted up. See that you are well rooted for such stand firm in storms. And bring forth most[8] fruit. And see that you indulge not a _____[9] at the will in _____[10] [des]troy all.

6. Page is torn here.
7. Page is torn here: perhaps "power."
8. Or perhaps "much."
9. Page is torn here.
10. Page is torn here.

Appendix D

Transcription of Gilbert Tennent's Sermon Manuscript 12

[no date]

Ps. 122:1, 2

Ps. 27:4: "One thing have I desired of the LORD, that will I seek after, that I may dwell in the house of the LORD all the days of my life, to behold the beauty of the LORD, and to enquire in his temple."

It cannot certainly be determined to what danger which David was in that this psalm has a reference, nor is it of much consequence for us to know it, but it is of importance to observe from the series [?] of this psalm how a devout mind comforts and supports itself in danger by confiding in its God and breathing [?] after communion with him in the ordinances of his worship. Particularly the words of our text we have a beautiful representation of the temper and character of a good man expressed in relation to his desires as to their object, mode and end, or in other words, we are here told what it is he desires after and how he desires and why. These particulars I purpose to discourse upon and then proceed to the improvement.

1. As to the object or matter of his desires, it is that he may dwell in the house of the Lord all the days of his life. Here observe that the house of God in Scripture is used to represent both the church militant and triumphant, or the church of God on earth and the church of the first-born in heaven.

The tabernacle at first, and the temple afterwards, are frequently called the house of God, for there God dwelt in a peculiar manner, and there he promised his presence to his people who convened at stated seasons to worship him; to this purpose speaks the psalmist. Ps. 42:4 and Ps. 122:[1–]2. "I had gone with the multitude, I went with them to the house of God with the voice of joy and praise, with a multitude that kept holy day." "I was glad when they said unto me, let us go into the house of the Lord. Our feet shall stand within thy gates, O Jerusalem!" The material temple is a house of God in which he dwelt and was worshiped by the Jewish people, was a representation of the spiritual houses or spiritual societies of believers in which he would dwell in future times after the temple was destroyed. In the New Testament, for the most part the house of God and a worshiping assembly of professing Christians or believers are the same thing. I Pet. 2:5. "Ye also, as lively stones, and built up a spiritual house." I Tim. 3: 5, 15. "That thou mayest know how thou oughtest to behave thyself in the house of God, which is the church of the living God," "for if a man know not how to rule his own house, how shall he take care of the church of God?" Without regard to any ceremonial sanctity of place or largeness of number, the blessed Jesus promises that when two or three of his people are met together he will be in the midst of them. From what has been said we may conclude that the house of God in our text in general signifies to us Christians, the church of God, or the assemblies of his people engaged in public worship. The psalmist desired that he might duly and constantly attend upon the public worship of God with other faithful Israelites, according as the duty of every day required, and therefore he longed to see an end of the wars in which he was engaged—not that he might live at ease in his own palace, but that he might have leisure and privilege to attend constantly at the stated seasons upon the worship of God in his courts. Thus Hezekiah, a genuine son of David, wished for the recovery of his health—not that he might go up to the thrones of judgment, but that he might "go up to the house of the Lord." Is. 38:22. That I may dwell in the house of the Lord all the days of my life: Observe truly pious persons not only desire to go to God's house, but [also] to dwell there all the days of their lives. They want not to sojourn there as a wayfaring man that turns aside to tarry but for a night or to dwell there for a time only, as the servant that abideth not in the house forever, but to dwell there all the days of their life: for there the Son abideth ever. Seeing that worship is to be the blessedness of eternity, it should be the business of time. It is true in this world we cannot consistently with the other duties of life be always engaged in God's immediate service, but certainly they should be all performed with a reference to this as their end, viz., to prepare us for it, and assist us in it, and such as are truly religious will persevere to the end of life in esteem of, a relish for, and attendance upon the duties of public worship. They forget not the assembling of themselves together as the manner of some is, who are puffed up and with Jeshurun being waxen fat, kick with the heel of contempt against the doctrine and discipline of the word of God.[1]

---

1. See Deut. 32:15.

2. The house of God may denote the state of glory in Heaven. The spirit of God in Scripture delights to set forth heaven under a variety of similitudes, to assist our conceptions of it, and fire our hearts upon it; it's called a country, a better country, Heb. 11:14, 16. A kingdom that God hath prepared for them that love him, Jam. 2:5. A city that hath foundations—a house in which are many mansions; John 14:2 'Tis a country for largeness and extent, a paradise for pleasure, a kingdom for grandeur, a city for order, and a house for the warmth and familiarity allowed to the blessed inhabitants; 'tis a house of God in which all his people shall live as children in the same family, members of the society and hold a common dependence upon the same Father, showing the greatest love to him and to each other. Under this notion the Apostle speaks of Heaven and comforts himself with it in view of his dissolution; 2 Cor. 5:1 "For we know that if our earthly house of this tabernacle were dissolved, we have a building of God, a house not made with hands eternal in the heavens." This may well be called the house of God, being one of his own contriving and building, for the house of his kingdom and the honor of his majesty and of consequence a so noble work of his power and wisdom, answerable to the glorious ends for which it was designed.

The firmament so thick set and adorned with stars is but the pavement of the outer court of this house of God. The glory and magnificence of this does therefore intimate the inconceivable beauty and brightness of the third heaven, the grand emporium, the seat of the divine residence; where Jehovah is eminently present, continually defusing the richest beams of his glory and goodness to all the inhabitants of that blessed abode! Surely eye hath not seen neither hath ear heard, wither can it enter into the heart of men to conceive, what God hath laid up for you that love him! Now we are the sons of God[,] saith the apostle John, but it doth not yet appear what we shall be! This therefore is what the psalmist and every saint further means by the house of God, which he was so intent upon, and desirous to dwell in, he would abide not only in the church under the enjoyment of the means of grace here below, but [also] in the state of glory above! 'Twas this he ultimately aimed at, and would not take up with anything short of at his home or rest! He desired to dwell in the church of God on earth, but it was that he might be prepared for heaven to dwell there; he was thankful for ordinances, and mad[e] conscience [?] of attending upon [them] but was looking and longing for a world when he shandn't need them, but behold Jehovah without a glass. A saint esteems the ordinances of God's worship more than necessary food, and cannot live without them upon earth. But yet these cannot be to him instead of Heaven, while he lives upon earth he desires to live in the church of God but he would not live here forever, there being a better house of God in Heaven. 'Tis there he hopes and longs to dwell forever. The glory of the Lord sometimes fills his house below, and he manifests himself to his people so as he does not to the rest of the world; but there are brighter manifestations made to his favorites above, which therefore they are allowed to expect, and so cannot but desire after them. Those doubtless the psalmist had in view in our text, which he _____[2] expresses his regard to, as his final happiness! Ps. 17:15 "As for me, I will behold thy face in righteousness; I shall be satisfied, when I awake, with thy likeness!" How much so ever he valued the discovery God was pleased to vouchsafe in his sanctuary, he received them but as earnest and pledge, of something higher to succeed, he was doubtless sensible of the present weakness of his capacities, and that this state, when raised to the highest, was but a state of probation and therefore he stretches his view beyond the grave. There is a river that makes glad the city of God,[3] so that it is good to draw near to him in his house below, but the fullness of joy is in the presence of his glory above. There they are, fully satisfied with the fatness of his house. There they drink of the rivers of pleasure that flow at his right hand forevermore! But I proceed to the

2. Prop.[-osition] which was to them how a child of God desires to dwell in the house of God forever, of what are the properties of his desire. I answer they are

1. Sincere and real, and not in pretense and profession only[;] they are such as they can appeal to God about, and speak of before him, one thing have I desired of the Lord.

2. Supreme. One thing have I desired, one thing above and before all others, that I may dwell in the house of the Lord. He disregards all other things in comparison of this [bent page] desires them only in order to it, and so far as they were consistent with it, this one thing had the first and choice place in his affections. If he has this he is well, easy and thankful, as if he needed no more. But in want of this nothing can quiet his restless soul. Ps. 42:1, 2 "As the hart panteth after the water brooks, so panteth my soul after thee, O God. My soul thirsteth for God, for the living God: when shall I come and appear before God?" Ps. 63:1, 2 "O God, . . . my soul thirsteth for thee, my flesh longeth for thee in a dry and thirsty land, where no water is; To see thy power and thy glory, as I have seen thee in the sanctuary." Ps. 84:1, 2 "How amiable are thy tabernacles, O LORD of Hosts! My soul longeth, yea, even fainteth for the courts of the LORD; my heart and my flesh crieth out for the living God." And v. 4 and 10 "Blessed are they that dwell in thy house: they will be still praising thee. [For] a day in thy courts is better than a thousand. I had rather be a doorkeeper in the house of [my] God than to dwell in [the] tents

2. This word is illegible.
3. See Ps. 46:4.

of wickedness." Ps. 26:[8] O "LORD I have loved the habitation of thy house, and the place where thine honour dwelleth."

3. Habitual and permanent. It is not a transient flash of good mood which soon expires, which is the case of hypocrites who begin in the spirit but end in the flesh, who hear the word for a time, hear with joy as Herod, but are by and by offended when their heroding [acting like Herod] is struck at; it is true [that] this love to the word and ordinances of God is not always in evidence [?] in good men, nor have they all arrived to a like desire of eminence therein, but the habit of it remains in the souls forever, it being a part of the new nature created in them by the Holy Ghost[,] which shall never die as long as Christ lives; they therefore desire to dwell in God's house all the days of their lives. The divine life is fed and nourished by the word and ordinances of God and therefore it is as natural for those that have it to desire after them and that frequently and steadily as for living man to desire after bread. It is therefore an argument of no spirit, life of no goodness to disrelish and desert them.

4. Influential and operative. Upon practice the soul that desires to dwell in the house of God will express it in prayer to him and follow it with his own endeavour. One thing have I desired of the Lord and that will I seek after, that I may dwell in his house all the days of my life. Whatever others say or do, I will, I am fully determined to seek after this with earnestness to my life's end. I'll submit to any difficulties so I may abide and dwell in God's house. I'll take all opportunities with pleasure at waiting upon him there.

3. D_____[4] which was to show why a child of God desires to dwell in his house and

1. One reason is that he may behold the beauty of the Lord. i. If by faith have a clear apprehension of the perfections of God's nature in general such as his wisdom, goodness, holiness, power, truth.

2. A discovery of the harmonious manifestation of these attributes in the way of salvation by Jesus Christ, or in other words, a view of the glory of God in the face of Jesus Christ. Wisdom contriving the scheme of redemption, which is what angels desire to look into and what the saints cry out with ravishment about "the depth of the riches both of the wisdom and knowledge of God." Rom. 11:33 To behold infinite goodness triumphant in the gift [sight?] of the son of God to suffering and death to save an undone world; herein is love—Surely the goodness of God is his glory, yea it is the beauty of his nature. Zech. 9:17 "For how great is his goodness, and how great is his beauty"—to behold his holiness expressed in the punishment of his own son when he stood in a sinner's place. Justly may we say with the seraphim

---

4. This word is illegible. The numbering of sections is convoluted from this point onward. The numbers appear here as they do in the manuscript.

on this occasion, holy, holy, holy is the Lord of hosts. Holiness, in particular the beauty of God. Ps. 110:3 "Thy people shall be willing in the day of thy power, in the beaut[ies] of holiness." To behold divine power overruling all, it respected the redeemer's sufferings as well as his support under them and in the conversion of sinners to him and their perseverance to salvation—To behold unshaken truth and faithfulness by which he infallibly performs all the promises he has spoken—To behold justice entirely satisfied by the sufferings and obedience of the son of God in our nature and mercy at the same time illustriously magnified in pardoning repentant transgressors.

3. It implies our discerning our property in them and that they are all engaged to promote our benefit, fills us with unspeakable sweetness and inspires us with the most affectionate gratitude, and when we can say, My Lord and my God[,] this disposes us to enquire[,] what shall I render to the Lord?[5] I may add that when we behold the beauty of the Lord[,] it transforms us into his image from glory to glory—

2. Another reason why a child of God desires to dwell in God's house is to enquire in his temple, respecting his duty to God and God's dealings toward him; he wants not only to be conformed to God's nature and to have communion in his love, but he wants [also] to be further instructed in the mind of God, respecting what is required of him. Lord[,] what wilt thou have me to do. He wants to know how to apply the general directions of the scriptures to particular cases and to find out how the promises are fulfilled in Providence. But in particular these things following excite good men to desire to dwell in God's house, viz.

1. The command of God. The injunction to some to preach the gospel, implies an injunction upon others to hear it, to heed how they hear supposes a command, without which preaching would be to no purpose. We should not therefore forget the assembling of ourselves together as the manner of some is now the will of God. In his word has a counterpart in the believer's heart. He therefore says, speak, Lord, for thy servant heareth, and when the Almighty says Seek ye my face, his heart replies, thy face, Lord, will I seek.

2. The honour of God. The Lord loves the gates of Zion more than all the dwellings of Jacob, i.e., he prefers public to private worship because he is thereby more glorified through the open and united acts of worship of his people. By this a sense of his being and perfection is professed in the world. Now the honour of God cannot but be dear to those that love him. They are, therefore, sorrowful for the solemn assembly, and to them the reproach of it is a burden. They are grieved when deprived of an opportunity of public worship as the Jews in the captivity were and burdened when they hear such

---

5. The page is torn here. This may be a citation of Ps. 27:4.

solemnities deserted or ridiculed. Such pious persons the Almighty promises to show favour to. Zeph. 3:18, 19 "I will gather them that are sorrowful for the solemn assembly, to whom the reproach of it was a burden. Behold, at that time I will undo all that afflict thee; and I will save her that halteth, and gather her that was driven out; and I will get them praise and fame in every Land where they have been put to shame."

3. The everlasting interest of mankind is exceedingly c___nd[6] in it. For this is appointed by God as the ordinary means of the conversion of sinners to him, and their edification, and hence we are told that faith comes by hearing—we preach Christ, says the Apostles, to the Jews a stumbling block—we are born again not of the corruptible seed but the incorruptible, the word of God which liveth and abideth forever. For this purpose a ministry was appointed as a standing order of men in the several ages of the church to turn sinners from darkness to light—and hence Cornelius was directed, though he had a vision of an angel to send to Peter to Joppa to come and instruct him, and Ananias was sent to convince Saul after his vision for the same purpose.

But the preached word which is a part of public worship is not only appointed as the ordinary mean of the conversion of sinners, but likewise as the stated mean of the edification and establishment of the saints. Eph. 4:11–15 "And he gave some, apostles; and some, prophets; and some, evangelists; and some, pastors and teachers; for the perfecting of the saints, for the work of the ministry, for the edifying of the Body of Christ: Till we all come in the unity of the faith, and of the knowledge of the Son of God unto a perfect man, unto the measure of the stature of the fullness of Christ: that we henceforth be no more children, tossed to and fro, and carried about with every wind of doctrine, by the sleight [of men,] and cunning craftiness whereby they lie in wait to deceive."

4. The promise of God, the blessed Jesus promises that when two or three are gathered together in his name he will be in the midst of them. Exod. 20:24 "In all places where I record my name I will come unto thee, and I will bless thee." This precious promise of the presence and blessing of God in places of public worship is a powerful inducement to our conscientious and constant attendance upon them.

5. The practice of God's people in all ages of the church. Cant. 1:7, 8 "Tell me, O thou whom my soul loveth, where thou feedest, where thou makest thy flock to rest at noon: for why should I be as one that turneth aside by the flocks of thy companions? If you know not, O thou fairest among women, go thy way forth by the footsteps of the flock, and feed thy kids beside the shepherds' tents." The tabernacles of God were amiable to the psalmist. He loved the place where God's honour dwelt, and in his solitude and separation from the house of God, envied the swallows that had their residence there.

---

6. Page is torn here; perhaps "contained."

Appendix E

Table of Contents, John Willison's
Sacramental Directory

Introduction—A Treatise concerning the Sanctification of a Communion
    Sabbath

Chap. I—Containing Directions how to prepare for a Communion Sabbath
    Direct. I—Concerning the Nature, Ends, and Uses of the Lord's Supper;
        and of the Work of communicating
    Direct. II—Concerning the Necessity of communicating, and the Sin of
        neglecting this Duty; Objections made against this Duty answered
    Direct. III—Concerning the Necessity of frequent communicating;
        Objections against Frequency answered
    Direct. IV—Concerning the Necessity of Solemn Preparation before our
        partaking
    Direct. V—Concerning habitual and actual Preparation
    Direct. VI—Concerning the Sin and Danger of unworthy communicating
    Direct. VII—Concerning sequestrating ourselves from the World before
        partaking
    Direct. VIII—Concerning Self-Examination before partaking
        1. Of the Examination of our State
        2. Of the Examination of our Sins
        3. Of the Examination of our Wants
        4. Of the Examination of our Ends
        5. Of the Examination of our Graces
        Objections of doubting Believers answered
    Direct. IX—Concerning Humiliation and mourning for Sin before
        partaking

Selected Bibliography

Primary Sources—Published Works

Beza, Theodore. *Master Bezaes Sermons Upon the Three First chapters of the Canticle of Canticles: Wherein are handled the chiefest points of religion controversed and debated between us and the adversarie at this day, especially touching the true Jesus Christ and the true church, and the certain & infallible marks both of the one and of the other.* Translated out of French into English by John Harmar, her Highnes Professor in the Greeke Toung in the Universitie of Oxford and felowe of the Newe College there. Oxford: Joseph Barnes, 1587.

Calvin, John. *Commentaries on the Epistles to Timothy, Titus, and Philemon.* Translated by William Pringle. Grand Rapids: Wm. B. Eerdmans Publishing Co., 1948.

———. *Commentary on the Epistle of Paul the Apostle to the Corinthians.* Translated by John Pringle. Vol. 1. Grand Rapids: Wm. B. Eerdmans Publishing Co., 1933.

———. *The Gospel according to St. John 11–21 and the First Epistle of John.* Edited by David W. Torrance and Thomas F. Torrance. Translated by T. H. L. Parker. Calvin's Commentaries. Edinburgh and London: Oliver & Boyd, 1961.

———. *Institutes of the Christian Religion.* Edited by John T. McNeill. Translated by Ford Lewis Battles. Library of Christian Classics 20–21. Philadelphia: Westminster Press, 1960.

———. *Short Treatise on the Holy Supper of Our Lord and Only Saviour Jesus Christ.* In *Calvin: Theological Treatises.* Translated with introduction and notes by J. K. S. Reid. Library of Christian Classics 22. Philadelphia: Westminster Press, 1954.

Gerson, Jean. *Early Works.* Translated and introduced by Brian Patrick McGuire. Preface by Bernard McGinn. Classics of Western Spirituality 92. New York and Mahwah, NJ: Paulist Press, 1998.

Hildegard of Bingen. *Scivias.* Translated by Mother Columba Hart, OSB, and Jane Bishop. New York and Mahwah, NJ: Paulist Press, 1990.

John of the Cross. *The Complete Works of Saint John of the Cross, Doctor of the Church.* Vol. 2. Translated and edited by E. Allison Peers from the critical edition of P. Silverio de Santa Teresa, CD. New ed. London: Burns, Oates & Washbourne, 1953.

Luther, Martin. *The Freedom of a Christian*. Translated by W. A. Lambert. Revised by Harold J. Grimm. From the American Edition of Luther's Works 31. In *Three Treatises*. Philadelphia: Fortress Press, 1986.

MacFarlan, Duncan. *The Revivals of the Eighteenth Century Particularly at Cambuslang, with three Sermons by the Rev. George Whitefield, taken in shorthand, compiled from original manuscripts and contemporary publications by D. MacFarlan*. London and Edinburgh: John Johnston, 1847. Reprint, Glasgow: Free Presbyterian Publications, 1988.

McGready, James. *The Posthumous Works of the Reverend and Pious James McGready, Late Minister of the Gospel in Henderson, Kentucky*. Edited by James Smith. Nashville: J. Smith's Steam Press, 1837.

[Moravian Church / Unitas Fratrum / United Brethren.] *A Collection of Hymns of the Children of God in all Ages, from the Beginning till now. In Two Parts. Designed chiefly for the Use of the Congregations in Union with the Brethren's Church*. London: Printed; and to be had at all the Brethren's chapels, 1754. 1754 MORA, Archives and Manuscript Department, Pitts Theology Library, Emory University.

Pears, Thomas C., Jr., "Sessional Records of the Presbyterian Church of Booth Bay, Maine, 1767–1778." *Journal of the Presbyterian Historical Society* 16 (1935): 203–40, 243–88, 308–55.

Schaff, Philip. *Reformed and Catholic: Selected Historical and Theological Writings of Philip Schaff*. Edited by Charles Yrigoyen Jr. and George M. Bricker. Pittsburgh Original Texts and Translations Series 4. Pittsburgh: Pickwick Press, 1979.

Shepard, Thomas. *The parable of the ten virgins opened & applied: Being the substance of divers sermons on Matth. 25.1, 13 . . . by Thomas Shepard, late worthy and faithfull pastor of the church of Christ at Cambridge in New-England*. London: Printed by J. H. for John Rothwell and Samuel Thomson, 1660.

Steuart, Walter, of Pardovan. *Collections and Observations Concerning the Worship, Discipline, and Government of the Church of Scotland*. 5th ed. Edinburgh: Edinburgh Printing Co., 1837.

Tennent, Gilbert. *Brotherly Love recommended, by the Argument of the Love of Christ: A Sermon, Preached at Philadelphia, January 1747–8. Before the Sacramental Solemnity. With some Enlargement*. Philadelphia: Benjamin Franklin and David Hall, 1748.

———. *The Danger of An Unconverted Ministry, Considered in a Sermon on Mark VI.34. Preached at Nottingham, in Pennsylvania, March 8. Anno 1739, 40*. 2nd ed. Philadelphia: Benjamin Franklin, 1740.

———. "The Divinity of the Sacred Scriptures Considered; And the Dangers of Covetousness Detected: In a Sermon, On Jeremiah 22.29. Preach'd at New-Brunswick in New-Jersey, April ult. 1738." In *Sermons on Sacramental Occasions by Divers Ministers*. Boston: J. Draper, for D. Henchman in Cornhill, 1739.

———. "The Duty of Self-Examination, considered in a Sermon, On I Cor. 11.28. Preached at Maiden-Head in New Jersey, October 22, 1737. Before the Celebration of the Lord's-Supper." In *Sermons on Sacramental Occasions by Divers Ministers*. Boston: J. Draper, for D. Henchman in Cornhill, 1739.

———. *The Espousals, or, A Passionate Perswasive to a Marriage with the Lamb of God, wherein The Sinners Misery and the Redeemers Glory is Unvailed in. A Sermon upon Gen. 24.49. Preached at N. Brunswyck, June the 22d, 1735*. New York: Printed by J. Peter Zenger, 1735.

———. *A Persuasive to the Right Use of the Passions in Religion, Or, The Nature of religious Zeal Explain'd, its Excellency and Importance Open'd and Urg'd, in a Sermon on Revelations iii.19. Preached at Philadelphia, January 26th, 1760*. Philadelphia: Printed and Sold by W. Dunlap, 1760.

———. "The Preciousness of Christ to Believers, Consider'd in a Sermon on I Pet. ii. 7. Preached at New-Brunswick in New-Jersey. The first Sabbath in August, before the Celebration of the Lord's-Supper, Anno Domini, 1738." In *Sermons on Sacramental Occasions by Divers Ministers*. Boston: J. Draper, for D. Henchman in Cornhill, 1739.

———. *A Sermon Upon Justification: Preached at New-Brunswick, on the Saturday before the Dispensing of the Holy Sacrament, which was the first Sabbath in August, Anno 1740*. Philadelphia: Printed and sold by Benjamin Franklin in Market Street, 1741.

———. "The Unsearchable Riches of Christ. Considered, in Two Sermons on Ephes. iii.8. Preached at New-Brunswick in New-Jersey, before the Celebration of the Lord's-Supper; which was the first Sabbath in August, 1737." In *Sermons on Sacramental Occasions by Divers Ministers*. Boston: J. Draper, for D. Henchman in Cornhill, 1739.

———. "The Unsearchable Riches of Christ: Sermon II." In *Sermons on Sacramental Occasions by Divers Ministers*. Boston: J. Draper, for D. Henchman in Cornhill, 1739.

Watson, John. *Letter to the clergy of the church known by the Name of Unitas Fratrum, or Moravians, Concerning a Remarkable Book of hymns Us'd in their Congregations; pointing out several inconsistencies, and Absurdities in the said Book*. London: printed for J. Payne, and sold by R. Whitworth, printer and bookseller in Manchester, 1756. 1756 WATS, Archives and Manuscripts Department, Pitts Theology Library, Emory University.

Watson, Thomas. *The Godly Man's Picture, Drawn with a Scripture Pensil, or, Some Characteristical Marks of a Man That Shall Go to Heaven*. London: printed for Thomas Parkhurst at the three Crowns, over against the great Conduit at the lower end of Cheapside, 1666. Reprint, *The Godly Man's Picture, Drawn with a Scripture Pencil, or, Some Characteristic Marks of a Man Who Is Going to Heaven*. Edinburgh: Banner of Truth Trust, 1992.

Westminster Assembly (1643–1652). *The Westminster Directory, Being a Directory for the Publique Worship of God in the Three Kingdomes*. Introduction by Ian Breward. Grove Liturgical Studies 21. Bramcote: Grove Books, 1980. Text reproduced from the original ed. in the British Library: *A Directory for the publique worship of God, throughout the three kingdoms of England, Scotland, and Ireland. Together with an ordinance of Parliament for the taking away of the Book of Common Prayer and for the establishing and observing of this present Directory throughout the kingdom of England, and Dominion of Wales*. London: printed for Evan Tyler, Alexander Fifield, Ralph Smith, and John Field, 1644.

Whitefield, George. *The Works of the Reverend George Whitefield, Late of Pembroke-College, Oxford, and Chaplain to the Rt. Hon. The Countess of Huntingdon, containing all his sermons and tracts which have been already published: With a select collection of letters written to his most intimate friends, and persons of distinction in England, Scotland, Ireland, and America, from the year 1734 to 1770, including the whole period of his ministry. Also, some other pieces on important subjects, never before printed, prepared by himself for the press. To which is prefixed, an account of his life, compiled from his original papers and letters.* Vol. V. London: Printed for Edward and Charles Dilly, in the Poultry, 1772.

Willison, John. *Balm of Gilead, consisting of Sermons Preached on Various Occasions. Likewise Sacramental Meditations and Advices. By the Reverend John Willison of Dundee.* Edinburgh: Printed by J. Pillans & Sons for John Bourns, 8 Greenside Street, 1819.

————. *One Hundred Gospel-Hymns, In Memory of Redeeming Love, and of the Death and Sufferings of the Lord Jesus Christ, for Perishing Sinners, Much adapted to Sacramental Occasions.* Dundee: H. Galbraith, 1767.

————. *A Sacramental Catechism, or, A Familiar Instructor for Young Communicants.* Glasgow: Printed by David Niven, 1794.

————. *A Sacramental Directory: Or, a Treatise concerning the Sanctification of a communion Sabbath. Containing Many proper directions, in order to our Preparing for, Receiving of, and right Behaving after, the Sacrament of the Lord's Supper.* Sixth edition, corrected and inlarged. Glasgow: Robert Duncan, 1769.

Primary Sources—Unpublished Works

Tennent, Gilbert. "De nuptiis cum Christo." Sermon manuscript 1. AMs, [17]53. The Gilbert Tennent manuscript collection, Henry Luce III Library, Princeton Theological Seminary, Princeton, NJ.

————. Untitled, undated sermon manuscript 4, on Canticles 4:16. AMs, [17]53. The Gilbert Tennent manuscript collection, Henry Luce III Library, Princeton Theological Seminary, Princeton, NJ.

————. Untitled, undated sermon manuscript 12. AMs, [17]53. The Gilbert Tennent manuscript collection, Henry Luce III Library, Princeton Theological Seminary, Princeton, NJ.

Secondary Sources—Books and Dissertations

Ahlstrom, Sydney E. *A Religious History of the American People.* New Haven, CT, and London: Yale University Press, 1972.

————, ed. *Theology in America: The Major Protestant Voices from Puritanism to Neo-Orthodoxy.* Indianapolis and New York: Bobbs-Merrill Co., 1967.

Alexander, Archibald. *Biographical Sketches of the Founder and Principal Alumni of the Log College: Together with an Account of the Revivals of Religion under Their Ministry.* Philadelphia: Presbyterian Board of Publication, 1851.

Armstrong, Maurice W., Lefferts A. Letscher, and Charles A. Anderson, eds. *The Presbyterian Enterprise: Sources of American Presbyterian History.* Philadelphia: Westminster Press, 1956.

Astell, Ann W. *The Song of Songs in the Middle Ages.* Ithaca, NY: Cornell University Press, 1990.

Atwood, Craig D. *Community of the Cross: Moravian Piety in Colonial Bethlehem.* University Park: Pennsylvania State University Press, 2004.

Bishop, Selma L. *Hymns and Spiritual Songs of Isaac Watts, 1707–1748: A Study in Early Eighteenth Century Language Changes.* London: Faith Press, 1962.

Blair, Anthony L. "Fire across the Water: Transatlantic Dimensions of the Great Awakening among Middle-Colony Presbyterians." PhD diss., Temple University, 2000. Paperback ed., Saarbrücken, Germany: LAP, Lambert Academic Publishing, 2010.

Bloch, Ariel, and Chana Bloch. *The Song of Songs*. New York: Random House, 1995.

Boles, John B. *The Great Revival: Beginnings of the Bible Belt*. Lexington: University Press of Kentucky, 1996. Originally published as *The Great Revival, 1787–1805: The Origins of the Southern Evangelical Mind*. Lexington: University Press of Kentucky, 1972.

Bouwsma, William J. *John Calvin: A Sixteenth Century Portrait*. New York: Oxford University Press, 1988.

Bowmer, John C. *The Sacrament of the Lord's Supper in Early Methodism*. London: Dacre Press, 1951.

Bradshaw, Paul. *The Search for the Origins of Christian Worship*. New York: Oxford University Press, 1992.

Brilioth, Yngve. *A Brief History of Preaching*. Philadelphia: Fortress Press, 1965.

Brown, Callum G. *The Social History of Religion in Scotland since 1730*. 2nd ed. Christianity and Society in the Modern World. London and New York: Methuen, 1987.

Burleigh, J. H. S. *A Church History of Scotland*. London: Oxford University Press, 1960.

Burnet, George B. *The Holy Communion in the Reformed Church of Scotland, 1560–1960*. Edinburgh and London: Oliver & Boyd, 1960.

Bynum, Caroline Walker. *Fragmentation and Redemption: Essays on Gender and the Human Body in Medieval Religion*. New York: Zone Books, 1991.

———. *Jesus as Mother: Studies in the Spirituality of the High Middle Ages*. Berkeley: University of California Press, 1982.

Campbell, Ted A. *The Religion of the Heart: A Study of European Religious Life in the Seventeenth and Eighteenth Centuries*. Columbia: University of South Carolina Press, 1991. Reprint, Eugene, OR: Wipf & Stock, 2000.

Casey, Michael. *Athirst for God: Spiritual Desire in Bernard of Clairvaux's Sermons on the Song of Songs*. Kalamazoo, MI: Cistercian Publications, 1988.

Cleveland, Catharine C. *The Great Revival in the West, 1797–1805*. Chicago: University of Chicago Press, 1916.

Coalter, Milton J., Jr. *Gilbert Tennent, Son of Thunder: A Case Study of Continental Pietism's Impact on the First Great Awakenings in the Middle Colonies*. Westport, CT: Greenwood Press, 1986.

Conkin, Paul K. *Cane Ridge: America's Pentecost*. Madison: University of Wisconsin Press, 1990.

Craighead, J. G. *Scotch and Irish Seeds in American Soil: The Early History of the Scotch and Irish Churches, and Their Relations to the Presbyterian Church of America*. Philadelphia: Presbyterian Board of Publication, 1878.

Davidson, Robert. *History of the Presbyterian Church in the State of Kentucky: With a Preliminary Sketch of the Churches in the Valley of Virginia*. New York: Robert Carter, 1847. Reprint, Greenwood, SC: Attic Press, 1974.

Davies, Horton. *Worship and Theology in England from Watts and Wesley to Martineau, 1690–1900*. Combined ed. Grand Rapids and Cambridge, UK: Wm. B. Eerdmans Publishing Co., 1996. Originally published as *From Watts and Wesley to Maurice, 1690–1850*. Princeton, NJ: Princeton University Press, 1961. And as *From Newman to Martineau, 1850–1900*. Princeton, NJ: Princeton University Press, 1962.

———. *Worship and Theology in England from Cranmer to Baxter and Fox, 1534–1690*. Combined ed. Grand Rapids and Cambridge, UK: Wm. B. Eerdmans Publishing Co., 1996. Originally published as *From Cranmer to Hooker, 1534–1603*. Princeton, NJ: Princeton University Press, 1970. And as *From Andrewes to Baxter and Fox, 1603–1690*. Princeton, NJ: Princeton University Press, 1975.

Dean, Kenda Creasy. *Practicing Passion: Youth and the Quest for a Passionate Church.* Grand Rapids: Wm. B. Eerdmans Publishing Co., 2004.

Erler, Mary C. *Women, Reading, and Piety in Late Medieval England.* Cambridge: Cambridge University Press, 2002.

Engammare, Max. *"Qu'il me baise des baisiers de sa bouche"* [Song 1:2]: *Le Cantique des cantiques à la Renaissance; Étude et bibliographie.* Geneva: Librairie Droz, 1993.

Eslinger, Ellen. *Citizens of Zion: The Social Origins of Camp Meeting Revivalism.* Knoxville: University of Tennessee Press, 1999.

Fawcett, Arthur. *The Cambuslang Revival: The Scottish Evangelical Revival of the Eighteenth Century.* Edinburgh and Carlisle, PA: Banner of Truth Trust, 1971.

Forrester, Duncan, and Douglas Murray, eds. *Studies in the History of Worship in Scotland.* Edinburgh: T&T Clark, 1985.

Fratt, Steven Douglas. "Scottish Theological Trends in the Eighteenth Century: Tensions between 'Head' and 'Heart.'" PhD diss., University of California, Santa Barbara, 1987.

Gaustad, Edwin S., and Leigh E. Schmidt. *A Religious History of America.* Rev. ed. New York: HarperCollins, 2002.

Gerrish, B. A. *Grace and Gratitude: The Eucharistic Theology of John Calvin.* Minneapolis: Fortress Press, 1993.

Hall, Stanley Robertson. "The American Presbyterian 'Directory for Worship': History of a Liturgical Strategy." PhD diss., University of Notre Dame, 1990.

Hambrick-Stowe, Charles E., ed. *Early New England Meditative Poetry: Anne Bradstreet and Edward Taylor.* New York and Mahwah, NJ: Paulist Press, 1988.

———. *The Practice of Piety: Puritan Devotional Disciplines in Seventeenth-Century New England.* Chapel Hill: University of North Carolina Press, 1982.

Hoffecker, W. Andrew. *Piety and the Princeton Theologians.* Phillipsburg, NJ: Presbyterian & Reformed Publishing Co., 1981.

Hoffman, Bengt R. *Theology of the Heart: The Role of Mysticism in the Theology of Martin Luther.* Edited by Pearl Willemssen Hoffman. Minneapolis: Kirk House Publishers, 1998.

Hoffman, Lawrence A. *Beyond the Text: A Holistic Approach to Liturgy.* Bloomington and Indianapolis: Indiana University Press, 1987.

Holifield, E. Brooks. *The Covenant Sealed: The Development of Puritan Sacramental Theology in Old and New England, 1570–1720.* New Haven, CT, and London: Yale University Press, 1974.

Hudson, Winthrop S. *Religion in America.* 4th ed. New York: Macmillan Publishing Co., 1987.

Irwin, Kevin W. *Context and Test: Method in Liturgical Theology.* Collegeville, MN: Liturgical Press, 1994.

Isaac, Rhys. *The Transformation of Virginia, 1740–1790.* Chapel Hill: University of North Carolina Press, 1982.

Jones, Cheslyn, Geoffrey Wainwright, and Edward Yarnold, eds. *The Study of Spirituality.* New York and Oxford: Oxford University Press, 1986.

Jones, Serene. *Calvin and the Rhetoric of Piety.* Columbia Series in Reformed Theology. Louisville, KY: Westminster John Knox Press, 1995.

Lambert, Frank. *Inventing the "Great Awakening."* Princeton, NJ: Princeton University Press, 1999.

Lane, Anthony N. S. *John Calvin: Student of the Church Fathers.* Grand Rapids: Baker Books, 1999.

Leith, John H., ed. *Calvin Studies VIII: The Westminster Confession in Current Thought; Presented at the Colloquium on Calvin Studies, held January 26–27, 1996, at Davidson College and the Davidson College Presbyterian Church, Davidson, NC.* Davidson, NC: Davidson College, Colloquium on Calvin Studies, 1996.

Lindenauer, Leslie J. *Piety and Power: Gender and Religious Culture in the American Colonies, 1630–1700.* New York and London: Routledge, 2002.

Lovejoy, David S. *Religious Enthusiasm in the New World: Heresy to Revolution.* Cambridge, MA, and London: Harvard University Press, 1985.

Maag, Karin, and John D. Witvliet, eds. *Worship in Medieval and Early Modern Europe: Change and Continuity in Religious Practice.* Notre Dame, IN: University of Notre Dame Press, 2004.

Matter, Ann E. *The Voice of My Beloved: The Song of Songs in Western Medieval Christianity.* Philadelphia: University of Pennsylvania Press, 1990.

Maxwell, William D. *A History of Worship in the Church of Scotland.* London: Oxford University Press, 1955.

———. *John Knox's Genevan Service Book 1556: The Liturgical Portions of the Genevan Service Book Used by John Knox While a Minister of the English Congregation of Marian Exiles at Geneva, 1556–1559.* Edinburgh and London: Oliver & Boyd, 1931.

———. *An Outline of Christian Worship.* Rev. ed. London: Oxford University Press, 1949.

Meeks, Wayne A. *The First Urban Christians: The Social World of the Apostle Paul.* New Haven, CT, and London: Yale University Press, 1983.

Murphy, Roland E. *The Song of Songs.* Edited by S. Dean McBride Jr. Minneapolis: Augsburg Fortress, 1990.

———. *Wisdom Literature and Psalms.* Nashville: Abingdon Press, 1983.

Oberman, Heiko. *The Dawn of the Reformation: Essays in Late Medieval and Early Reformation Thought.* Edinburgh: T&T Clark, 1986. Reprint, Grand Rapids: Wm. B. Eerdmans Publishing Co., 1992.

Old, Hughes Oliphant. *The Patristic Roots of Reformed Worship.* Zurich: Theologischer Verlag, 1975.

———. *The Reading and Preaching of the Scriptures in the Worship of the Christian Church.* Vol. 1, *The Biblical Period.* Grand Rapids and Cambridge, UK: Wm. B. Eerdmans Publishing Co., 1998.

———. *The Reading and Preaching of the Scriptures in the Worship of the Christian Church.* Vol. 3, *The Medieval Church.* Grand Rapids and Cambridge, UK: Wm. B. Eerdmans Publishing Co., 1999.

———. *The Reading and Preaching of the Scriptures in the Worship of the Christian Church.* Vol. 4, *The Age of the Reformation.* Grand Rapids and Cambridge, UK: Wm. B. Eerdmans Publishing Co., 2002.

Ozment, Steven E. *Homo Spiritualis: A Comparative Study of the Anthropology of Johannes Tauler, Jean Gerson and Martin Luther (1509–16) in the Context of Their Theological Thought.* Leiden: E. J. Brill, 1969.

Parker, T. H. L. *Calvin's Preaching.* Louisville, KY: Westminster/John Knox Press; Edinburgh: T&T Clark, 1992.

Pope, Marvin H. *Song of Songs.* New York: Doubleday, 1977.

Raitt, Jill. *The Eucharistic Theology of Theodore Beza: Development of the Reformed Doctrine.* AAR Studies in Religion 4. Chambersburg, PA: American Academy of Religion, 1972.

Rattenbury, J. Ernest. *The Eucharistic Hymns of John and Charles Wesley*. Edited by Timothy J. Crouch. American ed. Akron, OH: OSL Publications, 1990. 2nd American ed. Akron, OH: OSL Publications, 1996.

Richard, Lucien Joseph. *The Spirituality of John Calvin*. Atlanta: John Knox Press, 1974.

Roberts, Richard Owen, ed. *Scotland Saw His Glory: A History of Revivals in Scotland*. By W. J. Couper, James Burns, Mary Duncan, et al. Wheaton, IL: International Awakening Press, 1995.

Ruth, Lester. *A Little Heaven Below: Worship at Early Methodist Quarterly Meetings*. Nashville: Abingdon Press, 2000.

Schmidt, Leigh Eric. *Holy Fairs: Scotland and the Making of American Revivalism*. 2d ed. Princeton, NJ: Princeton University Press, 2001. Originally published as *Holy Fairs: Scottish Communions and American Revivals in the Early Modern Period*. Princeton, NJ: Princeton University Press, 1989.

Scott, John Thomas. "James McGready: Son of Thunder, Father of the Great Revival." PhD diss., The College of William and Mary, 1991.

Spinks, Bryan D. *Sacraments, Ceremonies and the Stuart Divines: Sacramental Theology and Liturgy in England and Scotland, 1603–1662*. Hants, UK, and Burlington, VT: Ashgate Publishing, 2002.

Stead, Geoffrey, and Margaret Stead. *The Exotic Plant: A History of the Moravian Church in Great Britain, 1742–2000*. Werrington, Peterborough: Epworth Press, 2003.

Stoeffler, Ernest. *Continental Pietism and Early American Christianity*. Grand Rapids: Wm. B. Eerdmans Publishing Co., 1976.

Tamburello, Dennis E. *Union with Christ: John Calvin and the Mysticism of St. Bernard*. Columbia Series in Reformed Theology. Louisville, KY: Westminster John Knox Press, 1994.

Thompson, Bard. *Humanists and Reformers: A History of the Renaissance and the Reformation*. Grand Rapids: Wm. B. Eerdmans Publishing Co., 1996.

Torrance, Thomas F. *Scottish Theology from John Knox to John McLeod Campbell*. Edinburgh: T&T Clark, 1996.

Trinterud, Leonard J. *The Forming of an American Tradition: A Re-examination of Colonial Presbyterianism*. Philadelphia: Westminster Press, 1949.

Turner, Denys. *Eros and Allegory: Medieval Exegesis of the Song of Songs*. Kalamazoo, MI: Cistercian Publications, 1995.

Wakefield, Gordon Stevens. *Puritan Devotion: Its Place in the Development of Christian Piety*. London: Epworth Press, 1957.

Wallace, Ronald S. *Calvin's Doctrine of the Word and Sacrament*. Grand Rapids: Wm. B. Eerdmans Publishing Co., 1957.

Walsh, Carey Ellen. *Exquisite Desire: Religion, the Erotic, and the Song of Songs*. Minneapolis: Augsburg Fortress Press, 2000.

Ward, W. R. *The Protestant Evangelical Awakening*. Cambridge: Cambridge University Press, 1992.

Westerkamp, Marilyn J. *Triumph of the Laity: Scots-Irish Piety and the Great Awakening, 1625–1760*. New York: Oxford University Press, 1988.

———. *Women and Religion in Early America, 1600–1850: The Puritan and Evangelical Traditions*. New York and London: Routledge, 1999.

Won, Jonathan Jong-Chun. "Communion with Christ: An Exposition and Comparison of the Doctrine of Union and Communion with Christ in Calvin and the English Puritans." PhD diss., Westminster Theological Seminary, 1989.

Secondary Sources—Articles

Bennett, James B. "'Love to Christ': Gilbert Tennent, Presbyterian Reunion, and a Sacramental Sermon." *American Presbyterians* 71, no. 2 (Summer 1993): 77–89.

Brauer, Jerald C. "Types of Puritan Piety." *Church History* 56 (1987): 39–58.

Butler, Jon. "Enthusiasm Described and Decried: The Great Awakening as Interpretive Fiction." *Journal of American History* 69 (September 1982): 306–9.

Cummings, Owen F. "Mystical Women and the Eucharist." *Antiphon: A Journal for Liturgical Renewal* 5, no. 3 (2000): 11–20.

Fishburn, Janet F. "Gilbert Tennent, Established 'Dissenter.'" *Church History* 63 (1994): 31–49.

———. "Pennsylvania 'Awakenings,' Sacramental Seasons, and Ministry." In *Scholarship, Sacraments, and Service: Historical Studies in Protestant Tradition; Essays in Honor of Bard Thompson*, edited by Daniel B. Clendenin and W. David Buschart, 59–87. Lewiston, NY: Edwin Mellen Press, 1990.

Fraser, James W. "The Great Awakening and New Patterns of Presbyterian Theological Education." *Journal of Presbyterian History* 60 (Fall 1982): 189–208.

Hudson, Winthrop S. "Mystical Religion in the Puritan Commonwealth." *Journal of Religion* 28 (1948): 51–56.

Kieckhefer, Richard. "Convention and Conversion: Patterns in Late Medieval Piety." *Church History* 67, no. 1 (March 1998): 32–51.

Long, Kimberly Bracken. "The Communion Sermons of James McGready: Sacramental Theology and Scots-Irish Piety on the Kentucky Frontier." *Journal of Presbyterian History* 80, no. 1 (Spring 2002): 3–16.

Maclean, Iain S. "The First Pietist: An Introduction and Translation of a Communion Sermon by Jodocus van Lodenstein." In *Calvin Studies VI: Colloquium on Calvin Studies at Davidson College and Davidson Presbyterian Church, Davidson, North Carolina, January 1992*, edited by John H. Leith, 15–31. Davidson, NC: Davidson College, Colloquium on Calvin Studies, 1992.

Marini, Stephen. "Hymnody as History: Early Evangelical Hymns and the Recovery of American Popular Religion." *Church History* 71, no. 2 (June 2002): 273–307.

McMillan, W. "Festivals and Saint Days in Scotland after the Reformation." In *Records of the Scottish Church History Society*, vol. 3, edited by W. J. Couper and Robert McKinlay. Edinburgh: Scottish Church History Society, 1929.

Meek, D. E. "Communion Seasons." In *Dictionary of Scottish Church History and Theology*. Edinburgh: T&T Clark, 1993: 200.

Old, Hughes Oliphant. "Gilbert Tennent and the Preaching of Piety in Colonial America: Newly Discovered Manuscripts in Speer Library." *Princeton Seminary Bulletin* 10, no. 2, new series (1989): 133–34.

Opie, James, Jr. "James McGready: Theologian of Frontier Revivalism." *Church History* 34 (1965): 445–56.

Searle, Mark. "New Tasks, New Methods: The Emergence of Pastoral Liturgical Studies." *Worship* 57 (1983): 291–308.

Taft, Robert. "Response to the Berakah Award: Anamnesis." *Worship* 59 (1985): 305–25.

Watkins, Keith. "The Sacramental Character of the Camp Meeting." *Discipliana* 54 (Spring 1994): 2–19.

Willison, John. "Willison's Sacramental Catechism." *Journal of Presbyterian History* 44 (June 1966): 81–82.

Index